EMOTIONAL LITERACY

Intelligence with a Heart

Claude Steiner, Ph.D.

Printed in United States of America

For information address:
Personhood Press
"Books for ALL that you are!"
Post Office Box 370
Fawnskin, California 92333
800.662.9662   email: personhoodpress@att.net

Library of Congress Cataloging-in-Publication Data
Claude Steiner, 1935

Emotional Literacy / by Claude Steiner
Library of Congress Catalog Card Number:

ISBN 1-932181-02-4

Original version published as *Achieving Emotional Literacy*
by Claude Steiner & Paul Perry. Avon Books 1997.

Visit our Web site at
http://www.personhhoodpress.com

Visit Claude Steiner's Web site at
http://www.emotional-literacy.com

cover: editing: interior design & layout by:
Linda J. Thille   Susan Remkus   www.madhof.com

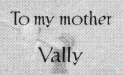

To my mother

Vally

whose heart I longed to touch

Table of Contents

ACKNOWLEDGMENTS
PREFACE

Book One
Emotional Literacy

INTRODUCTION XV

Emotions & Personal Power
Finding My Teachers
Enter Feminism and the Emotions
Four Discoveries That Made a Difference
Strokes and Love
The Power of the Critical Parent
The Safety of the Cooperative Contract
Paranoia and Awareness
Emotional Literacy in Everyday Life

CHAPTER 1 1
WHAT IS EMOTIONAL LITERACY?

An Intimate Dinner
Return of Common Sense
The Forgotten Heart
Hunger for Emotions; Love & Hate
Psychopaths & Empaths
EQ & IQ
Emotional Intelligence & Emotional Literacy
Heart-centered EQ
Summary: What Is Emotional Literacy?

CHAPTER 2 23
EMOTIONAL AWARENESS

Roots of Emotional Awareness
The Triune Brain
The Reptilian Brain

The Limbic Brain
The Emotional Awareness Scale
Beyond Awareness
Summary: Emotional Awareness

CHAPTER 3 47
TRAINING TO BE EMOTIONALLY LITERATE
The Appeal of an Emotionally Literate Life
The Training Process
An Energizing Process
Strategies of Emotional Literacy Training
Where to Start
Emotional Literacy; Training Steps
Summary: Training to Be Emotionally Literate

Book Two
Emotional Literacy Training

CHAPTER 4 57
OPENING THE HEART
The Power of Strokes
Trouble in Stroke City
The Stroke Economy & its Rules
Why People Accept Negative Strokes
The Emotional Literacy Training Program
Emotionally Literate Transaction #0:
    Ask for Permission
Emotionally Literate Transaction #1:
    Giving Strokes—Offering Honest & Truthful Statements
    of Affection
Stroke Enemy #1: The Critical Parent
The Poetry of Strokes
Emotionally Literate Transaction # 2:
    Asking for Strokes—Requesting the Affection That We Need
Emotionally Literate Transaction # 3:
    Accepting Strokes—Taking in Strokes We Want
Case Study in Acceptance
Emotionally Literate Transaction # 4:

Rejecting Unwanted Strokes—"Thanks but No Thanks"
Separating the Wheat from the Chaff
Emotionally Literate Transaction # 5:
    Giving Ourselves Strokes—Healthy Self-love
Self-strokes to Fight the Critical Parent
Summary: Opening the Heart

CHAPTER 5 83
SURVEYING THE EMOTIONAL LANDSCAPE
I Can Make You Feel, You Can Make Me Feel.
Emotionally Literate Transaction # 6:
    The Action/Feeling Statement
Action/Feeling Case Study
Action/Feeling Error 1:
    Confusing Action with Motivation
Action/Feeling Error 2:
    Confusing Feelings with Thoughts
Primary & Secondary Emotions
Action/Feeling Error 3:
    Ignoring the Intensity of an Emotion
Clarifying an Action/Feeling Statement
Emotionally Literate Transaction #7:
    Accepting an Action/Feeling Statement—Non-defensive
    Reception of Emotional Information
An Action/Feeling Transaction That Worked
Emotionally Literate Transaction #8:
    Revealing Our Intuitive Hunches—Getting a "Reality Check"
    on an Intuition about Another Person's Actions or Intentions
How Do Others Feel?
Intuition in Action, a Case Study
Discounting Intuition
Emotionally Literate Transaction #9:
    Validating an Intuitive Hunch—A Search for the Truth,
    No Matter How Small
The Payoff: Loving Emotional Cooperation
How Empathy Matures
One More Case Study of the Emotional Landscape:
    Putting it All Together
Summary: Surveying the Emotional Landscape

CHAPTER 6 119
THE MISTAKES WE MAKE AND WHY WE MAKE THEM
The Games People Play
Scripts: Decisions That Rule Our Lives
Rescuer, Persecutor, Victim
The Rescuer, Persecutor, Victim Merry-go-round
Role Switching
Summary: the Emotional Mistakes We Make

CHAPTER 7 135
TAKING RESPONSIBILITY
Personal Case in Point
Obstacles to Taking Responsibility
Emotionally Literate Transaction #10:
    Apologizing for Our Rescues
Emotionally Literate Transaction #11:
    Apologizing for Persecution
Messy & Neat
Apologies & Guilt
Requirements & Errors of an Apology
Emotionally Literate Transaction #12:
    Apologizing for Playing the Victim Role
Emotionally Literate Transaction #13:
    Accepting an Apology
Accepting Apology Error #1:
    Forgiving Too Easily
Accepting Apology Error #2:
    Bashing the Righteous
Acceptance of Apology with Conditions
Emotionally Literate Transaction #14:
    Rejection of an Apology
Case Study: Both Sides of Apology
Emotionally Literate Transaction# 15:
Begging Forgiveness—
    An Emotionally Literate Way of Apologizing for an Action
    That Has Deeply Hurt Another Person
Case Study: Begging Forgiveness
One That Didn't Work
Summary: Taking Responsibility

CHAPTER 8 167
EMOTIONAL LITERACY WITH COUPLES & CHILDREN
    Emotional Literacy with Couples
        Equality & Honesty in Intimate Relationships
        Equality
        Honesty
        Pre-nuptial Emotional Agreements
        Honesty Is the Best Policy
        Housekeeping Required
        Review, Review, Review
        Be Flexible
        A Walk in the Woods
    Emotional Literacy & Children
        The Wrong Way & the Right Way
        A Better Approach
        Emotional Literacy Guidelines for Children
        Keep the Heart Open
        Don't Power Play Your Children

CHAPTER 9 191
EMOTIONAL LITERACY IN THE WORKPLACE
    Practice What You Preach
    Start an Emotional Literacy Study & Support Group
    The Ten Commandments of Emotional Literacy

Book Three
The Emotional Warrior

CHAPTER 10 203
THE EMOTIONAL WARRIOR
    The Ancient Regime
    Understanding the Power of Control
    Avenues of Power
    The Many Faces of Power
    Our Inner Enemy—The Critical Parent
    Seven Sources of Power
    A Shift for the Millennium

CHAPTER 11 221
THE EMOTIONAL WARRIOR
ONE LAST WORD 221
NOTES FOR PHILOSOPHERS 223
    Love as a Fundamental Good
    Lying & Honesty
    The Truth
    Violence & the Dark Side
    Violence & Abuse
    The Critical Parent

APPENDIX A 233
    An Emotional Awareness Questionnaire

APPENDIX B 241
    Training Handouts

GLOSSARY 259

ABOUT THE AUTHOR 264

REFERENCES 265

INDEX 269

Acknowledgments

This book is the culmination of thirty-five years of work. Thanks are due, first and foremost, to Eric Berne for taking me on as a disciple and teaching me most of what I know as a psychotherapist.

More than any other book I have written, this book is the result of very closely knit teamwork. Thanks to Jude Hall, who besides editing these pages through many versions and revisions, has added examples, elaborations and ideas, made my language richer, and acted as my intellectual and philosophical conscience as this work took shape. Thanks to Paul Perry, who co-wrote the original version of this book. A very special thanks to Fred Jordan, who was available, one simple phone call away, to give his advice throughout the writing stages of the book. I consider myself blessed to have such a wise and kind maven on my team. I also thank Ron Levaco and Charles Rappleye, who in a similar capacity gave sage advice at some of the strategic crossroads of this book's journey. Thanks to Deirdre English and Gail Rebuck, who steadfastly supported my writing for many years before this book found an agent and a publisher. Thanks to Beth Roy, Mimi Steiner, Rod Coots, Bruce Carrol, Ron Levaco, and Saul Schultheis-Gerry for their reading of and many comments on the final manuscript, and to Ramona Ansolabehere and Michael Hannigan for useful critical commentary on the text. Adriane Rainer's reading, informed by many hours of previous editorial work on this material, was especially useful. Ann McKay Thoroman, my editor at Avon Books persevered with unflagging interest and hard work.

Thanks are due to all the people who over the years attended my seminars, workshops, and group and individual therapy, and all my friends and relatives who shared their life experiences with me and provided the information upon which to base the assertions I make in this book.

This is particularly true of my children Mimi, Eric, and Denali, my brother Miguel, my sister Katy, and finally Jude Hall, my wife, who for months was available to give a hand at a moment's notice in the final writing stages. In particular I want to thank the many Emotional Warriors around the globe, among them Marc Devos, Marielle Debouverie, Elisabeth Cleary, Elizabeth Edema, Michael Epple, Sylvia Cavalie, Becky Jenkins, Anne Kohlhaas-Reith, Ron Hurst, Denton Roberts, Beth Roy, Hartmut Oberdieck, Richard Reith, and Mimi Steiner.

Going back to the 1960s when these ideas were born, thanks are due to Nancy Graham for first uttering the term "emotional literacy," which I promptly scooped up and have used ever since. I thank Hogie Wyckoff for helping shape the concepts of Pig Parent (now the Critical Parent) and the Stroke Economy. Hogie was also the first to insist that honesty was an essential component of a cooperative way of life. Bob Schwebel deserves thanks for introducing cooperation to my thinking, and Marshall Rosenberg was the first to point out the importance of linking actions with feelings. Thanks are due to all the members of the RAP Center in Berkeley who contributed their lives and ideas to the theories presented in this book, in particular to Becky Jenkins, Carmen Kerr, Hogie Wyckoff, Robert Schwebel, Joy Marcus, Rick de Golia, Sarah Winter, and those who joined us later—Sandy Spiker, Eric Moore, Darca Nicholson, Melissa Farley, Mark Weston, Marion Oliker, JoAnn Costello, Beth Roy, Randy Dunigan, and Barbara Moulton. Finally, I thank David Geisinger for pointing out that a relationship is as good as its dialogue, Chris Moore for informing me on the latest philosophical arguments about the nature of truth, and Marc Devos for suggesting that emotional literacy training could be divided into three stages: an opening of the heart, a gathering of information, and taking of responsibility.

Preface

I have undertaken to rewrite *Achieving Emotional Literacy*,[1] five years after its publication in 1997 and fully in the twenty-first century. The book is longer and more elaborate, and it incorporates feedback originated by the original book. It integrates information from readers and clients, what I have gleaned from other books on emotional intelligence, from evolutionary psychology and neuroscience, and from what I have learned in my personal life over the last years; this work is, as most such work in psychology, the product of both science and personal predilection.

Since the publication of *Achieving Emotional Literacy* in 1997, emotional intelligence has passed from being a welcome, fresh way of thinking to becoming a number of widely disparate movements. The largest of these movements was a consultant's "growth business" with scores of companies offering to evaluate and improve people's EQs in the workplace. Regrettably, in that environment emotional intelligence became synonymous with "mature", "stable." and "hard-working." These are fine qualities, but they are vague and indistinguishable from all else that is desirable. No systematic methods of teaching emotional intelligence have been developed and no dramatic progress has been made in measuring EQ. Some questionnaires were developed which arguably have something to do with emotional intelligence and may actually help select better workers, but none can claim to yield any convincing measurements of EQ.

Twenty-five years ago, I conceived emotional literacy as a tool of human emancipation from stifling rationality and power. But the field of emotional intelligence, especially in the workplace has lost its edge; instead of liberating people's emotions, it is being used to help companies spot bright-eyed, self controlled, hard-working employees.

Emotional skills are a great deal more than positive attitudes and impulse control; they can humanize and improve any enterprise beyond anything that has been experienced so far and their potential is being squandered on diluted, half measures. I fear that emotional intelligence is morphing into yet another corporate, human engineering lubricant with little specific relationship to emotional literacy.

On the other hand, EQ has also become a subject matter in schools, where thousands of devoted teachers are applying one or more of the scores of EQ teaching aids developed by as many companies. Here the results seem more promising, because what is being taught is unquestionably beneficial. Children are being educated about their different feelings, how to speak about them and how to express and control them. They are being trained with a kind-hearted attitude and a focus on developing friendly, cooperative relationships. Evidence suggests that these efforts are having beneficial results, at least in terms of the decreasing amounts of aggression being seen in the schools that teach the subject.[2] Still, none of these programs focus on the heart centered techniques that are at the core of this book, techniques which in my opinion would greatly amplify the beneficial effects of emotional literacy training for children and adolescents.

EMOTIONAL LITERACY

The point of this book goes beyond workplace maturity or schoolyard aggression. Emotional literacy is a source of personal power indispensable for success in today's world.[3] The following five essential, thoroughly time-tested assertions must be understood to appreciate this work's scope:

▨ Emotional literacy is love-centered emotional intelligence.

▓ Loving (oneself and others) and being loved (by oneself and others) are the essential conditions of emotional literacy.

▓ The high skill of loving and accepting love, lost to most people, can be recovered and taught with five simple, precise, transactional exercises.

▓ In addition to improving loving skills, emotional literacy training involves three further skills of increasing difficulty; each one is supported by a further set of transactional exercises.

These skills are:

    a. Speaking about our emotions and what causes them,

    b. Developing our empathic, intuitive capacity, and

    c. Apologizing for the damage caused by our emotional mistakes.

Practice of these specific transactional exercises in personal relationships at home with friends and at work with others, will, over time, produce increased emotional literacy.

With these exercises you can become a more loving person, a person who feels love toward people and is able to love passionately in a sustained way; a person who is able to be affectionate and friendly. You will be better able to recognize, express, and control your emotions; you will realize when you are angry or joyful, ashamed or hopeful, and you will understand how to make your feelings known in a productive manner. You will become more empathic and will recognize the emotional states of others and respond to them compassionately. You will be able to take responsibility for the emotional damage caused by your mistakes and apologize for them effectively. Instead of undermining and defeating you, your emotions will empower you and enrich your life and the lives of those around you.

In Summary

Emotional literacy—intelligence with a heart—can be learned through the practice of specific transactional exercises that target the awareness of emotion in ourselves and others, the capacities to love others and ourselves while developing honesty and the ability to take responsibility for our actions.

BOOK ONE

Emotional Literacy

Introduction

Before getting to the substance of this book, I want to tell you what qualifies me to write on the subject.

This book is based on both on my professional and scientific training, enhanced by my experience as I struggle to understand my own emotional life. I believe that my combined professional, scientific, and personal experiences have translated into an understandable and productive text.

I was raised in a state of utter emotional illiteracy, as was expected and usual of the white, middle class boys destined to become professional men of my generation. I ignored my own emotions, believing that it was shameful, weak, and frightening to dwell on them. Equally, I disdained and ignored the emotions of others. All the while my emotions, especially my unacknowledged need for love, dictated and distorted most of my behavior. When I think back, sad to say, many of the things I did as I clumsily grasped for love were emotionally painful to the people in my life. I am told that people tolerated my hurtful ways because I made up with a naïve, narcissistic charm what I lacked in sensitivity.

You might think that I decided to study psychology because I was interested in people's feelings. In fact, my interest in psychology had to do with the belief that it would give me power over people: to be in a position to help, but also to dominate and control. As a student of psychology, emotions were the furthest thing from my mind. Actually, since the early 1900s, the emotions had been excluded from scientific psychology. Why? Because introspection, the method that was used to study emotions, was deemed to be hopelessly biased and subject to distortion.

Science is a discipline that encourages detachment and rationality uncluttered by emotion. A watershed event in my life happened when, as part of my training doing physiology experiments with animal muscles, I had to run a wire down the backbone of live frogs to destroy their spinal cords. As I performed this grisly task, I told myself that if I wanted to be a real scientist, it was important to suppress my horror. The decision to do so, added to the earlier cultural and personal training of my childhood and adolescence, affected my life from then on. To my ever-lasting embarrassment, I later participated in experiments in which rats were starved to learn about their responses to severe hunger.

As a result of my decision to suppress my emotions during this critical stage of my professional training, I became even less interested in my own feelings and the feelings of others. I had infatuations but no real attach-ments and little respect, regret, or guilt when it came to the way I treated the people in my life. I never felt sustained joy and I never cried. I lost friends and was prone to depres-sion and despair. Although I have a respectable IQ, when I look back at myself I see an emotionally illiterate young man with a very low emotional intelligence or EQ (emotional quotient).

When I finally stumbled upon my emotions (which I will discuss shortly), I was like an explorer discovering an exotic land, amazed, frightened, and captivated by the emotional landscape within and around me. Eventually, I decided to make emotions the subject of ongoing inquiry in my psychological practice, a pursuit that absorbs me to this day. Though at times arduous, I find this quest rewarding and empowering in my personal and working relationships.

EMOTIONS & PERSONAL POWER

Power is generally thought of as control, mainly the ability to control people and money. When we think of a powerful person, for example, we picture a man, a captain of industry, a major politician, or a superstar athlete who commands millions in salary: a masculine person with nerves of steel and the capacity to be emotionally detached and cool. We have trouble picturing a woman even though women are increasingly acquiring that sort of power.

We have come to expect certain attributes in powerful people, and even though most of us will never attain that kind of power we imitate powerful people in the belief that in the real world, emotions are best kept under tight rein.

But the sort of personal power derived from the security of satisfying relationships and fruitful work is ultimately incompatible with a tight rein on our emotions. On the contrary, personal power depends on having a comfortable relationship with emotions—ours and other people's. Emotional literacy requires that our emotions be listened to and expressed in a productive way.

Not everyone who suffers from emotional illiteracy is emotionally deaf and dumb, as I was. Another form of emotional powerlessness occurs when we are excessively emotional and out of control with our feelings. Instead of being out of touch with the world of emotions, we're all too aware and responsive to them as they hound and terrorize us.

Either extreme spells trouble. Whether tightly controlled or too loosely expressed, our emotions can reduce our power rather than empower us. Unfortunately, in today's world, the interpersonal experience is all too often laced with emotional pain. Emotional literacy training facilitates cooperative, harmonious relationships at home and at work and gives us the tools to avoid an increasingly dark, cynical view of life. Emotional literacy makes it possible for every conversation, every human contact, and every partnership—however brief or long-term—to yield the largest possible rewards for all involved. Even though it doesn't guarantee unlimited access to cash and things, emotional literacy is a key to personal power because emotions *are* powerful if you can make them work for you rather than against you.

What was it that put me in touch with the positive power of my emotions? My encounters and subsequent relationships with two different people, seven years apart: a rogue psychiatrist and a feminist partner.

The first person who significantly changed my life was Eric Berne, a 45-year-old psychiatrist at the time I met him in 1956. Berne's psychoanalytic training had recently ended because of differences with his training analyst. Since the early 1950s, he had been investigating and developing some radical departures from psycho-analysis that would later be known as Transactional Analysis.

In 1955, he started holding weekly meetings with a small group of professionals at his apartment a few blocks from San Francisco's Chinatown. I was taken to one of these meetings by Ben Handelman, a friend and coworker at the Berkeley Jewish Community Center. I found what Berne had to say very interesting and joined in the lively discussion. After the meeting, Berne asked me to return the following week, and I did. From then on, except for the years I was at the University of Michigan studying for a doctorate in clinical psychology, I rarely missed a meeting. I became Berne's disciple and learned everything he had to teach about his evolving theory of transactional analysis. Berne died in 1971 at the early age of sixty.

Transactional analysis (TA) is a technique that inves-tigates human relationships by focusing on the precise content of people's interactions. TA is a powerful way of analyzing how people deal with each other and how they can change their lives by correcting their behavioral mistakes.

TA was a sharp departure from traditional psycho-analysis, which focuses on what goes on *inside* of people, while TA attends to what happens *between* them. But the most radical idea of Berne's was that you could actually cure people of their emotional problems by showing them how to act differently with each other in their social transactions rather than by focusing on understanding why they were emotionally disturbed. The idea was that while understanding may be helpful, changing one's behavior is what would actually cure emotional troubles. A radical view in those highly psychoanalytically influenced times, this is now an accepted and commonplace understanding which is the basis for the cognitive-behavioral psychotherapies. Yet it remains controversial in some circles.

Emotions were not, at the time, our focus. In fact, we saw them as being largely irrelevant to our work, which was simply studying interpersonal transactions from a rational perspective. Yet Berne's concepts had everything to do with the eventual development of emotional literacy training. Two of his concepts were key: the ego states, especially the inner "Natural Child," which is the source of our emotional lives, and the concept of strokes.

Berne discovered in each normal person three parts or distinct modes of behavior, which he called the Child, the Parent, and the Adult. He called these three parts of the normal personality "ego states," and he believed that we act as one of them at any given time. You can learn about the ego states in one of the many books written about TA.[4,5,6] Suffice it to say for now that the Child is the creative and emotional part of the self, the Adult is a rational "human computer," and the Parent is composed of a set of protective attitudes about people. Berne taught us to pay close attention to the "social transactions" between people, because you can learn everything you need to know about a person by closely watching the interactions of their ego states.

The other very important concept developed by Berne he called "strokes." Strokes can be positive or negative because any transaction that acknowledges another person is a stroke no matter how it feels. A "stroke," in the way that we will use the term in this book, refers to a positive stroke, a show of affection. When you say to someone, "I like the way you look today," you are giving that person a positive stroke: a stroke, for short. By the same token, when you lovingly pat your child on the back or listen carefully to what your partner is saying, you are giving him or her a stroke, as well. Strokes can be physical or verbal and are defined as the basic unit of human recognition.

The kinds of strokes that people give and take are especially informative. Some people exchange mostly negative, even hateful strokes, and their lives are very different from those who manage to attain a dependable diet of positive, loving strokes. When people love themselves and others, their transactions will be governed by their loving hearts and they will neither give nor accept negative strokes.

These two concept—ego states and strokes—formed the theoretical foundation of the transactional analytic study of emotions.

ENTER FEMINISM & THE EMOTIONS

I never would have made the connection between TA and emotional literacy were it not for another life-changing relationship that plunged me into the world of feelings. Recently divorced and almost overnight, I became deeply involved with a feminist—Hogie Wyckoff—who for the next seven years taught me the essentials of emotionality. Basically, she demanded that I "come out" emotionally; that I be honest about my feelings, that I ask for what I want, and above all, that I learn to say "I love you" from the heart. None of these demands was easy for me to meet. In fact, they were excruciatingly difficult. Under Hogie's loving, watchful tutelage, however, I made great emotional strides. It was exhausting work for her and in the end she could endure the struggle no longer, but she left me a changed man.

I met Hogie in 1969 while teaching a course in Radical Psychiatry at the Free University in Berkeley. Eventually the two of us (and others I mention in the acknowledgments) established a RAP Center at the Berkeley Free Clinic. RAP stood for "Radical Approach to Psychiatry"[7] and was essentially a protest movement against the abuses of psychiatry as practiced in those days. We started a number of "contact" groups, in which participants were taught the principles of Transactional Analysis as it applied to cooperative relationships. The most popular contact group to evolve from this work was called "Stroke City." In this group we began to develop the techniques for learning emotional literacy.

FOUR DISCOVERIES THAT MADE A DIFFERENCE

1. STROKES & LOVE

Three times a week "Stroke City" gathered in a large room at the RAP Center. For two hours in the afternoon in this room, about 20 people could give strokes, accept strokes, ask for strokes, and even give themselves strokes in a safe, protected environment.

The leader of the group scrutinized every transaction. It was his or her job to make sure that people gave each other clean, positive strokes, unclouded by hidden or overt criticism. When needed, the leader helped the participants correct their transactions so that the strokes were heard and accepted when wanted.

We created these early meetings to teach people to get along in a competitive and harsh world. However, we soon observed an unexpected side effect. Participants would often look around after some time and declare that they "loved everyone in the room." They would speak of pervasive feelings of love as they placed their hand over their hearts and they left these meetings with a light step and a happy, loving glow on their faces.

We assumed that people were just cheered up by these activities in a manner similar to what happens at a good ball game. But upon closer examination it became clear that these exercises had a profound effect on the participants' loving emotions. They spoke of loving feelings, of having an open heart, of a transcendent experience of affection, or of an "oceanic" feeling. What had started as an exercise to practice how to be cooperative and positive turned out to be much more. It affected the participants' loving capacities in a powerful and heart-expanding way. It was then that we began to see the connection between strokes and love, and that learning how to exchange positive strokes might have an effect on people's overall capacity to love. Eventually it became clear that strokes and loving feelings are intimately related to each other.

2. THE POWER OF THE CRITICAL PARENT

During these Stroke City sessions, as we discovered the connection between strokes and love, we also discovered the pervasive activity of the Critical Parent. The Critical Parent (the "Pig Parent" as we called it in those days) is the internal oppressor, that inner voice that keeps us from thinking good thoughts about ourselves and others. For instance, when some of the participants tried to give or accept strokes, they would "hear voices in their heads" that told them why the strokes should not be given or taken. These inner voices told the participants, in subtle or overt ways, that they were stupid, bad, or crazy for getting involved in this strange exercise and that if they persisted they would be shunned and isolated from the group. We came to discover that virtually everyone has some kind of internal bully making him feel bad about himself. This phenomenon has been observed by many, who have given it different names: Freud called it the "harsh superego"; AA calls it "stinking thinking." It has been called low self-esteem, catastrophic expectations, negative ideation, the inert spirit, the dark side, the inner critic, and on and on. The fact remains that it is a pervasive, well-recognized presence, the cause of great distress in our lives and a common target of treatment in psychotherapy.

Eric Berne called this internal adversary the Critical Parent ego state. The Critical Parent does not necessarily have anything to do with our mothers or fathers, though it often does. It is, rather, a composite of all the put-downs that we received in childhood when people—parents, relatives, siblings, friends, teachers—tried to protect, control, and manipulate us. It is important to remember that the Critical Parent has an external source; it is like a tape recording of other people's thoughts and opinions. The Critical Parent is an external influence that is allowed to run (and sometimes ruin) our lives. It invaded our minds when we were young; fortunately, it is possible to turn it down or off, and effectively neutralize it when we grow up.

The Critical Parent is especially interested in preventing people from getting strokes. Why? Because when we get loving strokes in our lives we are much more likely to disregard the Critical Parent and its efforts to "protect" and control us.

Even though people need positive strokes to thrive, it became clear in Stroke City that when they tried to give, ask for, or accept strokes, they often experienced extreme, sometimes paralyzing anxiety, embarrassment, and even self-loathing. Some people hear a voice saying, "You're selfish. You don't deserve strokes," or "This is stupid, you'll make a fool of yourself; shut up"; others just feel anxious or self-conscious every time they give or ask for a stroke. In the face of such opposition, very few find it easy to exchange strokes.

Almost everyone has an internal bully who slanders him or her from time to time, especially when he or she is emotionally vulnerable. Part of the work of Stroke City—and emotional literacy training—is to recognize and neutralize the Critical Parent that not only attacks our self-esteem but also the self-esteem of the people around us. It became clear that defusing the Critical Parent was a priority when teaching people about strokes and love.

3. The Safety of the Cooperative Contract

Even though most people enjoyed Stroke City and wound up feeling good, there were always a few who felt bad, left out, afraid, or hurt. It became clear that they had succumbed to the attacks of the Critical Parent. To protect the participants from anything that triggered or supported the Critical Parent's activity, I decided to start each meeting with an agreement called a "cooperative (non-coercive) contract," which promised that the participants and the leader would never engage in any attempts to manipulate or power play anyone. It also specifically required that participants would never do anything they did not honestly want to do. The contract further promised that the leader would take responsibility to oversee these safety agreements and would not permit any transactions that came from the Critical Parent.

A contract of confidentiality was added to the cooperative contract in order to facilitate emotional safety and protection from the Critical Parent (see worksheets at the end of the book). These two agreements, cooperation and confidentiality, dramatically reduced the number of people who felt badly at the end of our Stroke City meetings. Consequently, more participants were able to enjoy the love-enhancing effects of the exercise.

These calming, trust-enhancing agreements are a very important aspect of emotional literacy training today. They keep the Critical Parent "out of the room" and establish a feeling of safety and trust. They are essential for the difficult and sometimes even frightening work that needs to be done to fully incorporate love and all the other feelings into our lives.

4. PARANOIA & AWARENESS

The RAP center eventually dissolved, but the essence of "Stroke City" continued in emotional literacy training workshops in the form of "Opening the Heart" exercises.

In these exercises, people often developed suspicions and fears about the motives and opinions of others in the group, sometimes to the point of paranoia. The standard psychiatric approach to paranoia was to disprove it point by point and to blame it on "projection." So, for example, if David thinks that Maria hates him, the traditional psychiatric wisdom presumes that it is David who hates Maria. Because he can't face his angry feelings in himself—so it is thought—he is "projecting" his hatred onto her.

This approach, in my opinion, made people more—rather than less—paranoid. I found in my work that paranoia generally builds itself around a grain of truth just as a pearl builds itself around a grain of sand. Our approach, in David's case, would be to search for some measure of validation for David's paranoid feelings. We found that once a grain of truth in the paranoid fantasy was acknowledged, the person was usually able to let go of his paranoid ideas.

So, if Maria admits that she is, in fact, angry at David's sloppiness, then David can let go of the idea that she hates him. That feeling, he can now see, is a paranoid exaggeration of her actual feelings of annoyance he sensed. David had simply picked up—intuitively—some hidden negative feelings from Maria and blown them up, out of proportion. When that happens, the Critical Parent usually gets involved and fans the fires of suspicion with its own negative messages. Once David sensed that Maria was angry at him, the Critical Parent could easily add: "Sure, she is mad at you, you are a slob."

This is important because in our emotional lives we often pick up hidden negative feelings from other people, which can be very disturbing. This validating method was inspired by the work of R. D. Laing, the Scottish psychiatrist who pointed out that when we invalidate or deny people's experiences, or how they see things, we make mental invalids of them. Ronald Laing[8] found that when our intuition is denied, we can be made to feel crazy even if we are perfectly mentally healthy.

For instance: A woman's husband is attracted to a neighbor and the woman picks up subtle clues about his hidden infatuation. If she confronts her husband with her suspicions and he denies them over and over while continuing his infatuated behavior, her nagging intuitive fears might build undaunted— with the help of the Critical Parent—to the point of paranoia.

Based on this information, we learned to search for the grain of truth when people developed intuitive, even paranoid, ideas rather than accusing them of being irrational or discounting their way of seeing things. By finding this truth, no matter how small, we could move a relationship away from suspicion, paranoia, and denial, back toward communication, feedback, and honesty. At the same time, by testing the validity of people's emotional intuitions and hunches, we trained their empathic capacities—which are essential to emotionally literate relationships. This approach is a basic aspect of emotional literacy training. We encourage people to express their hunches, intuitive perceptions, and paranoid fantasies and instead of discounting them, seek their validation, even if only with a small grain of truth.

These four ideas are the cornerstones of emotional literacy training:

    1) the connection between strokes and love,

    2) the importance of fighting the Critical Parent,

    3) the usefulness of safety contracts when learning emotional literacy,

4) the validation of intuitive, "paranoid" hunches as a way of training intuition and cleansing relationships of fear, suspicion, and Critical Parent influences.

EMOTIONAL LITERACY IN EVERYDAY LIFE

As I developed these techniques over the years, I have adopted them myself and invited my family members, friends, coworkers, and intimates to use them, as well. I wrote books, delivered lectures, and held workshops. All along, according to people around me, my emotional attitudes improved. I began to give and take love and affection more freely; I got in touch with my feelings, the feelings of others, and the reasons for their existence; I learned to be honest about how I felt and decreased my tendencies to be defensive when confronted. I was able to love and enjoy life more fully. Finally, I learned to acknowledge and sincerely apologize for my mistakes. Most important, however, is the realization that I am still a "work in progress," that I am still making improvements to my own emotional literacy.

One frequent super-stroke I get from friends and trainees is that I practice what I teach and that my behavior is congruent with my theories. That is not to say that I have achieved perfect emotional literacy, only that I continue to learn day by day.

The chapters you are about to read contain a training program that is a proven method of developing emotional intelligence. I have seen it work for me and people around me, so I know it can work for you.

Chapter 1

What Is Emotional Literacy?

To be emotionally literate is to be able to handle emotions in a way that improves your personal power and the quality of your life and—equally importantly—the quality of life of the people around you.

Emotional literacy helps your emotions work *for you* instead of against you. It improves relationships, creates loving possibilities between people, makes cooperative work possible, and facilitates the feeling of community.

We can all learn about our emotions; few are as smart in the area of emotions as they could be. As a long-time teacher of emotional literacy, I have seen the extreme discomfort some people, especially men, initially show at the mere mention of the word *emotions*. Men often fear that deep and painful secrets will be unleashed if they reveal their feelings. Most often, people think that emotional literacy training will lead to a loss of control and power in their personal and business lives.

1

There is some validity to the fear that a loosening of our emotional restraints could get us into trouble. But emotional literacy is not a mere unleashing of the emotions; it is also learning to understand, manage, and control them.

Emotions exist as an essential part of human nature. When we are cut away from them, we lose a fundamental aspect of our human capacities. By acknowledging and managing our feelings and by listening and responding to the emotions of others, we enhance our personal power. Being emotionally literate means that you know what emotions you and others have, how strong they are, and what causes them; it means that you know how to manage your emotions, because you understand them. With emotional literacy training, you will learn how to express your feelings, when and where to express them, and how they affect others. You will also develop empathy and will learn to take responsibility for the way your emotions affect others. Through this training, you will become aware of the texture, flavor, and aftertaste of your emotions. You will learn how to let your rational skills work hand-in-hand with your emotional skills, adding to your ability to relate to other people. Hence, you will become better at everything you do with others: parenting, partnering, working, playing, teaching, and loving.

Emotional Mistakes We Make

Emotional mistakes are very common and often very destructive. If you don't believe that is true, consider the following examples of emotional illiteracy I have gathered from the newspapers over the past years:

- When presented with a second-place award at a statewide high school competition, the bandleader threw the award into a garbage can. The school's director got into a verbal fight and insulted the judges, saying his band deserved first place.

- Following a football game in an upper-middle-class community, an irate mother shouted obscenities at one of the referees and then grabbed him from behind as he tried to walk away. Three men then joined in the attack, punching him in the face and breaking his jaw, which had to be wired shut for several weeks.

- Another parent actually killed the father of his grade school son's martial arts competitor and was sent to jail for many years as a consequence.

- In England, a wealthy magistrate and his wife lied under oath, saying the wife had been driving their Range Rover when it ran into a wall. The couple, who had been drinking, were worried the magistrate might lose his driver's license. The husband and wife were jailed for fifteen and nine months, respectively, when witnesses denied their story. And their marriage was wrecked by the stigma of being branded liars in their community.

- Top presidential adviser Dick Morris had to leave President Bill Clinton's campaign when it was reported that he shared state secrets with a prostitute in order to impress her.

- And let's not forget the historic mistake that President Bill Clinton committed when he allowed his need for sexual strokes to dominate his good judgment and involved himself in an intimate relationship with a 21-year-old White House aide. To the bitter disappointment of millions of his supporters, he gave his enemies an opportunity to nearly wreck his Presidency.

Daily newspapers are filled with stories such as these, accounts of successful and otherwise intelligent people making grave emotional mistakes. These are stories in which emotions like anger, fear, or shame make smart people behave stupidly, diminishing them and rendering them powerless.[9]

The truth is, we all make emotional mistakes, though perhaps not such extreme ones. Though our errors may not find their way into the newspapers, almost all of us would have to admit that at one time or another we have been inordinately moved by anger, fear, insecurity, sexual need, or jealousy, or have failed to take responsibility for an improper action. In the end, these mistakes weaken us and our loved ones.

An Intimate Dinner

Emotional literacy increases our personal power. I will make that point again and again throughout this book, but let me illustrate it here with a story.

Nancy and Jonathan, who'd been married for some time, had invited Robert for dinner. Nancy and Robert were old friends, going back to high school, when they had dated briefly. Nancy had prepared a lovely meal and had even brought out candles for the event. When they sat down to eat, however, Robert did not seem to care about the decor or the food in front of him. As he pushed his food around on the plate, Robert talked about his break up with his wife. She had come home from work one evening and announced that she was leaving the relationship. She assured Robert that there was no other man, but refused to give further explanations for her departure; she just did not want to be married any longer.

He was despondent and didn't know what would become of him. "Face it, she just doesn't want me anymore," Robert blurted out miserably, after two glasses of wine.

"Now how am I going to meet someone else? I'm not as good-looking as I used to be, and I don't look forward to cruising the bars and answering personal ads." Nancy understood perfectly what her old friend was talking about. The last year, she had spent more and more time in the mirror scrutinizing her face, worrying that she looked old beyond her years. Aging had made her feel a new sense of insecurity. She had a little more wine.

Jonathan's day had been a long and hard one so he excused himself and went to bed. Nancy and Robert found themselves alone. The two old friends talked more about Robert's failed marriage. Conversation then turned to the romantic beginning and long duration of their wonderful friendship. Then Robert made a remark about his fading attractiveness. Nancy, touched by his vulnerability, assured him that he was very handsome and should have no trouble finding another relationship. On the verge of tears, he squeezed Nancy's hand. She moved over on the couch and gave him a hug.

Then their cheeks and lips brushed, and they suddenly found themselves kissing each other passionately. After a few seconds Nancy sat up.

"Stop," she said. "We shouldn't do this."

Robert stood up, shaken. "I'd better leave," he said, too embarrassed to look at Nancy as he walked to the door. "I'm sorry." With one final glance at Nancy, he said good night and fled out the door.

Nancy slept fitfully. The next morning, after lying awake and thinking for a long time, she told her husband what had happened. She explained that they had both been tipsy and depressed, and that Robert seemed so needy that she had lost her common sense for a moment.

Jonathan's response was not as strong as she feared. He was upset at first, but then he remembered that they had a vow to be truthful with each other. He realized Nancy could have said nothing about the kiss and he might never have known. Yet he also imagined finding out in the worst possible way, a year from now, perhaps, when a guilty Robert confessed to Jonathan over a beer, or Nancy made a slip of the tongue.

Jonathan felt very secure about Nancy's love and he realized that Nancy meant to protect him by telling him about the incident. He could also see that she was very moved about Robert's predicament and also afraid that Jonathan would not forgive her for her loss of control. He realized that Nancy had been feeling insecure about her looks and his love for her and was vulnerable to Robert's attention. Although his first feeling was anger, he realized that making a scene wouldn't make him feel better or resolve the situation they were in. He realized he might turn a minor issue into a deep rift, damaging his marriage.

Rather than exploding with uncontrolled emotion or being overcome by jealousy, he tried to understand Nancy's actions from her point of view. Next he told Nancy of his anger, shame, and jealousy, but that he was able to overcome these feelings. He admitted that he had not been sufficiently attentive to her, wrapped his arms around her and hugged her warmly. Then, after explaining his intentions to Nancy and giving Robert a call, he drove across town to Robert's apartment.

"Nancy told me what happened," he said as he sat down on the couch in Robert's living room. "I don't like it but I understand. I'm not angry. I assume that this was a mistake and won't happen again, right?"

"God, no!" Robert assured him. "I'm so sorry."

"Thanks then," said Jonathan, offering his hand in friendship. "I think things will be okay."

An event that began innocently enough as a simple dinner party of old friends rapidly escalated into a sexual encounter. Emotional mistakes of this sort usually remain a dark secret, undermining all the relationships involved. Sometimes, if the truth comes out, the result is a fight (verbal or physical) leading to festering emotional wounds that eventually result in divorce and lost friendships. Handled badly, it could have led to the ugly sort of incident that we read about in the newspapers. It is the rare person who, like Jonathan, stops and thinks before deciding how to act on such an emotionally charged event. Yet Jonathan was able to speak about, sort out, and keep his feelings in check until he could express them in a productive manner and prevent his life from being damaged by emotions spinning out of control.

He was able to empathize with Nancy and with Robert's emotional state, realizing he might have done a similar thing in their place. As a result of their emotionally literate exchange, Jonathan and Nancy found a deeper respect for each other. They were able to open a dialogue about some of the rough spots developing in their current relationship, which actually strengthened their marriage. Talking about their emotions—expressing and controlling them—did not leave them feeling unprotected. Rather, it gave them a renewed sense of personal power and confidence about their relationship. It helped them flourish as a couple and enabled them to hold on to their friendship with Robert.

In many ways this story defines all the issues relevant to emotional literacy. Jonathan recognized his emotions; that he was quite angry and jealous. He understood the reasons for those feelings. He also empathized with Nancy's affection for Robert and with her wish to comfort him. Jonathan could understand that she was flattered by Robert's passionate attention especially since he, Jonathan, had been somewhat neglectful of her. In addition, he felt for Robert's sadness and fear of being alone and his attraction for Nancy. At the same time, Jonathan was very clear that he did not want the incident to reoccur.

On her part, Nancy was able to experience and then control her sexual impulses with Robert and later be honest with Jonathan. She was able to express her regret without being defensive or afraid.

Once he understood his feelings better, Jonathan was able to control his impulse to lash out. He recognized the importance for Nancy of keeping Robert's friendship. Finally, Jonathan realized the importance of keeping the vows of complete honesty with Nancy. All of this took skills that some people develop early in life, but that all of us can learn at any time. To devote time to learning these skills is to pursue emotional literacy.

The Forgotten Heart

Most people would not act the way Jonathan or Nancy did in the above story. Why is that? Why do so many smart people act in emotionally dim-witted ways? The answer is that we have lost touch with our feelings and never learned to deal with them. Why has this happened?

We are emotionally illiterate because we have suffered—and continue to suffer—so many painful emotional experiences. Our emotional systems have shut down. How does this happen? Let me begin with an example of physical injury.

Several years ago, Chuck, a young grape farmer on the ranch next to mine in Mendocino County, absent-mindedly reached into the rear of an operating hay baler. He felt a shock travel up his arm. He pulled his hand back and looked at it. With an odd lack of emotion or alarm, he wondered where his index and middle finger had gone. Rotating his hand, he saw the two fingers hanging by threads of skin.

At first, he felt nothing. Then the pain came thundering in, and at last he realized the two fingers had been cut off. Today, after many operations, Chuck's fingers—reattached to his hand but lifeless—constantly remind him of his accident. He is able to speak about the accident calmly even though others cringe just thinking about it.

Why did Chuck at first feel nothing and even now feel less than others when thinking about the dreadful accident? Because his nervous system, to keep him from being overwhelmed, temporarily went into shock and blocked the pain. The shock reaction is highly useful. Because Chuck didn't feel the pain, he had a few seconds to absorb what had happened, to think rationally about it.

Numbing is a natural response to trauma. Temporarily sparing us the pain of a wound gives us a chance to escape or to make life-saving decisions we could not make if we were blinded by agony and horror. However, the physical numbness that follows physical hurt is limited. It is short-lived, providing a brief period of anesthesia before the pain comes flooding in.

The numbness that invades us as the result of emotional hurt is similar. Physical trauma tends to occur as singular-incident events and the numbing it causes tends to be temporary. But in the case of cruelty and emotional trauma, when they persist, the numbing becomes chronic. We survive uncontrollable, ongoing psychological trauma by engaging defense mechanisms—psychological walls that insulate us from our painful emotions and separate us from hurtful people and the pain they cause us. Emotional trauma can be vividly re-experienced when we remember what happened. Emotional numbing keeps us from having tormenting thoughts, flashbacks, or nightmares. This may sound like a good thing, but it's a trade-off that can be very problematic. The psychological walls we erect to separate us from emotional pain can become permanent and also separate us from kind, loving people and feelings of joy, hope, or love. What keeps us from feeling emotional pain can also keep us from feeling emotional pleasure. In addition, the emotional walls we erect will, on occasion, collapse and we will be flooded by overcome chaotic, sometimes destructively strong emotions.

Some people oscillate between numbness and a disabling hypersensitivity to all emotions. Both these extremes are forms of emotional illiteracy. Whether emotions are absent or all too present, they fail to perform their powerfully helpful functions.

To recover from emotional damage it is important that we be allowed to repeatedly recall the traumas that caused our withdrawal and discuss them with sympathetic listeners. But typically we don't discuss and recover from such traumas. Instead, we just get used to a state of emotional numbness or chaos. Often emotional traumas such as parental abuse or alcoholism are often shrouded in shameful secrecy and don't get "talked out." Emotional traumas recur because we don't learn how to avoid the abusive, greedy, thoughtless, and selfish people who cause them; instead, we continue to relate to them and repeat patterns of emotional abuse. That is why the emotional traumas of a lifetime are likely to accumulate and fester in the dark recesses of the soul, crippling the victim's emotional heath.

My years of observation have persuaded me that not only sufferers of severe post-traumatic stress, but the majority of us, live in a state of semi-permanent emotional shock. Continually reinforced by recurring painful experiences, we have lost touch with most of our feelings. We forget traumatic incidents, don't remember how we felt, and don't know anyone who would listen patiently and sympathetically long enough to sort it all out. Consequently, we go through life emotionally anesthetized, with most of our feelings locked up in our hearts, constantly disappointed in a wary and unreceptive world.

Certainly not all of us come from abusive homes or have alcoholic parents. But even the commonplace ups and downs of coming of age and going through our workaday lives can be quite painful and result in a certain degree of self-protective numbness. Emotional shocks start early in childhood and continue throughout our lives. We are yelled at while playing an exciting game ("Will you shut up for a minute?"), or left alone when we are afraid ("You'll get over it."). Our parents may fight or simply ignore each other. We are hit or mocked by other children, sometimes even by those we think are our friends. We are capriciously scapegoated or cruelly snubbed.

Two examples well illustrate these types of silent trauma. One acquaintance of mine recalls how, when she was 12, her two most beloved friends handed her a letter in which they made fun of the way she looked and the way she danced, told her that she was stupid and stuck-up whale, and announced that they were dropping her as a friend. To this day she is flooded by feelings of sadness and anger when she thinks about that awful experience. Another friend relates how an older boy would come up to him every day while he waited in line for lunch in junior high school and make fun of his nose. He "went along" with the joke but was profoundly humiliated. This emotional torment went on for a whole school year.

Childhood can be full of emotional stress and even abuse. Often, the affection we crave is denied us or used to manipulate our behavior, given only if we are "good," withheld if we are "bad." While all this is going on, we are silently urged—within our families and at school—to conceal what we feel and long for. To "spill our guts" about our feelings, we are taught, would be rude, humiliating, or indiscreet. We are taught an emotional illiterate life style. To fit in, we must first close off from our emotions.

Often, our parents care only about our most obvious problems; whether a bully is after us or whether we are having trouble making friends. They are not often interested in our subtler agonies—rebuffs, embarrassments, romantic disappointments or feelings of inadequacy. Some parents are uncomfortable asking their children how they feel and rarely discuss their own emotions.

Hunger for Emotions, Love & Hate

At the center of all of this emotional confusion is love and its opposite, hate. We long to love and be loved. When instead of being loved we are treated hatefully, we are left to walk around with our thwarted needs and wounded feelings locked inside of us; we do not know what to do or who to speak to about them. We can't talk about our feelings, least of all about the love that we need. We don't understand the hatred that we feel and we understand the feelings of others even less. We hide our emotions or we lie about them or pretend not to feel them.

In our intimate relationships, where emotions are supposedly allowed free rein, many of us have been hurt so often that we remain subtly detached even in the throes of passionate love. Long-forgotten heartaches prevent us from fully letting go and giving ourselves to another without maintaining some secret, self-protective distance. We seldom allow ourselves the sweetest of emotional experiences—the vulnerable state of deeply loving someone without reservation. Instead, our resentments build upon our disappointments, sometimes developing to full-fledged hatreds. Once hatred is unleashed, it infects everything and love recedes completely.

Most of us sense that there should be more to life. We hunger for the intimacy of deep feeling. We hunger for a connection to others, to understand someone and be understood by him or her. In short, we long to love and be loved.

But how do we get there? We know in our hearts that being an emotional person, having heart-felt passions—loving, crying, rejoicing, even suffering—is a rich, valuable experience. In fact, we constantly seek indirect, artificial, or vicarious ways of having emotional experiences. We take drugs, or go to action, horror, and romantic movies; we watch sitcoms and soap operas on TV; we gamble, jump off bridges with bungee cords attached to our ankles, or parachute from airplanes all in search of emotional stimulation. These activities afford us a taste of what we long for and when we can't find the real thing we can eventually prefer them to the risks of real emotional participation.

A particularly horrifying example of this hunger for emotional experience is laid out by James Gilligan in his book, *Violence*.[10] Gilligan has worked for many years with prison inmates guilty of savage murders. These men, he has found, invariably live in a state of extreme emotional numbness. They report having almost no feelings, emotional or physical, to the point of thinking of themselves as living dead. The origin of these men's numbness is no mystery. Gilligan's research shows that in almost every case they were themselves victims of abuse, that they were battered by repeated physical and emotional traumas. They lived in a world devoid of reliable love and replete with hatred.

These men say that they commit their unspeakably violent acts hoping that such excesses will break through their numbness and cause them to feel something, anything. Such a person, having committed a brutal murder, may briefly feel that he has awakened from his deathlike anesthesia. But invariably, the emotions stirred up by the crime subside and the numbness returns.

This is a sobering example of how the trauma of lovelessness and hatred leads to numbness and deep emotional pathology. Left unchecked, this, hateful pathology passes down through generations.

There's an urgent need to break these cycles of lovelessness, violence, and emotional numbing. One way is by learning emotional awareness, to experience the emotion of love and eventually develop empathy—the open-hearted ability to feel what others are feeling and respond to it with compassion and kindness. Becoming aware of our loving feelings will also open us up to our angers, hatreds, and other negative emotions. To become emotionally literate we have to explore, understand, and learn to express all of them.

Psychopaths & Empaths

There are two kinds of people who seem destined to be powerful in the world: psychopaths, who feel nothing, and empaths, who are deeply in touch with the feelings of others. (Don't take these two extreme types too seriously; they are caricatures and are extremely rare in real life. I bring them up to make a point.)

Psychopaths can easily operate without the constraints that limit other mortals. They can lie, steal, extort, maim, and kill without guilt. When they get hold over other people, they can become enormously powerful. Consider Caligula, the Roman emperor, Adolf Hitler, Joseph Stalin, or Saddam Hussein. History is replete with obvious examples, but examples can be found everywhere, all around: in politics, business, gangs, and within certain families.

Empaths, on the other hand, gain power from their emotional skills. Born empaths have an innate gift for empathy that is fostered by their family and their teachers as they go through childhood and adolescence. Jesus Christ, Mahatma Ghandi, Mother Teresa, and countless others are historical and mythical examples of empaths. Their talent for loving others, fostering loving cooperation, for bringing out the best in people, gives them the power to get what people want most of all; more than money, more than political power or status, people want to love and be loved.

Again, these are two extremes; many powerful people are neither full-blown psychopaths nor empaths. But if you observe carefully, you will probably detect an individual's preference toward one or the other style. I, of course, am encouraging you to work toward the empathic ideal.

EQ & IQ

The value of being an emotional expert is not obvious to everyone, at least not as obvious as the value of being an intellectual expert. Research shows that if you have a high IQ (intelligence quotient), it's more likely you will do well in school and become productive, successful, and a good learner. Not only that, you'll probably enjoy long life and good health.[11] It seems that such happy results come from intelligence alone, but they don't. In his book *Emotional Intelligence*,[3] Daniel Goleman shows that emotional savvy is just as important in success as high IQ. Not only that, he shows that you need emotional intelligence to live a "good life"—one that allows you to enjoy the riches of the spirit. To live well, you need not only a high IQ but a high EQ (emotional quotient).

The term "EQ," though snappy, means less than you might think. It is a marketing concept, not a scientific term. An emotional quotient can't be measured and scored like an intelligence quotient. People have been rating IQ scientifically for nearly a century, though they argue about exactly what it means. Some say IQ precisely pegs an innate quality called intelligence. Others say it measures some less clear-cut quality of people who turn out to be successful in school, and eventually in life. Either way, you can validly and reliably measure a person's IQ, and it's proven an asset to have a high one.

EQ, on the other hand, can't be measured. True, researchers are pursuing the goal of measuring EQ, but no valid and reliable instruments exist at this time. So far, trying to rate somebody's EQ is like guessing how many beans there are in a jar: You can get a rough idea, but you can't be sure. Still, we can meaningfully speak of EQ as long as we don't claim to be able to measure it precisely. At the end of the book, there's a self-scoring questionnaire that will give you a rough idea of what your EQ might be, if it could be measured.

Emotional Intelligence & Emotional Literacy

The term "emotional intelligence" was coined by psychologists Peter Salovey and John Mayer.[12] Salovey and Mayer are research psychologists who are pursuing and slowly approaching the quantification of emotional intelligence. I coined the term "emotional literacy" 21 years ago, and it first appeared in print in my book *Healing Alcoholism* in 1979.[13]

What is the difference between emotional intelligence and emotional literacy? Briefly, as the title of this book indicates, emotional literacy is heart-centered emotional intelligence.

Emotional acumen can be organized around a variety of purposes. One extraordinarily successful version of emotional intelligence is the skill displayed by animators of feature films like "The Little Mermaid," "The Hunchback of Notre Dame," "Schreck," or "Monsters Inc." In these films, we see conveyed the most subtle, moving nuances in a wide gamut of emotions with only a few lines on a two-dimensional surface. These computer-designed emotional triggers are far cheaper and possibly more reliable than what any flesh and blood actor can provide. They are based on more than a century of research—beginning with Charles Darwin's 1872 book *The Expression of the Emotions in Man and Animals*,[14] in which he argued that all mammals show emotions in similar ways, thereby demonstrating their genetic commonality,[14] and culminating in a system of classification of 43 facial "action units" which combine into all the possible emotional expressions of the face.[15]

Another form of emotional intelligence is used when we want is to be able to influence people to buy or vote. We can use information available to sophisticated ad agencies which are quite successful in using people's emotions to accomplish their clients' goals.

As a far more dramatic example of the use of emotional intelligence, if what we want is to intimidate and terrorize people into compliance, there is intelligence that has been used from time immemorial and constantly updated by torturers around the world (the Inquisition, the Nazi Gestapo, the Communist NKVD, the Western Hemisphere Institute for Security Cooperation, formerly the School of the Americas) who achieve their purpose by emotional means.

On the personal level we can use our emotional skills to develop self-control or to soothe and isolate ourselves emotionally; or we can control others by creating guilt, fear, or depression. These skills can be seen as a form of emotional "intelligence," as well.

I see signs that many who agree that emotional intelligence is an important capacity have lost sight of what we really want: those emotional skills that improve people's lives—not just one person's or group's, but all people's. And the only emotional abilities that improve people's lives in that long-term, humane manner are the love-centered skills.

Heart-centered EQ

The avowed purpose of emotional literacy training is to help people work with each other cooperatively, free of manipulation and coercion, using emotions to empathically bind people together and enhance the collective quality of life. This purpose has caused me to organize emotional literacy training around the loving emotion.

The idea that love holds a central place in people's emotional lives is not a foregone conclusion. The classic book *The Emotional Brain; The Mysterious Underpinnings of Emotional Life*[16] by Joseph LeDoux fails to mention love even once in its index, while fear is mentioned more than 75 times. Daniel Goleman's *Emotional Intelligence*[3] has 20 index entries related to anger and only three index entries on love—and all in Chapter 1. Even as we all, deep in the heart, realize the importance of love, it is an emotion seldom discussed in detail by experts in the field.

Emotional literacy training is centered in the heart and consists of five principal skills:

1. KNOWING YOUR OWN FEELINGS

Do you know your true feelings? Many people can't define feelings of love, shame, or pride, nor can they tell the reason these undefined feelings are triggered. These same people are unable to tell how strong their emotions are, even if asked to categorize them as subtle, strong, or overwhelming. If you can't figure out what your feelings are or what their cause and strength are, you can't tell to what extent those feelings are affecting you and those around you.

2. HAVING A HEARTFELT SENSE OF EMPATHY

Do you recognize other people's feelings? Do you understand why others feel the way they do? Do you identify with another's situation or motives? This is the ability to "feel with" other people, to feel their emotions as we do our own. Most people have only the vaguest idea of what others are feeling. When we are empathic, people's emotions resonate within us. We intuitively sense what those feelings are, how strong they are, and what caused them.

3. LEARNING TO MANAGE OUR EMOTIONS

Are you in control of your emotions? Knowing our emotions and those of others is not sufficient to become emotionally literate. We need to know when and how emotional expression or the lack of it affects other people. We need to learn how to assert our positive feelings such as hope, love, and joy. And we need to know how to express our negative emotions such as anger, fear, or guilt, in a harmless and productive way or to postpone expressing them until a better time.

4. REPAIRING EMOTIONAL DAMAGE

Do you know how to apologize and make amends? Being human, we all make emotional mistakes and hurt others, but we seldom take steps to remedy our errors and prefer to "sweep them under the rug." We must learn to recognize what we have done wrong and fix it. To do this, we have to take responsibility, ask for forgiveness, and make amends. These tasks aren't easy, but if we don't carry them out, our unacknowledged mistakes will permanently poison our relationships.

5. PUTTING IT ALL TOGETHER

Eventually, if you learn sufficient skills, you develop an ability that I call "emotional interactivity." This means you can tune in to the feelings of people around you, sensing their emotional states and how to interact with them effectively.

As an example, Hannah used her emotional interactivity skills to avoid an emotional calamity at a Thanksgiving dinner I attended a few years ago.

When Hannah and her husband arrived at the dinner party, she immediately noticed that there was some sort of trouble. Everyone—the couple giving the party, their three grown children, and four young grandchildren—

seemed anxious. Jim, one of the sons-in-law, was off in a corner nursing a drink. Other family members were laughing tensely. The host and hostess seemed sad and dazed. Hannah took aside one of her friends and asked her why people seemed uneasy. It seemed that Jim had severely upset Judith, his wife's sister. Jim, a conservative thinker, had been arguing about child-rearing practices with Judith, who was much more liberal. The children had been horsing around and Jim, only half-jokingly, had told Judith she was spoiling her children and that they would turn into out-of-control teenagers, drug-addicted and sex-crazed. Judith got mad and told Jim in no uncertain terms to mind his own business. An uncomfortable feeling settled over the festivities.

Hannah took Judith aside and let her vent her anger about Jim's unwanted criticism. Then she spoke privately with Jim and listened to him express his feelings about bratty children and indulgent parents. But Jim saw, after talking to Hannah, that this argument was threatening to ruin everyone's Thanksgiving. Hannah brought the two of them together with Mark, one of the husbands who liked them both. Jim, Judith, Mark, and Hannah had a brief conversation in which hurt feelings were soothed and apologies exchanged. By the time dinner was ready, everybody was ready to sit down and enjoy the meal.

Hannah had done the right amount of talking to the right people to restore a pleasant emotional climate. She encouraged Jim and Judith to get together with her over lunch and further work out their conflict. She did all this easily and with a sense of loving good cheer.

How difficult is it to get to Hannah's level of emotional interactivity? It's a whole lot easier if you start while you are young. Like learning to speak French or to play the violin, you can acquire these skills far more easily in your youth, as you take advantage of the neurological "window of opportunity" for emotional learning. But if you didn't develop emotional skills during your youth. You can still learn them as an adult. In fact, most people acquire some emotional literacy skills early in life and add to them later. Now that you have this book, you have the chance to systematically improve your emotional literacy; study the lessons in these pages and put them into practice.

Summary

WHAT IS EMOTIONAL LITERACY?

When we are emotionally literate, we are able to make our emotions work *for* us and others around us instead of *against* us. We learn to handle the difficult emotional situations that often lead to fighting, lying, lashing out and hurting other people; instead, we learn to enjoy loving, hopeful, and joyful emotions.

Unfortunately, we are at constant risk of emotional trauma, most of it from simple everyday difficulties of living, some of it from betrayal and disappointment. Without an emotionally literate outlet, all of this emotional pain makes us freeze up to protect ourselves. When we hide within a protective emotional shell, we lose touch with our feelings and become powerless to understand or control them.

We hunger for emotional experience and we seek it in many ways. Emotional literacy training is a direct and effective method of reestablishing contact with our feelings and their power, especially the power of love.

CHAPTER 2

Emotional Awareness

Nearly everyone feels emotional distress when approached by a homeless beggar. Some of us try to shut off our feelings, preferring to pretend that she doesn't exist or somehow deserves her fate. Others feel guilt, and may think that they should be giving more money to charity. Still others will actually feel indignant and hostile toward beggars, treating them as unwelcome intruder into their lives.

My own reaction varies. Sometimes I feel fearful or embarrassed, while at other times I feel guilty or angry. If I decide against helping, I look away and quicken my pace. If I decide to help I hand over some coins without looking the beggar in the eyes. If he says, "God bless you," I don't feel blessed. The situation brings me too many unpleasant thoughts about what it must be like to be destitute. In the end I am happy to block the encounter from my mind. If I don't, I will feel off-balance and agitated for some time. Small wonder that I will go out of my way to avoid the homeless, even if it means crossing the street to do so.

This minute analysis of my emotional response may seem exaggerated and overdone, but think of your own experience. How much of what I describe goes through your mind when you run into a similar situation? How much of it do you experience without fully realizing your feelings? Most of us are not aware of the strong initial reaction that we quickly suppress in such situations. Is there an emotional aftermath for you after these kinds of encounters? Do they leave you shaken or indifferent? Angry, guilty, or self-righteous? Do they bring thoughts of "heartless" Republicans, "tax-and-spend" Democrats, or welfare cheats?

Although we don't usually notice it, most of us navigate through such challenging emotional seas daily. A driver cuts us off on a busy highway, a sales clerk is rude, a friend acts cold and distant, our partner rebuffs our advances. We are flooded by emotions and yet we may or may not be aware of the emotions we go through. Let us examine the roots of these emotional experiences in order to increase our awareness of them.

Roots of Emotional Awareness

Eric Berne, originally a psychoanalyst, gave birth to transactional analysis 50 years ago when he divided people's behavior (the ego in psychoanalytic parlance) into two portions:[30] the archeopsyche, which he called "the Child" for short and the neopsyche, which he called "the Adult." The Child was allied with our emotional nature and the Adult was rational and untrammeled by emotion.

Berne assumed that the two ego states, and later a third one which he called the Parent, had "specific anatomical representations" within the brain—in particular, that the Adult was located in the neocortex while the Child was located in a more primitive portion of the brain. He postulated that within short spans of time the ego states can become dominant—one at a time—and can be easily recognized by the average person.

Berne's ego state theory is firmly rooted in two major scientific trends: evolution and neuroscience. More recently, writers in evolutionary psychology have postulated that the mind is composed of "modules," which have evolved because of their adaptive benefits. These modules where first suggested by Noam Chomsky when he postulated that there exists a genetic grammar inborn in all humans that generates all human language.[17] The language module has been confirmed by ensuing developments in neuroscience and evolutionary theory. Further study has shown that there are similar modules for many other distinct traits such as how we process visual information or how we treat biological offspring. Steve Pinker in his book *How the Mind Works*[18] gives an excellent account of evolutionary psychology's mental modules . The ego states are three such hypothetical, distinct modules to be added to a human toolbox of adaptive capacities.

THE TRILINE BRAIN

In 1973, a quarter of a century after Berne postulated the three ego states, Paul MacLean,[19] senior research scientist at the National Institute of Mental Health, proposed that the brain is made up of three distinct subdivisions corresponding to three consecutive evolutionary eras: the reptilian, the limbic, and the neocortical.

These findings, very much in vogue for some years, have recently been questioned by neuroscientists who point out that the brain does not function as a collection of separate functional units but rather as a set of interlaced networks which evolve in intimate connection with each other. In spite of this objection it can be said without violating any neuro-anatomical dicta that the two evolutionary stages—reptilian and limbic—are distinguishable from each other and from the neocortex that developed later. At the end of the present stage of human evolution, larger and larger still size led to the full development of the neocortex.

The Reptilian Brain

The reptilian brain, the first highly complex neural bundle to appear in evolutionary history, supports the basic physiological functions: circulation, respiration, digestion, elimination. It is also involved in mating and territorial behavior—pecking order, defense, aggression, and the emotions of anger and fear.[20] In the human being it sits atop the spinal cord, and while it has evolved from its original form in lizards and snakes, it performs similar functions while at the same time communicating with the two subsequently developing brains, the limbic and the neo-cortical.

The Limbic Brain

Not concerned with its offspring, reptiles have no protective behavior repertoire and will abandon or even eat their own eggs as soon as they issue from the female. As evolution progressed and protection of the offspring became an effective survival strategy, the limbic brain, according to Lewis et al. in *A General Theory of Love*,[21] developed to fulfill that function. Protection of the young within a territory secured by reptilian function is the limbic brain's purpose. Protection required an affiliative drive, based on a hunger for contact and mutual recognition. This hunger for contact (strokes in transactional analysis terminology) maintained the bond between mother and offspring and generated closely knit groupings, all of which maximized survival of the young. The emotions of love, sadness, jealousy, and hope have their source in the limbic brain and can be observed in "higher" species such as cats, dogs, horses, and other warm-blooded animals.

According to this view, emotions are inborn, generated automatically in the most primitive—reptilian and limbic—portions of our brain. Fear, anger, sadness, love, hope, and happiness serve as constant reminders of our animal nature. These emotions are changed and shaped by the experiences that surround us throughout our lives.

The emotions are essential to our survival. They are instinctive responses to situations that call for action. We need them to make decisions, as Antonio Damasio[22] has shown in his research. Yet, most of us have little awareness of how strong our emotions are or even what triggers them. In fact, few of us even know what emotions we feel. Without such awareness, we cannot hope to develop the empathic and interactive skills that are the highest achievement of emotional literacy.

The Emotional Awareness Scale

Awareness of our emotions, a function of the Adult ego state located in the neocortex of the brain is the subject of this chapter. But first let me introduce the Emotional Awareness Scale (next page, figure 1).

The two extremes of the scale (zero awareness and total awareness) are unlikely to occur in real life but the places in between can be fruitfully explored. What follows is a description of each level of the scale. If you want to get an idea of where you stand on this scale, you may want to take the Emotional Awareness Questionnaire at the end of the book.

NUMBNESS. People in this state are not aware of anything they call feelings. This is true even if they are under the influence of strong emotions. Strangely, other people are often more aware of the numb person's feelings than she is. While a person in this state may not feel her

THE EMOTIONAL AWARENESS SCALE

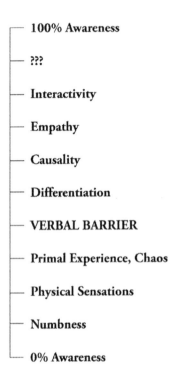

— 100% Awareness

— ???

— Interactivity

— Empathy

— Causality

— Differentiation

— VERBAL BARRIER

— Primal Experience, Chaos

— Physical Sensations

— Numbness

— 0% Awareness

own emotions, those around her can perceive them from cues such as facial expression, blushing, and tone of voice; however, she is likely to report only coldness or numbness when asked how she feels. Her emotions are in a sort of deep freeze, unavailable to awareness. Her experience is similar to that of an anaesthetized patient with a numb feeling covering up the pain of a dental procedure.

For example, Lucas was a successful 38-year-old accountant, whom I met, along with his wife, Clara, during a mediation of their marital difficulties. Clara had just given a tight-lipped, tearful account of her anger and hurt about the way things were between them. I turned to Lucas. He looked stiff and uncomfortable.

"How do you feel, Lucas?"

"Well, I feel that she is being unfair."

"Okay. We can talk about the fairness of what she says later, when we get to your point of view. But how does the way she talks about you make you feel, emotionally?"

He hesitates, wriggles in his chair, gives me a quizzical look, thinks. Finally, looking embarrassed, he says: "I guess I don't feel anything."

"I wonder. Let's see, do you have any sensations in your body? Some people feel butterflies in their stomach, lumps in their throat, a painful tingling feeling, or dizziness."

"Well, I feel sort of numb all over. Not now so much but when she was talking."

"You don't feel anything?"

"Not really. In fact, I feel really distant, as if I were in a fog."

For someone like Lucas, this state of unawareness is a common experience that comes over him in situations in which others might have a strong emotional reaction. On occasion, however, the emotional barrier he lives behind breaks down and his anger breaks through. Once or twice a year Lucas goes on a drinking spree. When that happens he becomes nasty, emotionally abusive, and on occasion breaks some furniture. Then he sobers up and goes through a period of guilt and self-abuse. These outbursts leave him feeling shaken and guilty, but he is too bewildered by his own emotions to arrive at any insight about them.

Eventually, renewed numbness returns and he becomes a detached, hard-working accountant again. In psychiatric terms, this state of emotional numbing is known as *alexithymia*.

PHYSICAL SENSATIONS. At this level of emotional awareness, the physical sensations that accompany emotions are experienced, but not the emotions themselves. In psychiatric terms, this is called *somatization*.

A person might feel his quickened heartbeat but is not aware that he is afraid. She may notice a pressure in her chest but does not identify it as sadness and depression. He might experience a hot flash, a chill, a knot in his stomach, or ringing in his ears, tingling sensations, even shooting pains. She may feel all of these sensations of the emotion, but not be aware of the emotion itself.

People can be helped to move into a more heightened state of awareness, anywhere on this scale. Lucas, for instance, is generally numb but he can be made conscious of physical sensations if he is questioned. As Lucas describes his numb state, I pursue my questioning:

"Good, that is a clear description of what happens to you emotionally when your wife complains about you. But let's look into your reaction further. Do you have any of the other physical sensations I described before? What else is going on?"

"Actually, I also feel a tight band around my forehead."

"Anything else?" I scrutinize his face. "Do you feel a headache?"

"Not really, but I have a feeling that I'm going to get one. I get pretty bad headaches. I'm going to have to take some double-strength painkillers when we leave here."

When people live in this state of emotional illiteracy, they often consume drugs that target physical sensations with an emotional origin. Although these drugs can have detrimental side effects, they do work temporarily for the person who is trying to cope with his emotional conflicts. They do so by eliminating anxiety, headaches, stomach aches, and other physical sensations that would remind them of emotional problems that need attention. Consequently, the conflicts don't go away, and the emotional issues remain unresolved. The drugs may temporarily erase or improve the unpleasant sensations, but they throw the body's chemistry out of balance and can lead to harmful short- and long-term effects.

Lucas, as an example, drinks alcohol and coffee and takes over-the-counter painkillers for his sore back and headaches. His doctor has warned him that ibuprofen and acetaminophen taken with alcohol can cause liver damage, so he takes aspirin, which gives him an upset stomach, for which he takes an antacid. He drinks two cups of strong coffee in the morning to wake up, then drinks caffeinated diet cola all day to keep himself alert. He also smokes to deal with tension and anxiety. At night he likes to have "a glass or two" of wine "for his health" and to help him unwind and get to sleep. None of this self-medication leaves him feeling very good, but at least it makes his discomfort manageable.

When people take large quantities of drugs and/or alcohol regularly, they can no longer accurately interpret their bodily experiences. Are these experiences emotional or chemical, exaggerated or understated, healthy or diseased? When a person is so frequently and heavily medicated, it is very difficult to tell exactly what is going on emotionally.

While in this state of emotional unawareness, people are able to inflict great emotional damage on others. Strong emotions that are unacknowledged can explode into irrational behavior. People act out, emotionally or physically abuse their friends and family, feel extreme guilt, then shut down. This pained narrowing of emotional awareness and creating a familiar cycle of abuse, pain, numbness, and increased emotional illiteracy.

EMOTIONAL CHAOS OR PRIMAL EXPERIENCE. In this stage, people are conscious of emotions, which are experienced as a heightened level of energy that is not understood and cannot be put into words. That is why I call it primal, because it is similar to the emotional experience of babies and lower mammals who clearly experience emotions but would not be able to name them.

A person in this emotional state is very vulnerable and responsive to emotions but not necessarily able to comprehend or control them. A person in the primal experience level of awareness is more likely to have ongoing uncontrolled emotional outbursts and fits of impulsiveness or depression than the person whose emotions are frozen out of awareness

Persons in the primal awareness level will usually be the ones to fall apart first when stress bears down on a whole group. They'll get scared, cry, miss work, drink excessively. Lucas, as an example of the opposite, works in an extremely high-pressure and stressful environment. At tax time, he is acknowledged as a "cool head" and trusted with crucial decision-making. His coworkers and supervisors do not find his coldness particularly likable, but he is highly valued by his employers for his efficiency.

Given the apparent risks of emotionality, some people conclude that emotional awareness and responsiveness are handicaps. However, in the long run, achieving high emotional literacy skills and awareness of emotional information will lead to personal effectiveness and power—even in our emotionally illiterate world. This is because a highly emotionally literate person will know how to control her feelings when necessary—when and how to hold them back or when and how to express them in most situations.

Of course, there are situations where ruthless lack of empathy and emotional coldness are required; jobs like contract killer, executive in charge of downsizing, or certain military Special Forces. In these situations a high level of emotional awareness would make it impossible to perform effectively. Obviously, a person aspiring to emotional literacy needs to avoid these types of activities.

THE VERBAL BARRIER. The emotions are generated deep in the primitive portions of our brain, while the awareness of emotions requires that we utilize our more evolved brain, the neocortex—essential to language, abstract thinking, and reasoning.

Mammals who have not developed the higher functions of speech, language, imitation, speaking, writing, planning, and symbolic reasoning are not able to transcend the chaotic or primal level of feeling. Human beings, whose neocortex makes those verbal skills possible, are able to develop higher levels of emotional awareness. Antonio Damasio, in his extraordinary book, *The Feeling of What Happens; Body, Emotion and the Making of Consciousness*[23] provides an excellent account of the neuro-biology of this process.

Awareness of emotions and the capacity to apply them in an emotionally literate manner depends on the ability to speak about what we feel and why. The language of emotions elaborately deals with the exchange of strokes, with the identification of emotions and the clarification of their causes, and with the expression of regret and the desire for forgiveness.

Crossing this linguistic barrier requires social environment with people who are friendly to emotional discourse. Once a person is able to talk about his emotions with fellow human beings, he can develop an increasing awareness of his feelings.

Learning emotional literacy is like learning a new language. In fact, learning emotional literacy is like learning a dialect of English, as different from spoken standard English spoken as, say, Ebonics (Black English Vernacular).

Ebonics, an African American dialect, uses English words but is definitely different from standard English with different syntactic structures and words not found in standard dictionaries that are required to express desired meanings. Likewise with emotionally literate language, a different tone of voice is used, words are combined into strange-sounding sentences, and a number of neologisms are used to communicate the desired emotional content.

Emotionally literate expression may not make sense to the listener who doesn't speak the "emotional language" and might conclude that what is being said is nonsense. It's easier for an Ebonics speaker to speak to other Ebonics speakers; they find and speak to each other with pleasure. Likewise, being able to speak in an emotionally literate language is a pleasant, safe, and soothing experience in a world that is not hospitable to the emotions.

Let me now elaborate the upper end of the scale, beyond the verbal barrier where we can develop an emotionally literate discourse.

DIFFERENTIATION. As we discuss our feelings with others, we begin to recognize different emotions and their intensity, as well as learn how to speak about them to others. At this stage, we become aware of the differences between basic emotions like anger, love, sadness, hope, shame, joy or hatred. We realize that any feeling can occur at various intensities. Fear can vary from apprehension to terror. Anger can range from irritation to hatred. Love can be felt at many levels, from affection to passion.

We begin to recognize that we often have several feelings at once. Some of these feelings are strong and obvious, while others are weak and hidden. Some are brief while others are long-lasting. For example, when we are feeling overwhelmed by jealousy, we may realize that the main feeling is anger combined with weaker feelings of unrequited love, tinged by shame. Someone else might experience jealousy as feelings of fear combined with intense hate.

Let's continue to pursue our troubled accountant, Lucas. When I asked him why he responded so strongly to his wife's recriminations, he said, "Because I was a little annoyed, I suppose."

"How about sad?" I asked.

"I guess so. Yeah, sad too," he said with emphasis, "and afraid that I'll lose control and retaliate and hurt her feelings. She is so thin-skinned."

"How angry do you feel?" I asked again.

"Not very angry, just annoyed."

"But if you are not that angry, why would you lose control?"

"I suppose I am angry." He was quiet for a moment, during which I noticed his color redden. "Yeah, I guess I am."

"Furious?"

There followed a long silence. By now Lucas's face was very red. Turning to his wife, his voice full of guilt and apprehension, Lucas finally said, "Yeah, thinking it over, I would say that I do feel very strongly about it."

I questioned Lucas further, making sure that I was not putting words in his mouth. As I helped him become aware of his emotions, it turned out that Lucas felt intense, blinding anger about his wife's accusations and was extremely afraid of "losing it" and "blowing up at her." And when he thought about it, he also felt despondent and afraid. Quite a bit going on for someone who initially felt nothing.

CAUSALITY. As we begin to understand the exact nature of our feelings, we also begin to understand the causes of those feelings: the event that triggered our emotional response, why we feel strong pride or hate, whence our fear.

To illustrate, Peter began feeling jealous the night he noticed his girlfriend, Jennifer, laughing at their friend Michael's jokes. At first he was unwilling to admit feeling jealous, even to himself, because he prided himself on being confident and secure. But he caught himself being irritable with Jennifer and had to admit that he was probably jealous.

This highlights the inevitability of emotional inter-connections between people. Some will disagree, but we can cause feelings in others and they can cause feelings in us. We begin to discover the alchemy of emotions: how our emotional tendencies (to be thin-skinned, assertive, or jealous) combine with the emotional tendencies and behavior of others. Eventually we are able to investigate, and in most cases understand, why we feel what we feel.

In this case, Jennifer's apparent flirtation with Michael made Peter jealous. Peter, feeling embarrassed, explained his jealousy to Jennifer. She told him she never meant to make him feel that. She explained that after a hard week at work she enjoyed a good laugh. Now that she was aware of Peter's feelings of jealousy, she decided to make an effort to pay more attention to Peter while Michael entertained them.

EMPATHY. As we learn the different emotions that we have, the various intensities with which we feel them, and the reasons for them, our awareness of our own emotions becomes textured and subtle. We then begin to perceive and intuit similar texture and subtlety in the emotions of those around us.

Empathy is a form of intuition, specifically about emotions. The workings of empathy can at times feel like clairvoyance. When being empathic, we don't figure out or think about, see, or hear other people's emotions. We just know, directly, what the other person is feeling. It has been suggested that empathy is actually a sixth sense with which we perceive emotional energies in the same manner in which the eye perceives light. If that is the case, then empathy takes place on an intuitive sense-channel, separate from the other five senses, and goes directly to our awareness.

Emotional illiteracy results when we fail, in our form-ative years, to adequately develop that sixth sense. The constant lying about and discounting of feelings that are commonplace to childhood experiences and the systematic refusal to acknowledge our intuitions result in the defeat of our inborn intuitive sense. Some people are born empaths with high sensitivity to emotions, and others are emotionally tone deaf,[24] if you will. Most of us are somewhere in the middle, and all of us can learn or relearn empathic awareness.

There is risk inherent in empathic awareness. The empathic response is a complex event. We may or may not respond empathically to other people's emotions, and if we do, we may or may not be aware of our own response. From this point of view the ideal two-person relationship is one in which both are empaths, aware of their emotions. Most difficult is the relationship between an empath and an "unpath," in which one person reacts to emotions the other is not even aware of. This latter situation can be very unsettling and when chronic, can be maddening for the empath.

Empathy, like all intuition, is imprecise and of little value until we develop ways of objectively confirming the accuracy of our perceptions. For example, returning to Peter and Jennifer's situation, Jennifer had begun to suspect that Peter was becoming more and more uncomfortable around Michael. Her intuition told her, even though Peter denied it at first, that he felt jealous. She couldn't understand why he would feel this way, since she was very affectionate and attentive toward him during their private time together. She thought that Peter's jealousy might have to do with Michael's good looks, and began to wonder if Peter was insecure about his appearance.

Jennifer had been reading about emotional literacy and learning some of the techniques, which she had described to Peter. When Jennifer decided to ask Peter if he was feeling jealous, Peter's first impulse was to deny it. He thought his jealousy was childish and was embarrassed to admit to it.

"Be honest, please," Jennifer requested, reassuring Peter she wouldn't think less of him.

"All right, I do feel a little jealous," he admitted at last.

"But Michael isn't especially attractive to me. I'm much more attracted to you."

"No, that's not it. You've made it pretty clear how much you like me," he said, smiling sheepishly. "But you know how tongue-tied I get sometimes. Michael is so at ease and funny; aren't you kind of attracted to that?"

Jennifer thought a moment. "Well, I guess so. But you're just as funny in your own way, when we're alone. Anyway, it's fun hanging out with someone like him, but you're the person I want to be in a relationship with. There are always going to be other people we both know who have qualities we like, but I am with you because I love you." She gave him a hug and they embraced happily for a moment.

But now there was something Peter needed to clear up. "Can I ask you a question about this?"

Jennifer agreed eagerly.

"I feel like you keep your distance from me when he's around. Actually, I am afraid you lose interest in me when the three of us get together."

She was shocked. "Not at all!" But thinking it over, she realized why he might feel that way. "I guess I've always thought it's rude to be affectionate with a partner in front of someone who's single."

"I can see that," Peter nodded thoughtfully.

She added, "But you may be right, perhaps I've gone too far. I think we could hold hands sometimes or sit closer together without making Michael feel bad. I'll try to do that more. I just was being very careful to be considerate."

Peter's intuition that Jennifer was attracted to something about Michael was confirmed. Also confirmed was that she was avoiding contact with Peter when the three were together. But his fear that she was romantically interested in Michael, or that Michael had eclipsed him, turned out to be untrue. Instead, he was pleased to learn how much she wanted to fit in with his friends and how hard she tried to be considerate of other people's feelings. An important aspect of his intuition was validated, his fears allayed, and he discovered something new about Jennifer—her thoughtfulness toward his friends—which he found very lovable.

Peter had sometimes dismissed Jennifer's declarations of love as exaggerations, but hearing her talk calmly about why she'd chosen to be with him, he suddenly felt more sure of her love. By following up her hunch about Peter's jealousy, and by initiating a discussion with him, Jennifer was forging a stronger, more emotionally literate connection between herself and Peter. Her intuition proved correct, and that gave her a chance to change in a way that helped Peter feel better—just a sample of the many fruits of an emotionally literate dialogue.

We hone our awareness of other people's emotions by asking questions; if the other person is unwilling to be honest and supply truthful feedback, we cannot make progress. *Honest feedback is the sole means of heightening one's empathic intuitions.* The process of truthful discussion and feedback greatly improves the accuracy of our subsequent empathic perceptions. Awareness of our own emotions is a prerequisite for empathy, and we learn to become aware of the intensity of other people's feelings. We also learn to understand why these feelings occur, sometimes as clearly as we understand our own feelings. Eventually, as our emotional literacy improves, our empathic perceptions become more accurate and reliable. We learn to trust our feelings and perceptions and to be more open about them. This transformation is achieved through a continual formulation of our perceptions, gathering feedback to check them out, and correcting our misinterpretations.

It is important here to draw a distinction between empathy and sympathy. Sympathy is an intellectual process with which we can deduce and even visualize another person's emotional state. That helps us understand and even predict how he or she might feel and act. However, sympathy is not an emotional but a mental process. It stands in relation to empathy as a paint-by-the-numbers canvas stands to an artist's rendering. We can fill in the proper spaces with the rights colors or emotions to get a reasonable facsimile of the real thing without actually involving ourselves in the emotional process.

Empathy is quite different. It involves our own emotions: We understand what others feel because we feel it in our hearts, as well as visualize it in our minds. Many people are not able to empathize with certain emotions in other people. In such cases, sympathy is clearly better than a total lack of awareness of other people's feelings and emotions. Sympathy is a minimal form of emotional intelligence. To move to the next level of emotional awareness, true empathy is required.

INTERACTIVITY. As I have mentioned, being "merely" an empathic person, an "empath" if you will, has its disadvantages. The empath is keenly aware of a complex universe of emotional information not largely perceived by others, some of it painful, perhaps even unbearably so.

Knowing how others feel does not necessarily mean we know what to do about it. People's emotional behavior seems to call for a response; but a response may not be wanted, welcome, or possible. Being highly empathic in a largely emotionally illiterate world can literally drive a person mad; an empathic person needs to know what to do with his or her awareness.

Emotional interactivity requires knowing how people will respond to each other's emotions and when that interaction might escalate for better or for worse. It means knowing people's emotions well enough to know how one person will react to anger or fear or sadness and how another will respond to love, sexuality, joy, or hope. Emotional inter-activity is based on the most sophisticated level of aware-ness, the ability to realize what you are feeling and what others are feeling, and to anticipate how emotions will interact. This further enables you to anticipate how two different people, given their usual emotional proclivities, will react in a given situation.

Emotions merge, fade, grow, and shrink in each other's presence and over time. Interactive awareness has to do with understanding the way emotions, like chemi-cals, combine to create new substances that one could not have guessed at from examining the component parts. These combinations can be creative, inert, or explosive, as in the chemist's laboratory. The ability to predict these reactions can come only from a great deal of accumulated experience or wisdom. The complicated awareness of how emotions combine—with each other, within people, and between people—is the highest level of emotional sophis-tication.

While this sounds very complex, a simple example of this wisdom at work is the way my friend David intro-duced his new love interest, Ramona, to his teenage daughter, Robyn, who tended to be shy and resentful of her father's female friends. Knowing that a face-to-face meeting over dinner might be hard for Robyn, David instead decided that his new girlfriend should come along while he drove his daughter to another city to visit her mother. This gave Robyn a chance to observe him with his new partner while she sat in the back seat, safely out of sight. This way Robyn learned about her potential step-mother-to-be. She had a better chance to get to know and like Ramona than she could at a potentially difficult dinner, where she might be nervous about being in the limelight. David's sense that the back seat drive was a better option than a three-way dinner arose from his heightened aware-ness of emotional interactions.

Another more complicated example is John and Dawn, a couple who had been in a month-long conflict. John was angry because Dawn was spending more and more time at her new job, which was the first job she had ever had that really excited and fully challenged her. John was used to being the principal wage earner and was feeling inexplicable jealousy and envy. He had always been prone to emotional outbursts, and lately he felt dangerously close to losing his temper. John and Dawn had a good relationship of many years, and John knew that Dawn loved and trusted him. However, she was easily frightened by his displays of anger.

They had had a number of unproductive emotionally charged conversations, and Dawn was beginning to retreat emotionally from him. John was feeling increasingly at a loss. Brooding about what to do, John remembered the time he and Dawn had had a heated disagreement while dining with her sister Marsha. Marsha's presence helped John control his temper, and Marsha had acted as a calm advocate for Dawn, which seemed to embolden Dawn to hold her own in the debate. John decided that it would be a good idea to invite Marsha over for Sunday brunch, explaining that he wanted her help to discuss Dawn's work. He talked the idea over with Marsha and with her approval called Dawn. All three on a good time and after a pleasant meal John gently suggested that Marsha sit near Dawn while he told her how he had been feeling. John knew that if he let his feelings loose under less protected circumstances he might get angry and Dawn would feel overpowered. He might get her to cut back on her work, but not without creating serious emotional repercussions later.

Marsha was a good choice for a mediator because she liked both of them and was not scared of John. Her self-assured, calming influence gave John the confidence to speak out clearly and gave Dawn the strength to stand up to his demands without being intimidated.

On the other hand, if Dawn was a different sort of a person, not afraid to hear John's emotional point of view even if he got excited and raised his voice, the situation would be very different and would call for a different, perhaps more direct approach that would not require a third person to mediate. John was aware of his own feelings and tendencies and equally aware of Dawn's. He knew from experience how their different styles were likely to interact, namely, that he would raise his voice in excitement and that she would likely comply but later be unhappy and irritable. He took steps to prevent the problems that would result if he acted impulsively. This kind of deliberate analysis of the emotional landscape of a relationship is the hallmark of emotionally literate interactivity.

Interactivity is a much-used concept in the communication age. In that context, it refers to intelligent interaction instead of passive acceptance. The same is true of emotional interactivity. Interactive awareness enables us to register the emotions within and around us, and to begin to see how they can be molded to creative ends, instead of going unnoticed and being allowed to run out of control. We can use our emotional awareness to have easier, more positive and productive interactions. Interactivity empowers empaths to use their awareness to navigate powerful emotional situations in a skillful way. Interactivity is the link between emotional awareness, which is the subject of this chapter, and the larger topic of emotional literacy, the subject of this book.

???. I have added this category of as yet unknown level or levels of emotional awareness to indicate a higher aspect of emotional awareness is quite possible. Perhaps there is awareness of the emotions of animals or other living things, which for most people is beyond the pale. Perhaps you, dear reader, are privy to such awareness. If that is the case I would be thankful if you communicated it to me via my web site: www.emotional-literacy.com.

Beyond Awareness

Neocortical, Adult activity, in addition to language and symbolic thinking, is also involved in the modulation and even modification of the lower brains' functions. Rational control of the procreative, aggressive, protective, and affiliative drives are one of the byproducts of human neocortical evolution. However, as Joseph LeDoux points out in *The Emotional Brain*,[16] there is a distinct asymmetry in the way these two portions of the brain affect each other, namely that the reptilian and limbic brain have a far greater influence upon the neocortical brain than vice versa, "making it possible for emotional arousal to dominate and control thinking." "Although thoughts can easily trigger emotions, Le Doux writes we are not very effective at turning emotions off."

Certain emotional disturbances are in effect situations in which an emotion has gone out of control. Anxiety disorders, like phobias and social anxiety, are instances of fear being triggered, in a seemingly uncontrollable way, by events that normally cause little anxiety. Major depression is a case of sadness gone out of control. Anger out of control can lead to pathologically antisocial behavior.

In those cases emotional literacy seeks to reverse the dominance of the emotions by equalizing the influence of the neocortex and the lower brain and bringing Adult control over the emotions. When the problem is that the emotions are squelched the goal is to release the feelings from Adult or Parent dominance.

Awareness is an essential aspect of personal power, but as we have seen, it is not sufficient by itself to produce the changes that emotional literacy requires. As a person's emotional awareness expands, he or she is able to learn the additional skills of emotional regulation necessary to act in an increasingly emotionally literate way. Learning awareness and literacy are essential lessons in this book.

Summary

EMOTIONAL AWARENESS

Awareness is an essential part of emotional literacy. You can question yourself on an emotional awareness scale and see where you stand.

The scale, from lowest to highest awareness, is as follows:

NUMBNESS: You haven't any awareness of your feelings.

PHYSICAL SENSATIONS: You experience chaotic emotions but you don't know what they are. You can't discuss them or understand them.

CHAOTIC EXPERIENCE: You are aware of an emotional charge but you can't understand, explain or talk about it.

VERBAL BARRIER: The boundary between chaotic experience and the capacity to understand emotions.

DIFFERENTIATION: By crossing the verbal barrier and talking about your feelings, you learn to differentiate between anger, love, shame, joy, and hatred.

CAUSALITY: Not only can you tell emotions apart, you also understand what causes them.

EMPATHY: You are aware of other people's emotions.

INTERACTIVITY: You are sensitive to the ebb and flow of emotions around you and how they interact.

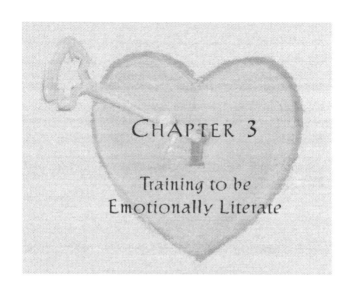

CHAPTER 3

Training to be
Emotionally Literate

You don't have to live in a state of emotional numbness, nor are you doomed to go through life feeling dejected, irritable, anxious, tortured by impulses, or emotionally out of control. And if you are an openly responsive empath, you don't need to be enslaved by other people's feelings. With a supportive environment and the transactional techniques outlined in this book, you can turn your emotions from a liability to a source of power.

Research shows you can heal the emotional chaos[25] of even extreme trauma in an environment that lets you express your strong feelings. In an emotionally literate environment, you can go right to the heart of any problem and if you are suffering from an emotional trauma, slowly but surely deal with its overwhelming emotions. The feelings that result from emotional trauma, including flashbacks, nightmares, anxiety attacks, and depression will lessen in time or even vanish when discussed with sympathetic friends, family, counselors, or therapy group members. Not only that, but you will discover a new emotional self and your relationships with others will be transformed.

It might seem that pursuing your emotional self is a fool-hardy adventure in a world such as ours. Those people around you who keep their strong feelings out of sight seem to have an advantage—they can stay the course when others are swamped by feelings. But in the long run, a truly productive life requires that we include emotional information in our choices. From a routine discussion of the news over breakfast to a critical decision such as marriage, you vitally need emotional knowledge for a well-rounded, effective approach to life.

The Appeal of an Emotionally Literate Life

Few things are as exciting as the rediscovery or refinement of our emotional selves. It is this excitement that fuels people's interest in emotional literacy workshops and training. When people glimpse the implications of an emotionally literate life they are often struck by its potential beauty. This drives some people to become Emotional Warriors in a crusade against emotional illiteracy.

For instance, a recently widowed grandmother of 55 who took one of my workshops in Germany wrote me as follows:

"Since I was a child I have known that life can be lived differently and I always had the vague idea that it had to do with honesty about feelings and no compromise about what I want, together with a strong love of people. I have tried to love people, I love my daughters and my grandchildren, but I see now that love is not enough. It can go very wrong, as in my marriage. From now on I will be a crusader for emotional honesty. Nothing less will do. Thanks for showing me the way."

This woman has set her goal very high. She can reach it, not all at once, but over time. The key is to work systematically. At the end of this chapter I briefly describe the three training stages I have developed to teach emotional literacy: Opening the Heart, Surveying the Emotional Landscape, and Taking Responsibility.

The Training Process

But first, let's take a look at the process that this training follows. It is possible to begin emotional literacy training by paying attention to any of the emotions, but over the years I have found that the most effective gateway through our emotional barriers is the expression our loving nature. Emotional literacy training begins and ends with the heart.

In my work with couples, women often complain that men do not love them or don't love them enough, that they do not express loving feelings, or that they gladly take affection but don't give it. (See Hogie Wyckoff's article "The stroke economy in women's scripts".[26]) To be sure, there are always a few men who simply don't love their wives (or partners). But more often than not, men do love them but suffer from an inability to express their love convincingly. These men often wonder, eventually, why it is that they can't be more loving in their actions. Women make this complaint often about men, but men can have the same grievance about women—that they are cold and don't show affection. This inability to show love is one example of emotional numbness. Emotional numbness is by no means exclusive to men, though research shows that their emotional range is, in the whole, more restricted. But no matter which gender is involved, the solution is the same: loosen the fetters upon your heart.

Let me give an example: Jack and Gina came to my office and were very upset. After a long courtship and a year and a half of blissful marriage, things were falling apart. They were "fighting about everything," and their fights were getting so bad that their relationship seemed destined to end in disaster.

In a very brief preliminary discussion, I could tell that they were still in love. They had always been unable to deal effectively with certain typical emotional issues. But these issues—having to do with sex and money—were now piling up between them. I could have spent quite a bit of time asking questions about their childhood or trying to mediate their arguments, but instead—because I could see that there was a lot of good emotional capital between them—I suggested that they start talking about the good things in one another that made them fall in love in the first place.

This calmed them down and got them back onto common ground. Soon they were speaking civilly to each other and their feelings of love were reawakened as they remembered the "good old days" of their relationship. In essence, they had reopened their hearts to each other. Over the next month, I had them explore their emotional makeup. Using emotional literacy training transactions, I asked them to talk about their feelings for each other, revealing their anger, their deepest fears, and their greatest hopes.

By the time they finished exploring each other's hereto hidden emotional landscape, they had a new understanding and appreciation for one another. This new understanding provided a way to recognize how they had damaged their relationship with a series of hurtful missteps that needed to be corrected. Now they were ready to accept responsibility for their actions. Painfully, they admitted their wrongdoings and accepted each other's apologies. This was difficult but it brought them great relief, often mixed with tears of joy and hope. Their mutual love had returned and their relationship was strengthened. The above discussion, in a nutshell, shows the process behind this program. Following is a discussion of each of the three steps in the training process:

1. OPENING THE HEART: This comes first because the heart is the virtual seat of our emotions. It is in our hearts that we feel good when we are happy, in love, or joyful. It is here that we feel bad when we are sad, angry, and heartbroken. So I start by freeing the center of our feelings from the restrictive impulses and influences that keep us from showing love for one another.

2. SURVEYING THE EMOTIONAL LANDSCAPE: Once the basic heart-opening groundwork is done, you can look around and take note of the emotional terrain in which you live. You can learn to know just what you are feeling, how strongly, and why. You become aware of the ebb and flow of your emotions. With your loving feelings as a secure base you note the emotions being experienced by others and see how their feelings are affected by your actions. You develop empathy. You begin to understand how all the emotions interact and sometimes create feelings that can flood over you and others. In short, you become more aware of and wiser about your own feelings and those of people around you.

3. TAKING RESPONSIBILITY: People make mistakes in their relationships, little ones and big ones. When you make a damaging mistake you need to apologize and take responsibility for your actions. It also stands to reason that you should make amends and correct your behavior so the mistake won't happen again. Taking responsibility for our actions and correcting our behavior is the final phase of emotional literacy training.

An Energizing Process

What I have described may seem like a lot of work. You may think the process will drain you. However, at the end of the day it will, in fact, energize you. We squander huge stocks of emotional energy when we block the expression of our emotions. Whether it's keeping silent about a shameful trauma, holding in our affectionate enthusiasm so we do not embarrass ourselves, or locking away a painful memory, we waste shocking amounts of energy hiding and repressing our feelings. Letting go of these feelings not only releases the power of our emotions, it also gives us back the energy we wasted keeping them pushed down. And letting others express their emotions brings them closer to us, energizing both parties with love and affection. That's why those who learn these lessons report such dramatic energy-enhancing effects.

It's an exciting prospect, isn't it? But we shouldn't rush forward blindly; it's best to go about it in a thoughtful and systematic way. I'll show you just how to do this using clearly explained, step-by-step, transactional exercises.

Strategies of Emotional Literacy Training

If you practice the three emotional strategies discussed in this book: Opening the Heart, Surveying the Emotional Landscape, and Taking Responsibility, you will see dramatic changes in your emotional awareness, attitude, and effectiveness. In particular, you will learn:

▨ How to know what you want and what you feel; how to be truthful about your emotions; how to pursue fulfillment of your emotional needs.

▨ How to manage your emotions creatively; when to hold back and when to express your feelings.

▨ How to deal with emotional numbness or turmoil.

▨ How to apply your knowledge of emotions at work, at home, in school, in social groups, and "on the street."

▨ How to improve and deepen your relationships and forge long-lasting, honest connections with people.

▨ How to practice a love-centered approach to personal power in a society that is moving in the direction of mistrust, loneliness, anxiety, and depression.

Where to Start

What follows are the three stages, each made up of four steps of emotional literacy training. This set of emotionally literate transactions is arranged in order of difficulty. You may find that you already have some skills with transactions 3 or 4 and want to start with transaction 5. Or you may feel confident with all 15 but need to fine-tune your skills. But it will be useful to understand all the components of emotional literacy training before you can begin to practice it effectively. If you know where you are going, it will be easier to keep a steady course and find your way.

The stages and transactions of this process are like a road map to emotional transformation. Each step is a specific, emotionally literate transaction. As you learn each transaction and practice it in your everyday life, you will learn the elements of an emotionally literate communication and emotional style. Some of these transactions will be familiar to you; some will seem outlandish. Some of them will be easy, some extremely difficult. The transactions early in the list are generally easier than the ones toward the end. The first transaction—asking for permission—has been numbered "zero" because it is different from the others in that it is suggested that it be used every time that an emotionally charged exchange is planned. Here are the transactions and stages that will be covered in detail in the chapters ahead:

EMOTIONAL LITERACY, TRAINING STEPS
0. Asking for permission.

STAGE ONE: OPENING THE HEART
1. Giving Strokes
2. Asking for Strokes
3. Accepting Strokes
4. Rejecting Strokes
5. Giving Ourselves Strokes

STAGE TWO: SURVEYING THE EMOTIONAL LANDSCAPE
6. Action/Feeling Statements
7. Accepting an Action/Feeling Statement
8. Revealing Our Intuitive Hunches
9. Validating an Intuitive Hunch

STAGE THREE: TAKING RESPONSIBILITY
10. Apologizing for Our Mistakes
11. Accepting Apologies
12. Rejecting Apologies
13. Asking for Forgiveness
14. Granting Forgiveness
15. Denying Forgiveness

Summary

TRAINING TO BE EMOTIONALLY LITERATE

You don't have to go through life emotionally numb or tyrannized by your emotions. In the right environment, with supportive people, you can learn a more satisfying emotional existence.

You'll find the quest for emotional literacy exciting and satisfying. The process will energize you as you experience the power of your emotions and as you stop wasting energy to repress or hide them. To do so, you must practice with others who share your emotional goals.

OPENING THE HEART: With supportive people and friends, you take part in simple acts of mutual affection.

SURVEYING THE EMOTIONAL LANDSCAPE: You focus on the ebb and flow of your own emotions and those of the people around you. Listening with an open heart, you strive to understand emotions and their reasons.

TAKING RESPONSIBILITY: You admit that your minor or major mistakes have hurt people in your life. You lovingly apologize and make amends.

BOOK TWO

Emotional
Literacy
Training

CHAPTER 4

Opening the Heart

An open heart is the foundation of emotional literacy and a prerequisite for the next two stages of emotional literacy training: Surveying the Emotional Landscape and Taking Responsibility. In the heart-opening portion of the training, we apply the findings of the original Stroke City exercise, namely that *by the simple act of exchanging positive strokes in a safe environment we can cultivate our inborn loving capacities.* That is why the training starts here, by learning how to give and take affection—or in plain English, by learning to love.

The Power of Strokes

Scientific evidence strongly suggests that to maintain emotional and physical health, we need strokes and have to know how to procure them. The undeniable evidence is that love and intimacy affect health and recovery from illness. This finding has been elaborated by Dean

Cornish, MD in *Love and Survival: The Scientific Basis for the Healing Power of Intimacy.*[28] He writes:

> "Love and intimacy are at the root of what makes us sick and what makes us well; I am not aware of any factor in medicine—not diet, not smoking, not stress, not genetics, not drugs, not surgery—that has greater impact on our quality of life, incidence of illness and premature death from all causes."

The procurement of strokes is the motivation for interaction. People seek love; love is exchanged transactionally, through strokes. Strokes can be physical or verbal. Physical strokes are any form of touch: hugs, kisses, caresses, backrubs, holding hands, or being held. Verbal strokes are statements that acknowledge some feature of another person in a positive way. Verbal strokes can be about a person's looks, clothing, intelligence, generosity, creativity, emotional literacy, kindness, integrity, work ethic, practical skills, dignity, leadership ability, artistic talent, sexual responsiveness or prowess, honesty, playfulness, practical wisdom, elegance, tact, or any other attribute the person possesses. Listening carefully as someone speaks, or giving someone you love a bunch of beautiful flowers can be a powerful form of stroking; "action strokes" if you will.

Marcel and Carry are a good example of how important action strokes can be. Marcel is a very busy teacher. He has a full teaching schedule and a great deal of committee work. He brings work home from school and is always busy.

Marcel is not very good at giving verbal strokes, but Carry, his wife, has accepted this shortcoming and his busy lifestyle because he is very good at giving her action strokes. He makes sure that when she needs to talk to him he pulls himself away from his work and listens with complete attention. He brings her breakfast in bed on weekends and he buys her little surprise presents. In short, he is constantly showing her affection with his actions, in addition to the physical strokes they exchange whenever time permits. Even though Carry would like to have longer conversations and more quality time with Marcel, she loves him and gives him action strokes just by being there with a loving attitude and supporting him in his work.

They both feel stroked, even though they exchange few verbal strokes and would like more. They have, for the time being, adjusted to the situation.

Another example of actions strokes is Thomas and Louis, two lifelong friends who exchange strokes almost exclusively at the action level. They get together regularly, talk about sports and cars, go fishing, or have a beer or two. There is no question of their mutual affection and respect, and yet they never exchange physical strokes, and exchange verbal strokes only by complimenting each other's truck or prize catch. Both men get strokes they need from each other's friendship. Their wonderful friendship could be further improved if they opened their hearts more and learned to give each other verbal and even physical strokes, but they are both well satisfied with each other.

Strokes can vary in their intensity or in the kind of reaction they cause. Some strokes are "super strokes" because they are especially wanted. One teenager I knew longed to hear that he was good-looking. It took years for him to ask the question of someone and when he finally did he was lucky to receive a major life-long boost in self-confidence. A super stroke can also be a stroke that comes from a special person, like a revered teacher, our spouse, or a person we have a crush on.

The attributes that receive positive comment are not always obvious or expected. We learn about ourselves from the strokes we get. For example, Jane has asked David to give her some strokes about something other than her looks. Jane is surprised when he tells her, "I envy the way you get so emotional. I wish I felt as sure about what I feel as you do. I like it that you have such strong emotions." Jane had assumed that her tendency to cry at movies or during arguments was annoying. She learned something about herself and was surprised (and pleased) to find that David admired her for this sometimes dubiously positive ability to show her emotions.

On the other hand, there are negative strokes. These can be obvious insults, such as "Why can't you do anything right?" or subtle, hurtful remarks couched as jokes. Sometimes negative strokes can come disguised as compliments when they are based on a comparison between two people. For example, Jean's mother frequently said to her, "You have all the looks in the family, and your sister Sara has all of the brains." A statement like this was noxious to both of the girls, who came to resent their mother for pigeon-holing them. It took Jean years to realize that they were *both* good-looking *and* smart and that their mother had badly confused them with her devious compliments. Her sister Sara still hasn't gotten over believing that she is ugly.

Another example of a stroke that could feel good but be toxic would be a comparison such as, "You are my most loyal friend." Again, this might seem like a positive stroke, but it is actually harmful, because it denigrates the person's other friends. Far better would be to say something like: "I appreciate your loyalty. It's pure as gold."

Sometimes a stroke that we actually want can be delivered too strongly, making it unpleasant. An affectionate grandmother who smothers her grandchildren with wet kisses or a spouse who showers more physical attention to his wife than she may want at times are both examples of good strokes gone awry.

Finally, strokes are sometimes given insincerely. These strokes are supposed to feel good but rarely do. They are sometimes called "plastic fuzzies" (as opposed to "warm fuzzies"). You may want to read *The Warm Fuzzy Tale*,[29] my fairy tale about "warm fuzzies" and "cold pricklies" that makes these distinctions perfectly clear. Even though they feed our hunger for recognition and we do better with them than with no strokes at all, negative strokes are toxic. The fact that the term "warm fuzzy," which I "invented," is being used by politicians, captains of industry as well as teachers and actors is a super stroke for me.

Trouble in Stroke City

Our basic nature cries out for abundant strokes. Unfortunately, positive strokes don't always flow freely, even among people who love one another. It should be simple and pleasurable both to give and to get them. But when most of us try to pass strokes back and forth, we fumble. This vexing problem was exemplified by one of my clients, Thomas, who found that whenever he tried to say something loving to his wife, he felt as if he were being choked by an invisible hand. Though he knew what he wanted to say, he literally couldn't get the words out. On one occasion, when confronted by his wife's frequent question, "Do you love me?" he did manage to force the words from his mouth. But all he could do was utter a barely understandable, froglike croak: "High ghoulu."

Fortunately, his wife had a rich sense of humor, and much to his relief, burst out laughing.

"What?" she asked.

"I love you, I love you," he replied sheepishly, undercutting the powerful message by his hurried, embarrassed tone of voice. This farcical example of a common problem shows the fear and even physical difficulty we run into when we try to speak about our loving emotions.

People's evasions take many forms. "You know I love you," they may say. Or, "How many times do I have to tell you that I love you?" Or "Would I be here if I didn't love you?" Sometimes the sentiment is ruined just by the tone of voice—ironic, irritated, or dismissive: "Yes, dear, of course I love you." In any case, the loving stroke that one partner wanted and the other actually had was not truly delivered. This occurs commonly because few of us are truly free to love and to speak of love openly. Even though we talk and listen to talk about love constantly, we are inhibited about giving, asking for, or accepting strokes. We are especially uptight about giving strokes to ourselves. What restricts us?

Most of us follow unwritten rules about the exchange of strokes. When we break these rules, we are likely to experience disapproval or even harassment. If you warmly hug a loved one on a busy sidewalk, chances are that some people will look away uncomfortably. If you are over a certain age and kiss or cuddle each other on a bus, other passengers may look embarrassed or frown. If you call your wife or husband from your office and say, "I love you," you open yourself up to remarks from the person at the next cubicle. But these prohibitions don't come only from outsiders who disapprove. They are also severely enforced inside each of us by our inner Critical Parent.

What are the unwritten rules about giving and taking strokes? Where do they come from? I first became aware of the prohibitions placed on stroking at one of Eric Berne's weekly meetings. We would try different "psychological experiments" as a form of recreation after our "scientific" meeting. On one occasion, I suggested we try one of the "games" played at that time by members of Synanon, a drug-treatment organization. In this game, group members would go at each other with savage criticism. They did this because they believed that the drug addict's character required that type of tough approach for change to happen.

Following Synanon's example, we went at it with glee and the nasty comments—some offered supposedly in jest—flowed freely. I found the experiment quite disturbing. My feelings had been hurt by some of the things said about me, but of course I did not tell the others of my distress. I would have been too embarrassed to admit how badly I'd been hurt and how much I wanted the affection and respect of the group. Instead, I proposed that the next week we do just the opposite of what we had done and say positive, loving things about each other.

Everyone agreed. But at the next meeting, no one could think of much to say. Though we eventually muddled through, it was clear that producing positive strokes was hard, while producing negative ones was easy. Not only were people inhibited about giving strokes, I discovered, but also about asking for them or even accepting them. Giving oneself strokes was definitely taboo.

Years later, Diana, a group therapy member, helped me see this problem even more clearly. I noticed one afternoon that she seemed uneasy when someone in the group offered her a compliment. I asked her about her uneasiness.

"When Robert said something about me being pretty," she explained, "I was afraid that other people in the group might be thinking, 'I don't think so.' That if I smiled too much, or was moved, they would think I looked needy and pathetic and pity me."

I thought it would be interesting if I suggested that, as an experiment, she ask Robert to give her the stroke again. "But it would seem so pathetic and needy," she insisted, squirming in her chair.

Emboldened, I suggested, "Well, then, how about giving yourself the same stroke? Would you be willing to tell yourself that you are pretty?"

This was a shocking idea and by now, there were tears in her eyes. I feared that I had made her cry and asked if I had been too demanding. I asked her why she was crying; she said that Robert's compliment had shaken her up. She wanted to believe him and to thank him, but was terrified of allowing herself to look pleased. I asked her to reflect on why she might be feeling this way. After thinking about it, she remembered that when she was in grammar school and high school, the unpopular kids were always most likely to be made fun of when they acted pleased with themselves. Seeing this over and over had taught her to be afraid to accept strokes, especially a stroke that she really wanted. She felt that it might cause her to become emotional in public and therefore—in her mind—make her seem ridiculous. Asking for strokes or giving herself strokes frightened her even more.

Diana had no trouble giving strokes, but she had severe inhibitions against accepting them, asking for them, or giving them to herself. Unfortunately, Diana was not unusual. Some of us reject any strokes that are given to us. Many of us, like Thomas, choke up when we try to deliver them. All of these reactions keep us from being close to people.

THE STROKE ECONOMY & ITS RULES

Have you ever felt a great desire to tell someone that you liked or loved him or her and found yourself unable to do so? Or have you found yourself wondering if a friend, family member, lover, or spouse really loves or likes you and if so, in what way and for what reasons? Have you thought of coming right out and asking, only to dismiss the idea? Do you put yourself down, giving yourself negative strokes as a way to fish for positive strokes, hoping that somebody will contradict you? All of these are the result of our submission to the rules of the Stroke Economy.

The Stroke Economy is a set of rules enforced by people around us, but even more importantly, by our own Critical Parent, that critical voice we hear inside that keeps us from giving and accepting positive strokes. The Critical Parent would have us live by these Stroke Economy rules:

- Don't give strokes you want to give.
- Don't ask for strokes you want.
- Don't accept strokes you want.
- Don't reject strokes you don't want.
- Don't give yourself strokes.

Why People Accept Negative Strokes

When all the people in a social group follow the dictates of the Stroke Economy to a certain extent, the quantity and quality of strokes exchanged are dramatically reduced. People will become stroke-starved. One very important and damaging side effect is that stroke-hungry people begin to accept or even seek negative strokes because they can't get positive ones. In the same way that people dying of hunger or thirst will eat rotten food and drink polluted water, people will also accept and take in negative strokes when they get sufficiently stroke-hungry. But negative strokes, like salt water and rotten food, make people sick. Getting healthy, life-affirming strokes is a major human predicament and pursuit.

As I have said, one of the most important discoveries I made in the 20 years I have been teaching emotional literacy is that by systematically breaking the rules of the Stroke Economy and providing people with a steady diet of positive strokes, people's hearts will automatically open. They will experience loving feelings they have not before experienced and the effect will spread out from them to their families and friends. I have seen many people (myself among them) develop their loving capacities over time, simply by giving strokes, asking for strokes, accepting the strokes they want, rejecting the ones they don't want, and giving themselves strokes.

Opening the Heart

Let me now introduce step by step the emotionally literate transactions which, if used when appropriate over a period of time, will effectively open your heart:

The first transaction of Opening the Heart is giving strokes, but before you start opening your heart, let me introduce an even more important transaction: asking for permission.

EMOTIONALLY LITERATE TRANSACTION #0: ASK FOR PERMISSION

I number this transaction "zero" because it a special transaction which should always precede any of the others. Why? Because any emotional communication can be a daunting experience. It is not uncommon in emotional literacy training to see people cry when they are given a much-desired stroke, asked a particular question, or given a needed apology.

When about to speak about strokes or any other emotional issues, asking the other person's permission:

- Gives a warning that a difficult communication is coming and provides an opportunity to prepare and be ready to listen.

- Allows the receptionist a choice about dealing with the issue at this time (he may have a splitting headache or a big exam in the morning).

When we follow this approach, we ensure that our statements will fall on fertile soil and generate productive responses. By asking for permission every time we are about to engage in an emotion-laden transaction, we avoid possible shock, defensiveness, fear, and even anger in the other person.

Most important, though, the recipient has to be given a genuine choice. We need to be willing to accept that the timing of our statement might not be particularly good, and if so, be ready to wait for a better moment. By going slow and easy, we prepare ourselves and the other person for the strong emotional response that might occur.

The most important first step toward learning emotional literacy is finding one or more persons to learn it with. Once you have found a person who is interested in an affectionate, thoughtful dialogue and you are planning to give a stroke or address an emotional issue, give him or her an idea of what you are about to say with a comment like:

"Can I tell you something I like about you?"

"I would like to talk about a feeling I had when we talked the other night."

"I have been wanting to apologize to you for something I said a while ago."

"May I tell you what my favorite thing about you is?"

"I have been feeling upset lately. May I explain?"

"There is something going on between us that I don't like. Are you interested in talking about it?"

Many people find these preambles highly awkward. That is because what needs to be done is unusual and sometimes seems unnatural and likely to be ridiculed as nauseatingly "California-ish." Emotional discourse can be dismissed as "psychobabble" or laughed at by people who are uncomfortable with their emotions. Nonetheless, these are important methods that produce the changes we are trying to make. Although asking permission to make any kind of emotion-laden statement might seem odd, practice will remove this strangeness over time and will improve your interactions.

EMOTIONALLY LITERATE TRANSACTION # 1:
GIVING STROKES—OFFERING HONEST & TRUTHFUL STATEMENTS
OF AFFECTION

Throughout this book, the theme of honesty will come up again and again. The fact is that heart-based emotional literacy cannot develop in an environment of lies or subtle dishonesty. For people to feel the trust and confidence in each other to acquire the skills I teach here, they have to make a commitment to truthfulness and honesty. (See "Notes for Philosophers" at the end of this book.)

Giving strokes is the first opportunity to practice the all-important principle of truthfulness. A stroke has to be honest, not manufactured. Anything else will be confusing and counterproductive. As our hearts open, so do our intuitive powers. It is confusing to our intuition to receive a stroke that is presented as heartfelt and sincere but instead (at the intuitive level) feels phony and unreal. When we decide to give a stroke, we must make sure it is authentic. For some people, honesty is easy because they know how they truly feel. For others, that is where the learning begins.

For instance, Daphne was taught early in life that being nice and saying nice things to people was important, even if that was not the way she felt. After years of saying nice things and never considering their truth, Daphne doesn't really know how she feels about people or what it is that she likes or doesn't like about them. Therefore, she has to concentrate to become aware of her true feelings. Sometimes, when she is being truthful with herself, she realizes she has nothing complimentary to say. When that happens, she cannot honestly give a verbal stroke. At such times, her Critical Parent makes her feel very guilty and she reverts to the values she was raised with and invents a stroke. This prevents her from understanding that simply listening to people, touching them lightly, or smiling can be a stroke, as well—an action stroke. Daphne could sit back and tune in to how she feels and resist the nagging of her Critical Parent, who urges her to "Say something nice, stupid!" Unless she is true to herself, she cannot be true to others. And others will intuit when she is not telling the truth and treat her with hidden suspicion, dismissing her.

STROKE ENEMY # 1:
THE CRITICAL PARENT

The main problem in giving strokes is our Critical Parent, who acts like an emotional prison guard, giving us discouraging messages that keep us from getting in touch with our true feelings. Here are some of the messages our Critical Parent whispers or shouts to stop us from giving strokes:

- If the stroke is not wanted, you will look foolish.

- The stroke you have is inappropriate, badly worded, and clumsy. If you say it, you will only make a fool of yourself.

- It will seem like a sexual advance.

- It will just seem like insincere politeness anyway, so why take the risk?

- Someone will think you are needy and desperate for friendship.

- If you get overemotional, you will just make everyone feel awkward, and then you might really get upset.

The Critical Parent concocts complicated damning scenarios. For example, "If I tell my sister that I really miss her, I might start crying. Then she'll be embarrassed, I'll be embarrassed, and we'll both feel stupid and everyone will think that we are from a stupid family." Or if I ask my friend if he loves me, he might think that I am gay and panic and avoid me forever." Notice, however, that all these scenarios end up in the same way: not okay, rejected, alone, loveless, and excluded from the tribe, group, or family.

By giving strokes in spite of these Critical Parent injunctions, we see the appreciation for our strokes and begin to get strokes back. We feed our hunger for strokes. We realize how wrong the stroke economy rules really are. When that happens, the voice of the Critical Parent gradually loses its power to inhibit us.

For example, Melanie is shy about giving strokes. This is another way of saying that her Critical Parent harasses her whenever she tries. She wishes she could be more generous; she would like to give some strokes to her friend, Janelle, who is moving away to New York. Overcoming her Critical Parent, who enjoins her to be cautious, she tells Janelle that she thinks her new, short hairstyle really becomes her.

"I love it. You should keep it like that!" Melanie says enthusiastically.

Janelle laughs nervously and says, "Oh, I think it's too short."

"Seriously, it's perfect for you," Melanie adds, chastened.

Still no response. Having stuck her neck out to give a sincere stroke, Melanie is sad and disappointed. Her Critical Parent tells her that Janelle hated the stroke, that it was inappropriate and may have been construed as a sexual advance. Later, after Melanie rejects her Critical Parent's harassment and thinks with her Adult ego state, she realizes she gave that stroke quite abruptly, without preparing Janelle for her unusual enthusiasm. Maybe Janelle is uneasy about her appearance and doesn't quite believe Melanie's flattering remarks.

She resolves to ask for permission. The next time they talk, Janelle tells a very funny joke.

"You know something?" Melanie says, still laughing.

"What?" Janelle asks, worried.

"May I tell you something I like about you?"

"Okay," Janelle says, cautiously.

"I really like your sense of humor. At least we can still laugh together on the phone after you move."

Janelle smiles, looking a little sad. Ignoring the sadness, Melanie is encouraged; finally, she has hit on a stroke that Janelle is able to respond to.

Emboldened by her success, Melanie addresses Janelle again. "May I tell you something else?" After Janelle's silent agreement, Melanie says, "You know, you're like a sister to me; I'm going to miss you so much!"

Now Janelle doesn't know what to say. She smiles nervously, then looks serious. She promises to call as soon as she arrives in New York. Again, Melanie is disappointed. What went wrong? Does Janelle feel guilty for leaving? Do emotional goodbyes make her self-conscious? Her Critical Parent pitches in with: "You never leave well enough alone. You are always pushing for more. You spoil every situation with your greediness."

Next day Melanie goes out and buys a card for Janelle. She writes: "Dear Janelle, I had the feeling last night that when I said you were like a sister to me and I'd miss you, I made you uncomfortable. I'm not sure how you took what I said, but all that's important to me is that I let you know what a great time I always have with you, and how smart and funny I think you are. Best wishes in your new home."

To Melanie's delight, Janelle wrote her a postcard two weeks later:

"Dear Melanie, Got your sweet card. I love you too. Very busy. Let's stay in touch. Your New York sister, Janelle."

By starting out slowly, learning to ask for permission, being honest with her feelings of affection and refusing to go along with her Critical Parent and Janelle's, Melanie was gradually learning the fine art of exchanging strokes.

She was desensitizing herself to the initial fear and awkwardness her Critical Parent always exploited and working her way up from simple to more profound expressions of positive, loving emotions. Over time, both she and Janelle became freer in their ability to give and receive affection. This happened because Melanie decided that she wanted to give Janelle strokes and was not dissuaded by her own Critical Parent or by Janelle's initial inability to receive them. With practice, Melanie will find giving and accepting strokes easier and easier.

The Poetry of Strokes

A stroke should always aspire to be a love poem. Brief and shy perhaps, or full throated and showy, one word or a long paragraph, but from the heart and always hopeful and sincere. Even if it is an action stroke without words or physical contact, a stroke works because it is a heartfelt act of kindness and love extended to another person.

To open up our hearts, we need to examine our lives and ask ourselves how many times in a day we actually perform this basic function of human nature—expressing love to another person, whether within our family, at work, or on the street. We need to ask ourselves how we express this love: Is it done almost imperceptibly, passionately, or somewhere in between? And if we discover, as is often the case, that we are depriving others of the love we have for them, we must resolve to do something about it and then go ahead and do it.

EMOTIONALLY LITERATE TRANSACTION #2:
ASKING FOR STROKES—REQUESTING THE AFFECTION THAT WE NEED

It's nice to get strokes, but sometimes they aren't available or the ones that are available are not the ones we want. We can spend years silently and timidly waiting to learn whether the people in our lives think we are smart, creative, good-looking, or kind. We try to guess if they find these positive qualities in us. We seldom, if ever, simply ask. We have become so obedient to the Critical Parent that the idea doesn't even occur to us. But there are times when we need to ask for strokes. At such times, we need to decide what to ask for and from whom.

Asking for strokes is riskier than giving them. We can never be completely sure that the strokes we want are going to come our way. The other person may not honestly be able to tell us what we would like to hear. It is therefore more hazardous to ask for a specific stroke ("Do you like the way I sing?" or "Will you give me a hug?") than to ask for *any* stroke a person may have, physical or verbal. The risk of the latter request is that we might get a stroke we don't want. The reality, however, is that in most situations, with most people, when we ask, we can get what we need.

For example: "Hi, Daphne. I'm having a really bad day. I feel embarrassed saying this, but I could really use some moral support about my writing. Do you have any strokes that you can give me?" Such conversations are normally complicated, made almost impossible because people expect each other to lie out of politeness. That's why it's so important to find good friends, or a lover or spouse, someone who will be honest and gentle. With someone like that you can ask:

"I just bought these pants. Do you like them? Do you think that I look good in them?"

Or: "I wrote a letter to the editor of the *Times*. Would you read it and tell me if you like it?"

Or: "I just had a tough conversation with my teenager. I'm feeling unsure about being a good father. You've seen how I am with my daughter; can you give me some strokes about my parenting?"

Or: "I looked at myself in the mirror this morning and I can see some new wrinkles in my face. I'm afraid

I'm becoming old and ugly. Can you tell me something you like about my face?"

Or: "I've been feeling very lonely at this party. Everyone is having such a good time. Do you want to dance with me?"

And of course: "Do you love me?" "Why do you love me?" and "Why else do you love me?" "Will you tell me again?"

Again, the Critical Parent will be fiercely involved in making sure these questions aren't asked (or answered), throwing around all manner of objections such as:

"That's a silly question," "You are coming across real needy," "You'll never get an answer," "Don't be childish" and so on and on, *ad nauseum.*

EMOTIONALLY LITERATE TRANSACTION #3:
ACCEPTING STROKES—TAKING IN STROKES WE WANT

When we get stroke-starved, we need strokes in much the same way that we need food. We are like a starved, tired person coming home from work, considering a month-old drumstick from the back of the refrigerator. We may become confused about what strokes to take or to reject.

We may be stroke-starved because we simply are not getting any strokes at all. We may develop a sort of stroke anorexia, lose our appetite for strokes and allow ourselves to starve of stroke hunger. Or we may be extremely picky and refuse any but certain, sought-after strokes. On the other hand, strokes may be offered to us that are toxic but seem attractive on the surface, and we may take them. Or we may knowingly take bad strokes like a person drinking sea water who knows it will be deadly. Given all these complications, there is always the danger that we will take strokes we should reject or that we will discount and not accept a beneficial stroke that we actually want.

Case Study in Acceptance

In one of my training workshops, after I explained the Stroke Economy and established the ground rules (no power plays or pressure to do anything, and no lies), I invited the participants to go ahead and break any of the five rules of the Stroke Economy.

A thoughtful quiet ensued. After some of the people gave and took strokes for a while, Anna began to talk about how she had plenty of permission to give strokes but no permission to take them and even less to ask for them.

I asked her if she wanted to do something about it.

Shyly she agreed, and I asked her what she wanted to do.

"I would like to give everyone here a stroke," she said.

I responded that this would be very nice but it might be a bit too easy for her. How about asking everybody to give *her* a stroke?

She was taken aback by the suggestion and shook her head.

I said, "Well, in that case, what if just one person here gave you a stroke?"

After some thought she nodded, "Okay."

"Good!" I said. "I think you should ask."

She found the very thought of this very difficult but eventually, after some fretting, she said to the group, "I would like a stroke from anyone here."

Valery eagerly offered, "I am so glad you asked; can I give you a stroke?"

"Okay," said Anna.

"I have known you for some years now, and what I like about you most is how sweet and loving you are."

Anna's face darkened. "Thank you," she said.

I saw that something about the stroke did not work. "Can I ask you, Anna, did you take that stroke?"

Thinking about it, she said no. She explained that while she heard the stroke, she also heard her Critical Parent say, "She really doesn't know you. That sweetness is just an act, always being nice, never being yourself."

I turned to Valery and asked her if she agreed that she didn't know Anna. Valery responded, "I know that she is shy and sometimes doesn't speak her mind, but she is very loving, and I know that for a fact."

Turning to Anna, I asked if she believed Valery. Anna looked doubtful.

"Do you think she is lying?" I asked.

"Maybe to make me feel good."

"But we have a specific agreement not to do that. Do you really think that?"

Anna thought for a few seconds. "I guess not."

"You know what, Anna?" I asked. Anna looked at me curiously. "I think to do this right you need to apologize to Valery; she offered you this heartfelt stroke, and instead you listened to your Critical Parent and rejected it. Would you consider apologizing and asking her to give you the stroke again?"

Anna, shocked by this suggestion at first, agreed. She apologized and asked for the stroke again. This time she heard it, smiled happily and took a deep breath as a warm blush spread over her cheeks. Clearly, Anna had leaped a big hurdle and everyone was moved. It may be quite a struggle to convince someone to take a heartfelt stroke, but it is worth the effort. Giving a stroke that is rejected or discounted can be embarrassing and disappointing for both parties, so it is reasonable to gently persist. When we give a stroke and suspect that it hasn't been fully accepted, it is important to investigate:

"Did you hear what I said? Do you accept it? Do you believe me?"

"It seems that you did not quite take in my compliment, am I right?"

"Please take the stroke. I really mean it."

"Didn't you like what I said? Why? Is there some other way I can phrase it?"

Keep in mind that for stroke-starved people, strokes sometimes act like water on a parched houseplant. At first the strokes may sit on the surface or run right through and not be absorbed at all. Watering dry soil may take extra care, but eventually water will soak into it. Sometimes the process must be repeated before there is any effect. Therefore, it is important to watch people as you give them strokes.

A stroke is a transaction that involves both the giver and the taker—not just with words but biochemically. Because it is an emotional event that involves the whole body, it takes time to take its full course. You can tell from the recipient's body language if the stroke is accepted or rejected. A deep breath, a quietly satisfied look or a smile are the best signs that a stroke has been heard, and more important, fully taken in.

EMOTIONALLY LITERATE TRANSACTION #4:
REJECTING UNWANTED STROKES—"THANKS, BUT NO THANKS"

The most obvious example of unwanted strokes is sexual strokes from someone we are not interested in. Most people can attest that it is very hard to categorically reject certain unwanted sexual strokes. A woman may be unable to reject a sexual comment because she feels it would be impolite to ask the person to stop. A child may be repulsed by what seems to be a sexual stroke, but does not dare to take it that way. A man may feel it his manly duty to respond to a woman's advances.

Learning to reject unwanted strokes is an important skill. We need to stop the unwanted stroke to avoid an uncomfortable or even damaging situation. Furthermore, when adults or older children impose sexual strokes on young children, those strokes are undeniably harmful. Curiosity and hunger for attention can result in children seeming to consent to sexual strokes, which will damage them emotionally. When we teach kids about molestation, we are essentially teaching them how to reject injurious strokes, and if necessary, get away from (and report) someone who won't take no for an answer.

There are other unwanted strokes that are less obvious than the ones mentioned above. These are not toxic strokes; rather, they are strokes that seem to limit us. For example, a beautiful woman may eventually tire of being constantly told she's beautiful. When that stroke is offered to her, it may make her feel one-dimensional, as though that is all anyone ever notices about her. If she thinks that the affection of others is based only on her beauty, then she may feel trapped into always playing the part of the pretty woman. Actually, she may be starved to have attention paid to her ideas, her work, or her integrity. With emotional literacy training, she would learn to explain:

"I'm sorry but I've been feeling lately that you only compliment me for my looks. I guess I feel neglected in other ways. For instance, I really wanted you to congratulate me on my job promotion. I know you don't mean to offend or disappoint me. Instead of strokes about my looks, could you give me other compliments instead?"

Similarly, a hard-working man who is constantly praised for his hard work and responsibility may tire of such praise. Perhaps he would like to have more fun, and he feels that he is only appreciated for his willingness to work. Or perhaps he has other talents or admirable qualities that he feels no one notices, such as being good with his kids, or being sexy.

When people begin to resent a stroke they often receive, they usually think they must always play the same old role to be appreciated. Of course, rejecting an unwanted stroke can be uncomfortable and possibly even damage your relationship with the other person. After all, when a person gives you a compliment from the heart, he or she expects to hear at least a thank you. In these cases, it is important to decline the stroke gracefully. In an open-hearted manner, state what you would rather hear, and why, and ask for the stroke you really want.

Separating the Wheat from the Chaff

For some, the most difficult task in this enterprise is separating the strokes we do want from those we don't want, and separating the strokes that are good for us from those that may be harmful. When we don't seem to want a certain stroke, we need to ask ourselves: "Do I reject this stroke because it is not right for me or is this a perfectly good stroke that my Critical Parent doesn't want me to have?" When we decide that the stroke offered is good and we want it, we must fight our Critical Parent and accept it. If we figure out that it is bad or redundant, then we should reject it.

Lately there has been a society-wide movement to help people (mostly women and children) reject strokes they don't want. A positive development because it protects from the damage unwanted strokes can cause, the negative side of this movement is that we have built up additional barriers against all sorts of strokes. People are afraid that their heartfelt strokes will be misinterpreted and they will be perceived as being harmful or that in some cases simply holding a crying child or being friendly with a coworker will be construed as sexual behavior. This new stroke phobia is most evident in the way people who work with children are now refraining from any physical affection, no matter how innocuous. The fear of legal or social persecution reinforces the effects of the Stroke Economy and contributes greatly to the current emotional numbing of people and an increase in social alienation and depression. It would be far better if children learned to reject unwanted strokes, thus freeing grownups to be loving with them. This is why it has become even more important to teach this distinction between the desired strokes that are good for us from the unwanted strokes that are bad and should be rejected. The same is true of the work place where fear of sexual harassment accusations are severely inhibiting friendly and affectionate behavior so important to a good work situation.

EMOTIONALLY LITERATE TRANSACTION #5:
GIVING OURSELVES STROKES—HEALTHY SELF-LOVE

While there is no real substitute for getting strokes from others, knowing how to give ourselves strokes is an important skill that is very useful when we get into a difficult situation, away from people who will stroke us. Most of us have been conditioned to think of "patting ourselves on the back" as immodest and conceited or even needy, foolish and humiliating. There is nothing to be embarrassed about in giving yourself strokes, even if you are not in great need of them. There may be good things about you that others do not know, or perhaps people in your life have been stingy with their strokes and you need a few more than you are getting.

For instance, after everyone had devoured a meal that Colin made, he looked around the table and asked,

"Well, did you like the food?"

Everyone nodded and grunted appreciatively, but offered little in the way of detailed response. Somewhat disappointed by the lack of praise, Colin said,

"Well, if you ask me, I thought the chicken was really tender and the rice was spicy and fluffy. I can see you all enjoyed it. I'm really happy."

"Are you upset with us? We really did like it. I know I did," said Carrie, worried that Colin was reprimanding them for their meager responses.

"No, I was just giving myself a little pat on the back for a job well done," he declared. The others smiled approvingly, and everyone felt good about the exchange.

We especially need to be able to stroke ourselves to counteract the negative strokes we get from our Critical Parent telling us that we are stupid, bad, crazy, ugly, sick, or doomed. For this we need to understand how to respond when our Critical Parent attacks us.

If your Critical Parent says that you are stupid, unreliable, and can't be trusted, you need to be able to contradict this slander and tell yourself something like: "I am intelligent and a high achiever. Considering the fact that I have two well-cared-for children at home, I know I am reliable and can be trusted. I am proud of how smart, reliable, and trustworthy I am."

If your Critical Parent says that you are fat, ugly, and doomed, you need to be able to say, "So I don't have the looks of a model. But I have a nice healthy body and people have told me they find me handsome and attractive. I like the way I look and I am sure that I will meet the right partner for me." The same approach is useful when you are assaulted by other people's Critical Parents.

In Transactional Analysis, the source of this kind of positive "self talk" is called the "Nurturing Parent." Certain people are able to preserve a bedrock compassion toward themselves, despite criticism and ridicule from peers. This healthy self-love suggests a well-established, core confidence supported by the Nurturing Parent. However, no matter how good a Nurturing Parent we have, it can eventually run out of energy if it isn't replenished with strokes. The Nurturing Parent neutralizes the Critical Parent and is like a battery that is available as long as it is kept charged with a steady input of positive strokes.

Summary

Opening the Heart

We start this training by opening the heart because the heart is at the seat of love around which emotional literacy is built. We open our hearts and strengthen our bonds with others by giving and receiving strokes.

We all need positive strokes. There are physical strokes such as hugs and kisses; verbal strokes and action strokes, such as being attentive or helpful or showing empathy or affection.

The Stroke Economy is a set of rules that prevents us from giving and asking for strokes, accepting the strokes we want, and rejecting the ones we don't want. It also prevents us from giving ourselves strokes. The result is that we become stroke-starved and are willing to take whatever strokes we can get.

By releasing ourselves from the rules of the Stroke Economy, we free ourselves to be loving with each other and satisfy our need for strokes. We disobey the inner Critical Parent, which enforces the rules of the Stroke Economy and interferes with every attempt to gain emotional literacy.

We learn how to give people the strokes they want. We ask for the strokes we want. We learn how to accept or reject strokes. When we are stroke-starved, it's difficult to reject a stroke we don't want. That is one reason we need to learn to ask for and accept strokes we want. This keeps us stroke-nourished so that we are not tempted to take toxic strokes. We should reject toxic strokes, but when our Critical Parent prevents us from taking a stroke we want, we should defy this prohibition.

With our Nurturing Parent, we can give ourselves strokes to build our self-confidence. Still, we need to get strokes from others to keep our Nurturing Parent strong.

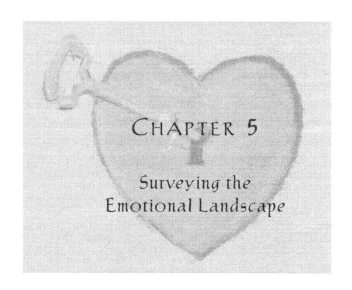

CHAPTER 5

Surveying the Emotional Landscape

Emotions can be classified as positive or negative depending on how they feel. If they feel good, they are positive; if they feel bad, they are negative. This is not to say that positive emotions are good and negative emotions are bad; all emotions are important and useful.

Opening the heart is concerned with the exchange of an exclusively positive emotion: love. Even so, the exercise can tap major negative emotions because of the Critical Parent's opposition to positive exchanges. Fear, anger, and shame can be triggered in the simple act of giving and taking strokes. Still, the basic currency of opening the heart is positive emotion. In the next step, surveying the emotional landscape, we squarely face and seek out not only positive emotions but negative emotions, as well.

We can discuss the nature and purpose of our emotions—negative or positive—and even whether they are our friends or enemies, but we cannot deny their existence. They affect us every minute of the day, whether we know it or not. Many of us are numb to our emotions, others too sensitive to them. We may be afraid of them or too ready to embrace them. The emotions can be calm and soothing; they can also be as threatening as a stormy sea. But if we are alive we will have emotions. How to become aware of our emotions and the emotions of others is the subject of this section. Here we will learn to recognize, map out, and navigate the emotional terrain.

The causes of our emotions are often unclear. We mistakenly tend to think of them as irrational. Every emotion we have has a definite cause; and that cause is, more often than not, someone else's behavior. We need to understand these causes if we are to be emotionally literate.

I Can Make You Feel, You Can Make Me Feel.

In the last two decades, popular psychology has led us to believe that we cannot cause feelings in others. You may have come to believe this false idea, which gained a foothold when the poem written by the psychologist Fritz Perls, the "Gestalt Prayer," gained acceptance as it was recited at thousands of human potential workshops across the Western world:

I do my thing, and you do your thing.
I am not in this world to live up to your
expectations
And you are not in this world to live up to mine.
You are you and I am I, if by chance we find each
other, it's beautiful.
If not, it can't be helped.

I believe that with his poem, Perls was trying to help people rid themselves of the excessive and guilt-based demands that people often make on themselves and one another. However, what he wrote became vulgarized into a call for emotional irresponsibility. In essence, it supported the belief that we are not responsible for the way others feel.

Another source for that belief is a particular interpretation of Buddhism which also deeply influenced the human potential movement in the U.S. It claims that we must strive to disconnect our emotions from the actions of others.

Whatever its source, the belief that we cannot make one another feel is the high point of emotional illiteracy. Years ago, I was so disturbed by the misguided implications in Perls's poem that I wrote a response to it:

If I do my thing and you do your thing
And if we don't live up to each other's expectations
We might live but the world will not survive.
You are you, and I am I,
and together, joining hands, not by chance,
We will find each other beautiful.
If not, we can't be helped.

What I was trying to say here is obvious to most feeling people: *We are responsible for each other.* Regarding emotions, we can indeed cause them in each other, and therefore we are often responsible for other people's feelings. However, there are those who vehemently disagree. At a lecture in which I was presenting my point of view on the subject, a man stood up and interrupted me.

"I completely disagree with you!" he exclaimed. "You cannot make me feel anything unless I let you."

I am embarrassed to admit that I took his bait. Faking anger, I stared at him and said: "That is the stupidest thing I have ever heard! Sit down!"

Stunned by my response, he turned bright red and sat down. From where I stood, he appeared to be scared and very sad.

"Now, may I ask you something?" Without waiting I smugly continued "What are you feeling right now?"

"Nothing," he insisted.

I was bewildered by his response. He was obviously shaken, yet he insisted that he was not. I turned to the rest of the audience and asked: "How about you? Did anybody feel anything?"

Many hands shot up. One by one, people voiced their feelings. I had made some of them angry with my fake attack. Others were embarrassed for my victim, while others felt afraid. Personally, I was left very uneasy because I believe it is wrong to power play or lie, and by faking anger I lied *and* attempted to power play my interlocutor. Yet I had proven my point. A number of people had been made to feel strong emotions by my staged response to my victim.

Clearly, if people can be made to feel fear, anger, shame, and other negative emotions, they can also be made to feel the emotions of joy, love, pride, and hope. That is ultimately what achieving emotional literacy is all about: giving people the tools to move from emotional numbness or frightening chaos to a positive, heart-centered, responsive and responsible, emotionally balanced life.

In this stage of the training we explore emotional awareness, which is the understanding of how emotions affect us every day. We will examine what we feel and what others feel, how strongly we feel those feelings, and why. The goal of this stage is to make us comfortable and well-oriented in the "emotional landscape."

We will look at:

▨ The connection between one person's actions and another person's feelings and

▨ The connection between a person's feelings and his or her own actions.

Both of these points relate to the fact that actions and feelings are closely related to each other and can't be kept apart. In fact, as mentioned before, it has been shown that actions will not occur without emotions. In addition, our actions can cause feelings in the people around us, which in turn can cause them to act in ways that will cause feelings in us, and so on and so on. In fact, the great majority of the emotions that we experience and the actions that they cause are the result of interactions with other people. True, some emotions are aroused by events (like being hit by a car or falling out of a boat) that are not directly related to other people's behavior. Other emotions are amplified by our own thoughts as when we develop social anxiety or phobias. But our emotional lives are largely the result of human interactions. The cycle of feelings and actions can be positive and constructive; it can also be vicious and destructive. In the next step, we will look at the connection between actions and feelings.

Emotionally Literate Transaction #6:
The Action/Feeling Statement

An action/feeling statement is a judgment-free method of exploring the connection between actions and feelings. It is a one-sentence description of the emotions we feel as the result of another person's action. This transaction provides a way of talking about our feelings that does not involve judgments, accusations, or theories. The boilerplate version is as follows:

"When you (describe action), I felt (name emotion)."

Very simple, isn't it? This statement is designed to tell another person about a feeling you had because of his or her behavior. By staying away from any judgments or accusations, it also helps to avoid placing blame or making someone defensive. An action/feeling statement simply says that the acknowledged action of one person resulted in an undeniable feeling in another.

Action / Feeling Case Study

John and Mary have a telephone conversation that Mary ends abruptly. John is upset by this sudden disconnection. The next day he calls Mary to tell her how her action made him feel. He asks if he can tell her something that is troubling him, and she agrees to listen. He explains, "When you suddenly wanted to stop talking on the phone last night, I felt angry at first, and then sad." Assuming that Mary can agree that she ended the telephone conversation abruptly, she now understands that John felt sad and angered by her action. That's all; no more, no less. This action/feeling statement successfully provides Mary with information about how John felt when she stopped the conversation.

A small goal you might say, but a critically important one in the learning of emotional literacy. It conveys information about John's feelings in connection with Mary's actions. It is also a way for John to express his feelings in a way that did not upset Mary.

A single action/feeling statement shows that an action resulted in a particular feeling. A series of action/feeling exchanges will have a dramatically clarifying effect on any emotional conflict. The reason for this is that action/feeling statements are a means of dissecting an emotional conflict, part by part. This is done by separating a conflict into two elements: what happened and what you felt.

In an emotionally literate relationship, no emotional event is too small to be dismissed. Invariably, once these seemingly trivial emotional events are explored, they reveal deeper emotional issues: personal insecurities, recurrent conflicts, real or perceived inequities, or persistent hurts in a relationship.

Action/feeling statements are not as easy to exchange as it might seem; errors can be made.

ACTION / FEELING ERROR # 1:
CONFUSING ACTION WITH MOTIVATION

When attempting to describe an action, it is possible to go beyond a simple statement:

"When you hung up the telephone"

"When you arrived late."

"When you interrupted me."

and add to it a judgment or interpretation of the action being described, such as:

"When you so rudely hung up on me"

"When you humiliated me by being late"

"When you showed your disregard for my opinion by interrupting me"

These statements put forward a theory about the other person's motivation (the intent to insult, humiliate, or disregard), rather than a simple description of an action. Elaborations like these confuse matters. They are often incorrect and will create unnecessary guilt, anger, and other disturbing feelings in the recipient. We will see later how to express these elaborations by stating our hunches and intuitions. For now we are dealing with the connection between one person's actions and another person's feelings.

ACTION/FEELING ERROR # 2:
CONFUSING FEELINGS WITH THOUGHTS

Another error that can occur in stating an action/feeling statement is confusing feeling and thinking. When we try to express a feeling, we often state a thought instead. For instance:

"When you interrupted our conversation, I felt that you were angry," or

"I felt that you weren't interested in what I had to say."

These are not feelings at all. Like the interpretations we looked at above, they are actually theories about what was going on in the other person's mind. Literacy has to do with language, and to confuse a feeling with an idea, thought, or theory is a common mistake that we need to avoid. In fact, any sentence that begins with "I feel *that*" is most likely to be about a thought perhaps best expressed by saying "I think that" or "I believe that."

To construct a good action/feeling statement, you need to focus on what you *feel*, not what you suspect or assume that the other person is thinking or feeling. The only thing you can know for sure is how you feel. If you want to know how others feel, you have to ask and make sure. Many arguments between people are based on this type of false assumption.

For instance, Frances believes the reason her husband doesn't look up from the paper when she talks is that he isn't interested in what she has to say. Actually, he is interested; the problem is that he tries to do two things he is interested in at the same time, something that doesn't work very well in most cases.

Frances can't be sure that her husband is not interested in what she has to say, but she is sure that when he splits his attention between her and the sports section she feels sad and eventually very angry. She might be tempted to say, "The way you read your paper while we eat makes me feel that you are not interested in me." Instead, it might be better if she said, "When you read the paper while we eat, it makes me sad and after a while I get angry."

Another more subtle version of this confusion of feeling with thought is a statement like:

"When you interrupted our conversation, I felt rejected."

This is an error, too, since "rejected" is not really an emotion but pertains to a *theory* about the other person's motivation. It does not explain to your listener what you are feeling. Were you angry? Were you sad? Were you embarrassed? Were you ashamed? These are feelings. When you say that you felt rejected, you are really saying that you believe that the other person rejected you—a theory about the person's motivation, and a theory that may well be incorrect. All the above errors involve either laying blame or trying to read the mind of the other person. Action/feeling statements teach us to stick to the facts and to stop assuming we can read other people's minds. *Keep the action/feeling statement simple: what happened and how you felt.*

Primary & Secondary Emotions

How do we know what we feel? Opinions vary on the definitive list of basic primary emotions. Fortunately, for all practical purposes, we have a pretty good understanding that anger, fear, sadness, and shame are primary negative emotions while love, joy, and hope are primary positive emotions. Again, saying that certain emotions are positive or negative does not imply that some emotions are better than others. In fact, all emotions are important; it's just that some feel good and others feel bad.

We must realize, however, that when we put a name and positive or negative valence (terror, apprehension, sadness, etc.) to an internal subjective experience, we are engaging in a rather arbitrary activity. The experience that occurs when we perceive a threat to our life—the heart beat, the tingling skin, the pressure in our head, the widening of our eyes, the paralysis of our limbs—all existed before somebody called it fear, *angst*, *miedo*, or *pavour*. The emotional/biochemical response to a life-threatening situation didn't need a whole lot of discussion.

Humans felt the need to call the fear response by a name, in order to talk about it, as in:

"When that big wave hit me and pulled me under, my heart beat fast. I was afraid."

Then another person could agree, "That's what happened when the volcano erupted. My heart beat fast and I was afraid."

And then somebody else might say, "I was not afraid." And he might get elected Chief of the tribe.

The more that fear becomes removed from life-threatening situations, the more important that we be able to talk about it. On the one hand, we may become terrified of harmless spiders. On the other hand, we may not feel fear when we are threatened with death or banishment from the tribe. Both situations are problematic for survival and both merit discussion. We seek to perfect our emotional dialogue in order to live in harmony with our emotions.

But speaking of the primary emotions is not sufficient to understand our emotional lives. Jealousy, hope, guilt, envy, hopelessness, or melancholy, to name a few, are secondary combinations of basic emotions and can't be understood in terms of just one emotion. When speaking about them, we should try to break them down into their primary component parts.

For instance, if Sam is feeling guilty, it might be helpful if he realized that his guilt is made up of shame and fear. Daria could explain her emotions more clearly when she is envious if she specified that her primary emotions are anger, sadness, and fear; doing so would expand her awareness of her emotional landscape. On the other hand, if a person says he feels humiliated, discounted, rejected, insulted, or loved, for instance, those are definitely not emotions but statements about what he believes others are doing to him. Such statements are potentially confusing rather than enlightening. They need to be reevaluated; the hidden emotional response needs to be discovered and stated. When a person says that he feels humiliated, he may actually be feeling ashamed and afraid while *believing* he was humiliated. When someone is "feeling" discounted, the actual feelings could be anger and sadness. "Insulted" may mean ashamed and angry, or sad and angry, or just plain angry. Feeling loved could be more complicated: It could be joy, it could be joy and hope, or it could be simply love.

Many questions remain about what the primary emotions are and how they combine into secondary emotions for different people. Is sex an emotion? How about hunger or thirst? Are psychological pain and hurt emotions? As of this writing, I am not sure. It remains to be seen. That should not prevent us from continuing to pursue emotional literacy by stating actions and feelings in as clear a manner as possible. As we do this, we will become more emotionally sophisticated and develop new and useful ways of communicating about our emotions.

On occasion it seems that people express emotions that are not genuine. It is possible to exaggerate emotions for the purpose of power playing others. These expressions of manufactured emotion are called "rackets" in transactional analysis. It is important to realize that unless an emotion is faked for the purpose of influencing others, all emotions are genuine no matter what the source or how "realistic" the connection between the feeling and its cause.

ACTION/FEELING ERROR #3:
IGNORING THE INTENSITY OF AN EMOTION.

Every primary emotion can be experienced in a range from weak to intense. Anger can go from irritation to fury, joy can range from contentment to ecstasy, fear can be apprehension and can be terror, love can be affection and can be heart-wrenching passion. Our tendency to understate and overstate the intensity of our emotional experiences can lead to misunderstanding and confusion.

Clarifying an Action/Feeling Statement

CLARIFYING THE FEELING

Sometimes you may need to help a person clarify how he or she felt when you did something. To do this successfully you will have to ignore judgments and accusations and help shape what is being said into the action/feeling formula. It is especially important to listen carefully and intuitively to understand the other person's feelings. In the above case of Mary and John, let's imagine that John said:

"When you so rudely hung up yesterday, I felt that you didn't care about me at all."

In order to extract a workable action/feeling statement from this comment, Mary might respond:

"Wait, let me get this straight. You are saying that when I stopped our conversation yesterday, which I remember doing, you felt something. But I can't tell what it was you felt. Were you angry?"

"No, I felt you were being rude."

"Okay, you thought I was being rude, but would you be willing to tell me how you felt? I am unclear about how you felt at the time."

"I don't know. I felt that you didn't like me."

"Well, okay, but you still haven't told me how you felt."

"What do you mean?"

"You are saying that I was rude and that I don't like you and I want to talk about that later. But I am trying to figure out what feeling, what emotion you felt. What were you feeling that made you think I didn't like you? Were you sad? Angry?"

"A bit. Actually, yeah, very sad. Then I started to feel angry."

"Okay, that's what I wanted to know. You felt sad and angry."

By now, dear reader, you may be saying: "People don't talk like that in the real world. Maybe they do in

California, but not anywhere else. I'm not willing to talk like that. I'd be embarrassed to death."

That's a fine action/feeling statement. To rephrase it slightly:

"When speaking in an emotionally literate way, I feel embarrassment." (Or more accurately, "I feel shame and fear.")

I recognize the problem and can only agree with you. For one thing, these examples sometimes don't reflect the pace of real-world conversations. But people just don't talk this way usually, and it is embarrassing and very difficult at times to do so. But it works. It creates a favorable climate for rational, emotional expression. It cools down unruly feelings, gives an opportunity to express these emotions that is less likely to result in further upset, and lays the groundwork for safe and productive emotional dialogue. It lets others know that how they feel is important to us—that we listen to them and value them enough to have an honest exchange. It informs people of each other's emotional terrain so that they can more easily find their way around it in the future.

Clarifying the Action

For an action/feeling statement to work, it is important that both persons agree that the action alluded to actually happened. Perhaps the recipient does not remember because it was long ago, or because there was too much going on at the time. Or perhaps the recipient remembers the situation but does not remember the action as described.

Example:

"When you changed Suzie's diaper while I was speaking, I felt angry."

"I don't remember; can you refresh my memory?"

"I was telling you about my upsetting conversation with Joe, and Suzie came in crying and you changed her diaper and never came back to our conversation."

"Okay, I remember now. I see: You felt angry then."

To be effective, an emotionally literate communication must be received as well as sent. When you are the recipient of an action/feeling statement, the emotionally literate thing to do is to take careful note of the emotions being described and your action that triggered them. This can be very difficult because when we are told that we may have made a mistake or that we have made another person feel bad, we are likely to respond with guilt and defensiveness.

Our first impulse will be to deny, explain, justify, or even apologize. I want to emphasize that it is important to simply absorb the information being given: the emotions caused in another person by your actions. The point is not how bad or wrong you were to act the way you did (that will be dealt with later in the book) but how what you did made the other person feel.

Nor is the point that you should apologize immediately or explain why you did what you did; there will be a time and place for that if necessary. The point is understanding the connection between your action and what the other person felt.

Remember, we are interested in understanding how we affect each other and how people respond emotionally thereby getting a map of the emotional terrain we live in, rather than placing or accepting responsibility or blame. Taking responsibility is important, but it comes later, after we understand each other well enough to apologize and make amends meaningfully and effectively.

Going back to John and Mary, she may already know that her behavior left John feeling angry and sad, or she might be surprised to hear it. She may understand why he feels this way, or she may be puzzled by it. In what she needs to do for now is to listen carefully, get the information, and acknowledge it. This acknowledgment can be in the form of a nod, or by saying, "I hear you" or "I understand that when I ended the conversation, you felt sad, and then angry."

By doing this, Mary learns about John's emotional responses to different types of situations, and she gives him an opportunity to let go of his unhappy feelings. This begins the process of emotional dialogue in which feelings are given proper recognition.

Again, accepting an action/feeling statement is not easy. The danger in receiving an action/feeling statement, especially if it is imperfectly formulated, is triggering a defensive response which results in your saying something like:

- "I thought you were finished talking; that's why I wanted to stop," or
- "Rude? You were being rude by talking on and on about your problems," or
- "Angry? You have a lot of nerve being angry. I should be angry about the waste of my time," or
- "Sad? Don't be so self-indulgent: Pull yourself together, it's not like I'm the meanest person in the world."

Every one of these responses is a defensive discount of John's feelings.

Discounts like these keep an emotionally literate dialogue from taking place. Most of the time we respond this way, we feel guilty about having hurt someone. If Mary feels guilty, misunderstood, or angry, she can talk about that later. For now what matters are John's feelings, not Mary's. It's just a matter of taking turns.

What is important at this point is that Mary acknowledge what John felt when she wanted to stop talking on the phone. Then she can talk about how she feels. Often this process calls for biting one's tongue and being patient. Keep in mind that silence can cool down the escalation of emotionally charged conversations. But more important, it is the only fair thing to do when a friend or loved one is in emotional distress. Why? Because it gives the person a chance to get his or her distress out and gives you a chance to exercise your love and empathy.

Of course, a defensive response can simply be a way of dismissing someone we don't want to deal with. When we encounter this kind of deliberately dismissive response, we have a special problem. Do we accept that we are dealing with someone who simply is not interested and that we are wasting our emotional energies, or do we try again to get an emotionally literate response? We'll explore ways of dealing with this dilemma in this chapter in "Revealing our Intuitive Hunches."

An Action / Feeling Transaction That Worked

Here's another example: Marianne and Mick had decided to watch a video together one evening. Mick was about to turn on the tape when the phone rang. "Hold on," Marianne said, "this may be Lilly and I want to talk to her for a minute. Is that okay?" Mick agreed.

Meanwhile, he had decided to put away some papers while he waited for her. When he looked up, he saw her laughing on the phone.

A funny show was on the TV and Mick got interested in it. Later, her phone conversation ended, Marianne stood near the couch waiting for Mick to start their movie.

After a while Mick turned to her. "When are you going to be ready?" he said with irritation.

"I've been ready," she said, surprised. "I've been right here, waiting for you."

"Fine, whatever, I just don't know what took so long," he said impatiently as he moved to turn on the movie.

This type of transaction had become a common experience between them. Mick's impatience surfaced several times a day in his interactions with Marianne.

Marianne was suddenly flooded with sadness and then felt a flash of anger. She often felt that she took the blame for their little conflicts, and that made her very unhappy.

She did not want to start their evening feeling sad and resentful. She decided to intervene with an action/feeling statement.

"Mick, I'm sorry but I need to talk to you before we start."

He looked at her with dismay, but agreed. Marianne proceeded:

"When you spoke to me just now in that tone, I felt pretty bad about it. It made me very sad and now I am angry."

"What was the tone?" Mick asked.

He had heard this type of complaint from friends and family before.

"Well, you sounded very annoyed."

"Well, that's true, I was annoyed." He thought for a few seconds. Then he said, "I see what happened now. When I talked with you in that annoyed-sounding tone, you felt bad." He looked in Marianne eyes and asked, "Is that right?"

She nodded. "Sad and angry," she said.

"I see," he said. After a thoughtful silence he stopped leaning impatiently toward the VCR for the first time during their conversation, put both arms around her waist gave her a tender kiss. The action/feeling transaction worked and they had a lovely evening.

The above suggestions are designed simply to bring out the feelings people have in response to other people's actions. It's important to know that when I did a certain thing, you had a certain feeling. But surely we can't speak very long without going deeper and dealing with people's motivations and intentions. The next step in emotionally literate dialogue is designed to accomplish that.

In our interactions, we are often not clear about what is going on in our own thoughts or emotions—let alone the other person's. We may not be concerned or even interested, and proceed as if everything is just fine. But if we do become interested in the other person's inner life, we could make a guess or assumption and easily misinterpret what is going on. Or we may guess accurately what the other is thinking or feeling and discount it.

Most of us like to think that what we say is logical and rational and comes from our Adult ego state. At a party, we may act childlike and happily acknowledge it. Or, when lecturing a whiny toddler, we may be parental and make no apology for it. But in most situations, we prefer to believe we are behaving in a logical and rational way—that is, "from our Adult."

We have a hard time admitting we may be acting irrationally, like a child, or reacting out of prejudice, like a punitive or even a nurturing parent. But a great deal of what people do and say comes from ego states other than the Adult. What is going on under cover of the Adult façade is accessible to our intuition.

The accurate use of our intuitive powers plays an absolutely central function in emotional literacy training. Intuition is your most important emotional tool. With it you can make powerful guesses when all the facts are not available.

It shouldn't be surprising that we can sometimes be fooled—or at least confused—by behaviors we observe in others. Let us pretend we are invisible and use our transactional analysis and intuition skills with a couple shopping at a supermarket:

Wife (noticing a six-pack in the shopping cart): "I didn't know we were buying beer."

Is this an Adult question or an expression of Parental disapproval?

Husband (responding): "Well, yeah!"

Is this also simply an Adult confirmation to his wife's Adult question or is it Child rebelliousness? How can you decide the ego states involved in this exchange?

Before Eric Berne developed Transactional Analysis, he became very interested in intuition. It was intuition, he said, that told him about the Inner Child behind what we do much of the time.[30] Following Eric Berne's example, we can use our intuition in making an initial guess whenever we are in the dark about someone's emotions or intentions. When in doubt, scientists, detectives, market analysts, psychologists, and psychotherapists use their intuition to guide their actions. What determines their success, however, is how accurately they check out their initial hunches. A detective who guesses the butler did it can't make the arrest without proof. A scientist who blindly follows his hunches without validating them will surely fail in the end. In the same way, if you use your intuition to discern people's feelings and thoughts, you must check out your hunch before acting on it.

In the case of the shopping couple, use your intuition and ask yourself what the husband-and-wife dialogue sounded like. Was it Adult to Adult ("You bought beer?"—"Yeah") or was it Parent to Child? ("Are you planning to get drunk?"—"Try and stop me!"). You will probably guess right, but a guess is not good enough. Evidence must be objectively collected.

It may help if you continue to observe and gather more information. Let's listen to the wife's response.

Wife: "Oh!" (smiling) "Okay!"

Her response seems to indicate that she accepts his answer as an Adult response to an Adult question. Nothing more is said on the subject and they go about their business.

Was this in fact an Adult to Adult transaction? Probably, but maybe not. If you could follow them home and continue to be invisible, it would eventually become clear.

Does he drink the whole six-pack before dinner? Does she throw a tantrum or go into a deep sulk? Or do they share a beer while they are having their hamburgers, and finish the six-pack over the next two weeks?

WHAT'S GOING ON HERE, A OR B?

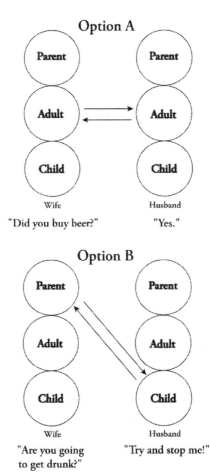

Option A

Wife — "Did you buy beer?"

Husband — "Yes."

Option B

Wife — "Are you going to get drunk?"

Husband — "Try and stop me!"

I invite you to become a transactional analyst and observe people's interactions at work, on the street, or in social situations and try to analyze the ego states and feelings being exhibited. In analyzing transactions we must take care not to jump to conclusions. Intuition is rarely completely correct or incorrect. It's not always possible, but to find out which intuitions are correct, it is necessary to check them against reality. How do we do that?

How Do Others Feel?

In our daily lives we are constantly trying to understand the behavior of others. When we are communicating badly with another person (which is often the case), we are forced to guess what is going on in his or her mind by using whatever information is available. We don't usually ask people why they are doing whatever they are doing. We probably would not get a reliable answer even if we did ask. When we want to figure out why people do what they do, we are often forced to largely rely on our intuition. But using something as fuzzy as intuition doesn't always make our conclusion usable or valid. Our intuitive hunches need to be crosschecked and modified to fit what is going on.

If much of what goes on in our emotional lives is dark and negative, our intuitions about people will be often dark and negative, as well. We fear that another person thinks that we are ugly or stupid, or that he would like to see us harmed, or that she would prefer not to be our friend at all. Often, these fears are exaggerated, but this does not make them completely inaccurate; they usually have a kernel of truth to them.

These negative intuitions, if left not checked against reality, can turn into "paranoid fantasies." They are fantasies because they are the product of a feverish mind, and paranoid because they are inaccurate exaggerations of a grain of truth. I am not talking here about the kind of persecution delusions that makes paranoia a form of madness. The type of garden variety paranoia I am talking about has its origin in a heightened but distorted awareness generated by our intuition.

We are aware of many things that are never spoken about, or are discounted and denied by others. Unless we reveal and check out our intuitions, we are left guessing at the motives of those others and these intuitions may develop into paranoid fantasies and unspoken resentments. That is why it is important to bring our intuitions into the open and check them out before they damage our relationships. The best way to do this is to simply inquire: Are you angry? Are you afraid? Do you dislike me?

Intuition in Action, a Case Study

Jane, upset about her coworker, Bettina, has been complaining to Marcus that she does not understand Bettina's behavior. Bettina seems spoiled to her and seems to have little respect for others. But Marcus is fond of Bettina and suspects that some kind of rivalry lurks behind Jane's complaints. When Jane begins to describe in excruciating detail how much time and attention her boss gives to Bettina, Marcus is sure that Jane is, in spite of her denials, somehow jealous of Bettina.

"It sounds as if you feel rejected by Bettina, and short-changed because she gets more attention than you," says Marcus.

"No, not at all," insists Jane. "Years ago, I felt that way, a little. I'm just worried about her behavior; I think she's alienating a lot of people."

"But she's very well-liked," says Marcus.

"I don't know how that can last, given the way she acts," declares Jane.

"I think the things you describe are not really that offensive, they're just assertive," says Marcus. "Are you sure you don't resent something about her that's influencing your judgment?" he asks as gently as he can.

"No, no, not at all," says Jane.

Marcus is stranded. His intuition is buzzing loudly, but Jane insists she doesn't harbor any bad feelings. The outcome is that Marcus feels less and less empathy for Jane's distress. The experience of having his intuition discounted is so unpleasant that he feels unable to connect with his friend emotionally. Marcus begins to look at his watch, longing for a change in the conversation.

In this case, having his intuition discounted made Marcus withdraw emotionally. When we sense something and it is denied, we have two options: Either we forget whatever it is that our intuition brought to our attention, or we persist in our idea. If we continue to get denials and dismissals of our intuitions, our efforts to figure out what is going on may lead us far off the mark, especially if we have an active imagination.

Discounting Intuition

Here is another example of intuition denied but eventually validated.

Donna has been having misgivings about her friendship with Craig for a long time. From the beginning of their friendship, she made it clear that she had no romantic interest, but over the past few months she has developed a hunch that Craig is becoming interested in her as more than a friend, which makes her uncomfortable. It annoys her that he always seems to have a hidden romantic agenda.

Donna and her longtime, on-again off-again boyfriend, Justin move in together. Suddenly Craig stops calling and does not return a couple of Donna's calls. Donna has come to feel so conflicted about Craig that she is almost relieved. Still, he is a dear friend and she really likes him. She doesn't want to lose his friendship. She sends him a card with a short note enclosed, hoping he will respond.

Still no phone call from Craig. So she calls him, feeling nervous. He has been depressed, he tells her, because of his highly unsatisfying job. She swallows hard and raises the dreaded subject:

"I've been noticing that you haven't called; I was wondering if you feel uncomfortable calling me here at my new apartment with Justin."

"Oh no, not at all," Craig quickly answers.

"Are you sure? Maybe you feel weird about meeting Justin for the first time over the phone?"

"No, not at all," says Craig.

"Are you upset with me? Is something else wrong?"

"No, no."

This response leaves Donna confused. Despite Craig's insistence that all is well, she still has a sense that there is something wrong with her dear friend. Emotionally, this is a minor catastrophe; it leaves her confused and distraught. Does she believe that he is really okay and only upset about work? Or is she angry because he is denying that something is wrong? Does she trust him? The questions his answer generates are enough to make her head spin.

What Craig did is called an "emotional discount." It denies Donna's intuition that Craig is angry or upset by dismissing it entirely. Confusion and increased paranoia are usually the result of such a response. It is dangerous to a relationship to dismiss someone's suspicions as wholly mistaken. The other person will rightly feel that he or she cannot be totally wrong, and may begin to suspect that you are being deceitful or that you are unaware of your motives.

Donna decides to take Craig at his word. But still no calls, no cards, no letters. Should she pursue him when the relationship is so fraught with unspoken friction? She decides to just leave it alone for a while.

By now Donna's mind is tangled in knots: Why would he choose to drop her as a friend now? Does he feel too humiliated to call? Is he jealous of Justin? If so, did he lie when he said he didn't feel bad about her move? Donna believes that she has given Craig an opportunity to be honest. Instead, he has negated her intuition in a baffling, deeply unpleasant way. Before long, there seems to be no remnant of the friendship of over four years. This is an example of how off-putting and bewildering it can be to have one's intuition negated.

EMOTIONALLY LITERATE TRANSACTION #9:
VALIDATING AN INTUITIVE HUNCH—A SEARCH FOR THE TRUTH, NO MATTER HOW SMALL

Most of us have fears that prevent us from admitting that another person's intuitions are true. We might consider such an admission a sign of excessive transparency and weakness on our part, or we may be reluctant to hurt another person's feelings. In any event, if an emotionally literate dialogue is to result, the person presented with another's intuition must overcome his reluctance and pursue its validation.

Let's revisit the above example and see what would have happened if Craig had been more faithful to his true feelings.

"Are you sure, maybe you feel weird about meeting Justin for the first time over the phone?" Donna once again asks.

This time, Craig chooses to validate instead of discount Donna's intuition.

"Well, okay, since you asked, I will admit that I was a little bothered years when you started dating Justin seriously and never introduced us."

Donna is taken aback. "I thought you understood that I'm reluctant to introduce my friends to each other sometimes. I told you about how I once introduced some people who really didn't like one another, and it was pretty awkward."

This may be true enough, but clearly there's more to be said; now it's Donna's turn to be honest.

"But, Craig, can I be honest, since you answered me honestly?" She waits to get Craig's permission to proceed. "I also was nervous about introducing you to Justin because I was interested in him romantically, and I have suspected for a long time that you were interested in me. I was afraid that you would feel jealous when I started dating Justin." Donna swallows hard. "Am I right that you have been jealous of us becoming a couple?"

This is the "moment of truth" for Craig. He can deny the whole thing, or he can explain to Donna that her intuition is off, that something else was going on that she never guessed. Or he might have to admit that he feels exactly as she suspects. Perhaps he feels both jealous of Justin and suspicious that Donna just doesn't like him enough to introduce Craig to her other friends. In any case, by finding out the truth about her intuition, Donna gets an emotionally literate dialogue going. In the earlier example, Craig's complete denial leads to an emotional stonewall that left Donna feeling bewildered and over-whelmed by unintelligible messages. After Craig's clarification of his feelings, Donna is deeply relieved and their relationship has a new chance to continue.

Sometimes, an entire intuition will be correct, not just part of it. For example, this conversation could easily have confirmed Donna's entire intuition. It could have gone like this:

"Actually, Donna, I am afraid you are right. I did harbor hopes of a relationship with you, and I was jealous of Justin when you moved in together."

Or in a different vein:

"Yes, Donna, I am angry with you. In fact, I've been really disappointed in our relationship lately. I'm not sure

I want to go on being friends. I've been wondering when you would get the hint and stop calling me." Harsh words indeed, and not very emotionally literate, but better for Donna to hear them clearly expressed than to have to live in a confusing and endlessly hurtful emotional climate.

Donna and Craig may go on to explore why he doesn't like her anymore, his hurt feelings, and what she did to hurt them. Or they may temporarily drop the matter and the friendship. Either way, they are several steps ahead in the process of understanding each other and living emotionally literate lives.

Usually, as in the case of Craig and Donna, matters are not nearly so far gone. Most problems of this sort are solvable, and when that is the case, this type of dialogue can work wonders to repair the little misunderstandings that otherwise erode a relationship.

The Payoff: Loving Emotional Cooperation

Being able to discuss each other's feelings can bring spectacular results, especially when both people are committed to frank emotional communication. In emotional literacy training workshops, I explain how intuition, when used in an effective and emotionally literate way, can greatly help us understand one another.

For example, Sarah and Julie were attending one of my workshops. There are hard feelings between them.

Julie is 27 years old, with a model-like figure. She is considered very beautiful, even though she dresses down in order not to attract attention. Sarah is 35 and having problems keeping down her weight. They are office mates and have been having some unpleasant arguments. They have been encouraged by their boss to attend the workshop. Julie is upset and has actually been feeling afraid of coming to work because of these disputes.

In the midst of a discussion about intuition, Julie asked Sarah if she could talk to her about a hunch that she had. Sarah agreed.

"I have a suspicion that you think that I am incompetent and willing to submit to anything that the administration dishes out. Is that true?"

Sarah shook her head and anxiously responded, "Not at all. I think you're very smart."

Julie slumped in her chair, discouraged. At this point I explained that there is usually some truth in people's hunches. Rather than flatly denying Julie's hunch and giving her a stroke instead of validation, it might be better for Sarah to think about what—if anything—may be true in Julie's fantasy.

"Emotional literacy involves honoring other people's intuition, rather than discounting it," I reminded the group. "You have to be willing to look deeply into your own motives." I let that thought soak in for a moment and then asked Sarah if there was any truth to Julie's intuition.

Sarah thought for several seconds and then nodded. "Julie, I guess your hunch is correct, in a way," she said nervously. "I do think that you're very smart, but I'm angry at you because I believe that you scare easily and go along with people who intimidate you. That makes me think you're weak. But I do believe you're very smart."

Julie felt better at hearing Sarah's true feelings and was able to agree that she was too easily intimidated. But she longed to learn to stand her ground the way Sarah did. Then she revealed another of her intuitions:

"I have another hunch, and this one is scary to bring up, but we agreed to be honest, so I feel I should. Do you want to hear what I am thinking?"

"Okay," Sarah said with a worried expression.

"Well," said Julie, I also am guessing that you resent that I'm younger and that the men around the office find me attractive. I worry that you seem to believe that I am some kind of bimbo."

Everyone in the workshop became very quiet, nervously looking at Sarah and wondering how she would respond I was worried, too; regardless of the number of workshops I have led, I become hyper-alert when a scary subject like this comes up, because the emotional safety of the group members is in my hands.

"This is not easy but I have to agree that I am jealous of the attention you get from the men around here," admitted Sarah. "That is part of my anger. I am not proud of that, but it's true."

The group fell silent as people wrestled with the awkwardness that they felt. Another group member named Mark finally broke in with an ice-breaking question. Eventually, Sarah and Julie got several heartfelt strokes for their courage and honesty. The group went on exploring the subtleties of relationships in the office. After a two-day workshop the group members left feeling empowered, and optimistic. Sarah and Julie had reconciled and given each other a long heartfelt hug.

As you can see, when we follow Opening the Heart with these two techniques—the Action/Feeling Statement and Validating an Intuitive Hunch—an emotionally literate dialogue ensues, in which suspicion, fear, recrimination, and guilt are avoided.

Through these dialogues, people learn to speak honestly and gather information about how they feel about each other. They discover how their actions affect one another's feelings, and how their intuitions reflect and distort reality. They do this without judgments, accusations, or emotional chaos, while working toward the possibility of trust. The end result is loving emotional cooperation in which everyone gets what they want: to love and be loved.

How Empathy Matures

In a relationship, as trust and frank communication develop, people routinely share their intuitive hunches and will find the grain of truth to validate other's intuitions. This ongoing dialogue fine-tunes people's understanding of each other's emotional terrain. People learn how others are likely to feel in certain situations: what worries them and what puts them at ease. With these transactions, practiced over time, intuition matures into a powerful empathic sense.

Intuition often starts as a vague understanding that we are barely aware of and can become a powerful searchlight illuminating the emotional landscape and rendering it familiar and accessible. This heart-centered capacity to feel with others is an essential component of the next stage of the training: Taking Responsibility.

ONE MORE CASE STUDY OF THE EMOTIONAL LANDSCAPE: PUTTING IT ALL TOGETHER

Now let's see how it works when we put together the steps we have covered so far.

Carter and Sandra work with each other. Sandra, the owner of the company, is Carter's boss. About six months ago, they became involved in a sexual relationship. Now, after months of romantic bliss, they have begun to argue. They have asked me, as a friend, to help them disentangle the conflicts and bad feelings that are plaguing them. I like both of them and worry that they have created an impossible muddle for themselves. My fear is that they will either have to stop working together or break up, or both. They want to see if they can keep their working rapport while preserving their romantic relationship.

Despite their recent difficulties, they both say they have strong feelings for each other and would like to forge a long-term commitment. Their fights began at work with arguments over business policy and customer relations. Carter is friendly and easygoing with clients, while Sandra tends to be more businesslike. This is usually a good balance, except that Carter has given extensive credit to three clients who aren't paying their bills. Sandra wants him to demand immediate payment, which he refuses to do. Both think the other is being unreasonable. Sandra feels that Carter is putting a strain on the company's finances, while Carter thinks that Sandra's attitude is going to alienate their clients. This conflict at work has spilled over into their private life. They seem to disagree about everything now. Their sexual relationship has all but ceased and the honeymoon appears to be over.

After several phone conversations, I invite them to dinner to talk things over. After dessert, I suggest we begin the discussion. Sandra seems sad and Carter appears to be angry, but neither speaks of how he or she feels. Instead, they criticize each other. Carter says that he feels constantly nagged and criticized. Sandra complains that Carter used to be passionate and is now sexually lazy.

After listening for a while I interject. "Listen, it's pretty clear that you are both quite upset. Don't you agree?"

Sandra nods. Carter, stone-faced, seems willing to hear me out.

"Let's begin by finding out what it is you like about each other. When people get in arguments like this, they forget what brings them together in the first place. Would you be willing to do that?"

They both agreed and interchanged their appreciation for each other. She spoke about how handsome and strong he was and he complimented her for her joy of life and intelligence. It was a pretty tight-lipped exchange but it relaxed them somewhat to realize that their dislike of each other was not as great as it seemed.

"Now I would like to help you both clarify why you are so upset, and to do that I suggest that we use what I call the action/feeling technique. Are you willing to try?"

They both nod. "It's very simple. You take turns filling in the blanks in an action/feeling statement, such as: "When you (describe an action), I felt (name an emotion)." The goal is to describe a specific action and the emotion (or emotions) that resulted. No frills, just those two facts: An action and the consequent feelings.

"Anyone want to start?" I ask. "Trust me, it will be interesting. The point is to get an idea of each other's emotional landscape and to explore what is going on between you. Before we start, one more thing." I explain how important it is to ask for permission every time something emotionally loaded is about to be said.

After an uncomfortable minute, Sandra takes the lead. "Can I tell you something I felt last night?" she asks Carter. After he agrees, she continues, "When you disappointed me last night, I felt you did not love me anymore."

"Whoa, Sandra, hold on!" I interrupt. "It will take some work to turn that into an action/feeling statement. Can I try?"

Sandra nods. "You say he disappointed you. That's not a clear-cut action. What did he do?"

"He knows; after leading me on all evening, he rolled over and went to sleep as soon as we went to bed," Sandra continues. "That was very disappointing and I felt he was no longer in love with me."

"What we are after here is a simple statement of emotions following actual behavior," I explain. "First, let's agree that he went to sleep." I look over to Carter and see that he did not dispute Sandra's statement. Turning to Sandra, I ask: "What exactly did you feel when he went to sleep? Let's talk in terms of primary emotions such as sad, mad, or ashamed."

"All three," she shoots back.

"Well, which was first and how strong?"

"Shame. I was ashamed of how sexually needy I was, then very sad, and now I'm angry, very angry." Tears well up in her eyes.

"Okay, now I'll make an action/feeling statement out of the information you've given me, cutting out the accusations: 'Last night when you fell asleep instead of making love to me, I felt ashamed, very sad, and then angry.' You see?" Sandra nods, drying her eyes.

Carter is sitting quietly with a blank expression. I turn to him. "Do you follow that, Carter?"

"Yeah, but I didn't really…"

"I'm sure that you have a lot to say about this situation," I interrupt. "But right now I just want you to tell me whether you understand what Sandra said. Namely, that she was ashamed, sad, and angry because you fell asleep as soon as you went to bed last night. It'll help clarify what's going on between you."

"Okay, I can see that. Can I say how I feel?"

"By all means."

"I feel that I have become Sandra's whipping boy. She criticizes me, and then she wants me to make passionate love to her. I can't do what she wants me to do at work or in bed, and I feel pushed around."

Again, I explained the problem with "feeling pushed around, feeling like her whipping boy" being non-feelings, and the need for a succinct statement relating actions to feelings. Eventually, Carter pinpointed several occasions in which Sandra had made critical statements. Then he was able to articulate the feelings that he experienced: anger, sadness.

They went back and forth. Sandra spoke of Carter's easygoing financial approach and how it scared her, while Carter addressed his feelings of embarrassment when Sandra made it clear that she owned the business and received a better education than he did. Though I encouraged them both to speak only about primary emotional states—feeling sad, ashamed, guilty, angry—more complicated emotional reactions kept coming up. In only about one hour, we had already gotten a lot of information out.

Then we moved on. I explained to them that complicated emotional reactions like these consist of simple, primary emotions that lead to negative intuitions. For example, Sandra's belief that she was being sexually teased and the fear that Carter no longer loved her, and Carter's belief that Sandra was critical of his lack of education and saw him as a sexual servant.

I told them that we were now ready to deal with these speculations, and asked each of them to state the suspicions I had before asked them to censor. I had just one rule, however: Listen to each other with an open mind. Instead of denying one another's accusations, look for the truth in them, however small.

I started off with a question: Did Sandra think of Carter as merely a sexy man without any brains? This was one of Carter's fears, which she categorically denied. Still, I invited her to think it over. "Sandra, let's assume that Carter isn't crazy and that if he believes these things, then there may be some truth to them," I said. "It does no good to discount what he experiences. Instead, why don't you think of what truth there may be in his fears, however small."

Her brow furrowed as she fell silent. Eventually she spoke. "It is true that I appreciate the way you make love to me, Carter. And it is also true that I want that kind of response from you as much as anything else that you give me. And I do think that when we make love you are wonderfully mindless. But I think you are right, that feeling becomes part of the way I see you all the time and that could be hurtful to you."

"It is," said Carter.

After a few moments of uncomfortable silence, Sandra asked Carter, "Can I tell you something I am afraid you think about me?" He agreed to hear what she had to say.

"This is very hard to say, but I'm afraid you think I'm frigid."

"Sexually, you mean?" he asked.

"Yes," said Sandra, on the verge of tears.

He thought for what seemed a long time. Then he looked at me with puzzled confusion.

"Think about it," I said. "Why would she get that impression? Do you think she is frigid or cold in some way?" I suggested.

"Well, yeah, I think she is cold sometimes," he said, turning to Sandra. "The way you want to treat the customers is cold, in a way. And sometimes you treat me that way, too. I have thought that. But in bed you're passionate when you want to be, or maybe I should say when you feel good about me."

Sandra agreed. "I guess that must have been what I was picking up, that you think I am cold in the way I deal with business. I hate that part of me," she said, again starting to cry.

Carter moved over and hugged her. "I don't hate it, I admire it. I admire the way you take care of business. Just don't close my account."

They both laughed. The conversation went on as we continued to map the feelings that they both had. We looked at how they had been busy drawing destructive conclusions from each other's actions, creating ugly emotions in both of them. I pointed out how relationships have a tendency to fall into channels or ruts that can take two possible directions, positive or negative.

Love, mutual consideration, trust, kindness, sexual abandon, and personal admiration can feed upon each other to create a good relationship just as anger, selfishness, resentment, and negative judgments feed on one another to ruin it. Sandra and Carter's relationship had shifted from a positive state—the honeymoon period of increasing affection and passion—to a negative one. It would take energy and effort to reinstate the positive cycle and eventually settle into it, but now they knew what they felt, how strongly, and why, and that would certainly help.

Sandra and Carter ended the conversation with a spontaneous hug and kiss and effusive thanks for me. They went on to couple's therapy and continued their emotional education. To this date they seem to be doing well and claim that our after-dinner conversation was the beginning of their renewed relationship.

Summary

SURVEYING THE EMOTIONAL LANDSCAPE

Despite what pop psychologists would have you believe, you can cause emotions in another person and vice versa. That's why the action/feeling statement is so valuable. You can use it to clarify the feelings that are caused by your and other people's actions without making accusations or being judgmental.

The format is simple: "When you (describe action), I felt (name the emotion)." If you correctly use action/feeling statements, you will over a period of time begin to illuminate the emotional landscape that surrounds you. You will have a tool to learn how people feel, how strongly, and why and how these feelings relate to other people's actions. Learning to hear and understand how we affect other people's feelings with our actions, without becoming defensive, is very important in this process.

As you improve your emotional literacy, you will be able to sense other people's thoughts and emotions, using your intuition. You will learn to state your intuitive hunches to people and as whatever truth resides in these hunches is validated through feedback, your intuition will mature into an empathic sense. This loving empathic sense is the foundation of emotionally literate behavior. With it we can confront difficult emotional situations head on and prevent them from escalating as we unlock the door to richer, more rewarding relationships.

CHAPTER 6

The Mistakes We Make
&
Why We Make Them

Before we move on to the third and most difficult portion of emotional literacy training, let us look at the emotional mistakes we make and why we make them.

We know that, sooner or later, we all make mistakes, big and small. We hurt the people we love; we lie to our friends; we betray people who trust us; we try to help and when we fail, we persecute the people who need us. When we make these mistakes and we realize that we have made them, we blame ourselves or we blame our victims or we make empty apologies. Most of the time, what we do to set things right does not work very well. We need to understand why we keep repeating these errors and then take effective steps to correct them.

Eric Berne, with his theory of games and scripts, gave us a very effective way to understand why we make the emotional mistakes we make and suggested a very effective method to stop making them. Let me explain.

The Games People Play

If you follow people around and watch their conversations, you'll notice that some people have the same unpleasant transaction over and over. Some people get mean and wind up scaring others. Some people turn every conversation into a joke. Others always depress anyone they talk with. Others yet bring up sexual or distressing themes, causing shock and consternation. Most of us have one such pattern, sometimes more than one, which we repeat over and over. These repetitive patterns are called games.

If we pay attention we can notice the feelings that result from these interactions. In conversations where people play games, one or more people wind up feeling bad: sad, angry, scared, hopeless and so on. Other conversations go smoothly and seem to make people feel good. They are probably free of games.

Either way, people are getting strokes. When people play games, they primarily exchange negative strokes. When interactions are free of games, the transactions are positive and the strokes are good. Berne discovered that there are different kinds of games. For instance, some people play depressing games like "Kick Me," others play angry games like "Now I've Got You," and yet others play self-destructive games like "Alcoholism."[31]

Why do people play these games? There are different theories. One is that the people playing a game are making a misguided attempt to get positive strokes, an attempt that backfires, producing negative strokes instead. I agree with this theory and have come to the conclusion that people play games because they are starved for strokes and will get them at any cost, even if all they get are bad strokes. I call this theory "stroke centered transactional analysis."

Scripts: Decisions That Rule Our Lives

Though games are failed, hurtful attempts to get positive strokes, every completed game gives the player strokes, even if they are negative. It also gives the player another payoff: The game confirms a certain view of the world that the player has come to adopt. This generates an "existential advantage" in that it enables the game player to see his life as coherent and intelligible, even though his worldview is negative.

Some typically negative worldviews are: "Nice guys always get the shaft," or "Never trust a woman (man)," or "Mess with me and you'll regret it." Such a view gives the player a sense that he understands the world, rotten though it is.

Early in life, people decide on their life expectations. These decisions become narratives, blueprints for living, or scripts similar to the scripts of movies or plays. Many people read their lines from these scripts for the rest of their lives. Every time a person plays a game to its conclusion, he or she gets a feeling of bittersweet satisfaction called the "script (or existential) payoff." This feeling tells her that even though she is all messed up, at least she knows who she is and what the meaning of her life is all about. Some very bad existential statements that nevertheless give meaning to life are "Born to lose," "Everybody hates me," "Nothing ever works out."

At the end of a terrible day, we can at least say to ourselves, "I knew it. Life is hell and then you die." And at the end of a terrible life it may reasonable to conclude: "Just as I thought. Life was hell and now I'm dying."

Games are part of these total life patterns or scripts. The "Why don't you. Yes, but." player has a depressive script; the "Kick Me" player has a Victim script; the angry player has a Persecutor script; the Alcoholic has a tragic, self-destructive script, and so on. The games we play and the strokes they obtain for us give significant shape to our lives.

One kind of script decision we make early in life deals with our emotions. Often, we head for one emotional extreme or its opposite. We cut off our feelings and wind up permanently numb, or we don't control our feelings and wind up living in emotional chaos. We decide not to love, and we become hard and cold; or we decide to love all the way and wind up constantly disappointed. We decide to avoid anger at all costs and become totally passive, or we decide to express anger freely and become violent. We decide to stop feeling or we decide to go with every feeling we have.

To get out of this fix we have to look beyond everyday vicissitudes and instead examine the patterns of our lives. Anyone who finds himself regularly in trouble with people will, upon reflection, probably see he is caught in a repetitive series of games that form a life script usually acquired in childhood.

Take the worker who regularly gets fired. Or the woman who gets dumped by her lovers over and over again. Or the man who repeatedly gets drunk. If you are always late, always in debt, always forgetting things, always lying to cover your mistakes, or always getting taken for your last penny, chances are these endless mishaps are part of a lifelong script. There are many theories that try to explain why our lives get as messed up as they do, why we get so depressed that we lose interest in life, why we go crazy, or why we become addicts or hurt people around us. Most of these theories blame our parents. Some theories blame our parents' genes, saying these troubles are hereditary. Others blame our parents' behavior, claiming they mistreated us and taught us to be depressed, crazy, or drunk.

All of these theories are somewhat true for some people and very true for others. There are hereditary aspects to alcoholism, madness, and depression. Some of us do learn from our parents to be depressed, dishonest, or angry, or to act crazy or to get high. Finally, some of us had difficult childhoods that have left us misinformed, confused, and frightened. Still, even if there is something in our genes that makes us act as we do, and even though our childhood or later occurrences may have damaged us badly, life is still made up of daily experiences that are shaped by our daily decisions and behavior. If we change those experiences by changing our decisions and behaviors and by rectifying our mistakes, our life can be changed, as well.

We can change the patterns of our lives by deciding to change our scripts and by finding meaning in a different kind of life plan, in which we are good to ourselves and other people instead of causing hurt. This is a decision in favor of emotional literacy and can have a transformative effect on us as well as those around us.

Rescuer, Persecutor, Victim

How do we break out of these emotional traps? Our scripts are not irrevocably hardwired into our brains; they are based on our own decisions and therefore we are not stuck with them, they can be re-decided. We can change them by changing our minds and acting in new, more productive ways.

The first requirement to change our scripts is to understand the three main destructive roles that people play in their games and life scripts. These roles are the Rescuer, the Persecutor, and the Victim. They are common to all games. When we are acting out our script, cycle through these three roles. If we stop playing the script games and their roles we literally starve the script by depriving it of the negative strokes it feeds on.

■ Rescuers take care of people who should take care of themselves, letting them off the hook, preventing them from making their own decisions or from finding their own way.

▨ Persecutors criticize, judge, preach, and punish.

▨ Victims let others run their lives and take care of them.

Why do we stick to these roles? Because we have learned to get strokes by playing them, and because the roles give meaning to our lives. Furthermore, Berne found that everyone who plays a game eventually plays all the roles of the game. That's why, in Transactional Analysis, as suggested by Stephen Karpman,[33] we arrange these three main roles in a triangle to show how people move from one role to the other in an endless merry-go-round.

In fact, these roles are so important to us that each of them has been legitimized by becoming the basis for a political ideology. The Persecutor role has been adopted by conservative extremists who want to abandon all responsibility for their fellow humans and would jail and disown every person who fails to be a "good" citizen. The Rescuer role is the pet attitude of "tax-and-spend" liberals who would sacrifice all our resources taking care of other people. The Victim is the preferred role for the members of groups that are embattled against society or unwilling to take care of themselves and who would prefer to be taken care of by others.

Now, this doesn't mean that these attitudes aren't sometimes legitimate. It is laudable to take care of other people. It is important to ask that people take care of themselves. It is reasonable to demand help when we are unable to go on. But when any of these approaches hardens into a political dogma that can't be challenged, or an inflexible role, it becomes harmful and unproductive.

One fruitful way of looking at this behavior is that the roles of Persecutor and Rescuer correspond to behaviors emanating from distinct portions of the triune brain

THE DRAMA TRIANGLE

as presented in Chapter 2. From this perspective the Persecutor role originates in the reptilian brain and the Rescue originates in the limbic brain. We switch between them depending on how we perceive the Victim. If the Victim seems helpless, we Rescue; if the Victim seems rebellious, we Persecute.

Politically, some people seem predisposed, innately or by their upbringing, to seeing powerless people as prone to take what is not legitimately theirs. They will react to powerless behavior with a territorial, reptilian response. ("What's mine is mine" and even "You can die for all I care"). Others are predisposed to seeing powerless people as helpless. They will react to powerlessness with a nurturing, limbic response. ("What's mine is yours" and even "Take it all if you must").

Clearly, any sort of unthinking, knee-jerk reaction to powerlessness is likely to be counterproductive. We need to use our neo-cortical Adult ego state to avoid Rescue or Persecution and to respond with nurturing or by defending our boundaries as is most beneficial for all involved.

How do you tear up your script, stop the games, and reclaim your natural, healthy life? The answer is that you have to give up the roles of Rescuer, Persecutor, and Victim. But when we do that, we have to be careful that we are not just jumping from one role to another. When a person tries to stop playing games, his first tendency is to move to a different role in the same game. If you are the Victim in a game of Alcoholism (that is, the helpless alcoholic), you may think you are changing by switching to the aggressive Persecutor or the kind Rescuer role, but that is not an improvement. It is merely the same game with a rearranged cast.

Eric Berne believed that most of us have an inborn tendency to find happiness and live mentally healthy lives. Hence, the famous saying, "I'm O.K., you're O.K." To make the necessary changes, each person needs to find the

"O.K. core" in him, or herself, and recognize it in the next person. There is no better way to find your O.K. core than to resolve to act differently from this moment on: to love and take care of yourself at the same time that you love and take care of others. In other words, not to Rescue, not to Persecute, and not to be a Victim. And nothing will better remind us of our previous mistakes than making a heartfelt apology and amends for them. This is why this last part of the program teaches you to apologize and make amends.

The Rescuer, Persecutor, Victim Merry-Go-Round

Let's look at these roles in more detail and how they work to keep us trapped in senseless, unproductive revolving and revolting melodramas.

THE RESCUER. A Rescue is a transactional event, part of a very common form of behavior known also as "co-dependence" or "enabling." It usually begins with an excessive willingness to be helpful that later causes problems and conflict. We play the Rescuer when we a.) do things for other people that we don't want to do, or b.) when we do more than our share. We are inspired to Rescue people when they seem to be unable to take responsibility for themselves. Some people are consistent Rescuers and will Rescue others at the slightest provocation, even if the other person has no real desire to be Rescued. When we do this it usually is because:

1. We like to feel needed.
2. We mistake competent people who are having difficulties for helpless people who are unable to take care of themselves.
3. We were raised to believe we have to keep people happy at all costs.

Alissa is a habitual Rescuer. She learns that her long-time neighbor Richard has AIDS. The next time she sees Richard, she feels compelled to be very thoughtful and to allude to his illness only with the utmost tact and concern. Eventually, the strain of working to make Richard avoid his painful condition and feel good makes it unpleasant for her even to see him. Alissa is vaguely aware that Richard is a self-sufficient and spiritually balanced man who doesn't really need her intense emotional output of pity. However, Rescuing is such a deeply ingrained habit she doesn't know how to stop. Richard, on his part, can be drawn by Alissa into conversations about his illness against his better judgment. Alissa's tendency to Rescue makes her dealings with Richard exhausting, to the point that she begins to avoid him. Still, even she knows she is making a bad situation worse for Richard and feels guilty about drawing Richard into the Victim role with her Rescue behavior.

This situation is typical for Alissa, who is constantly trying to do good for others but often is creating, rather than solving, problems for people. Rescues can also stem from a subtle desire to make others indebted to us, or an inability to say no when something is asked of us. When we fear that we are caught in a Rescue of our own making it can be difficult to be sure. Here are the two very specific criteria that define a Rescue transaction.

Again, we Rescue when we, either:
▨ Do something we don't want to do, or
▨ Do more than our share in a situation.

It is very important to distinguish rescuing as a humanitarian activity from Rescuing as an emotionally damaging role. That is why in transactional analysis we write them in lower case and capitals, respectively. Clearly, if someone is helpless and needs food, medical attention, or solace, we can be of help and should do so. If we come in at a crucial moment and literally save someone's life, we have rescued him or her in a profoundly positive way. Very often, however, in cases when we are "helping" others, we are actually causing harm, even though we believe that we are doing good.

A person who is a habitual Rescuer, always doing more than her share and engaging in activities that she doesn't really want to participate in, is most likely creating interpersonal problems for herself and others. Unwanted Rescuing fosters selfishness, dependence, and helpless behavior on the part of the Rescued/Victim. It also takes away the Rescued person's initiative and personal power, while it eventually creates anger and resentment in both the Rescuer and the Rescued. In addition, it ties the Rescuer and the Victim into a relationship of mutual dependence, or codependence, in which the Rescuer comes to need the Victim as much as, or even more than, the Victim needs the Rescuer.

THE PERSECUTOR. The Persecutor role is more easily spotted than the Rescuer role; it can be emotionally cold or involve anger, unfavorable criticism and judgment, and a superior attitude. Again, one characteristic of these three roles is that if you play one, you will eventually play the other two. For instance, it is inevitable that Rescuers will eventually Persecute their Victims when they become overwhelmed by the needs of those they are Rescuing. They will become tired of doing more than their share in taking care of others, and develop resentment and even hatred for those they have Rescued for needing and taking so much. That is why it is essential that we help someone we make sure that our help is given with an open and willing heart and that we never do more than our share in the process.

When the Rescuer becomes Persecutor he is not likely to become angry at himself, even though it was he who made the initial mistake by Rescuing. Instead, he will be angry at those he Rescued and to whom he has given so much. After all, he will ask, "Didn't I give everything and get nothing in return?" Let us look at an example of how Rescuers become Persecutors of their Victims.

Role Switching

Harry is an alcoholic. He drinks every day and gets drunk every weekend. His wife, Helen, drinks moderately, usually with him, and is a chain smoker.

After work, because his work is hard and he doesn't look forward to going home and dealing with his and Helen's troubles, Harry usually goes to the bar and has a couple of beers. When he gets home he is slightly drunk. He opens yet another beer and plops himself in front of the TV, hoping that Helen will come home and fix something to eat.

When she gets home, she cooks and eventually cleans up. Thinking that Harry's job is very stressful, she feels she should not nag him to help. Usually, by the time they go to bed, Harry is in a near coma from a couple of extra beers and a joint. They haven't had sex in years.

Harry and Helen's finances are strained from overspending on eating out and the interest on a loan they had to make for legal fees from Harry's drunk-driving arrest. Her income, which was supposed to help their quality of life, is barely enough to make ends meet.

Helen has been Rescuing and going along with Harry for years. One day she reads about codependency and decides to stop Rescuing Harry. She smashes all the liquor bottles in the house, changes the lock of the front door, and tells Harry that he can't come into the house if he is drinking. When Harry gets home from work after a few drinks at the bar, she refuses to let him in and calls the cops when he starts banging at the door. The cops arrive and eventually she lets Harry back in.

But Helen has had enough. She meets a nice, sober man at work and has sex with him, in part to get even with Harry. She likes this new man and a couple of months later, during a fight over the dishes, Helen announces to Harry that she is leaving him.

Harry is stunned by this reversal. He cries and begs and does not understand. He goes to the bar and talks to the bartender. He listens to Country-Western songs about the cruelty of women. He is now a full-fledged "helpless" Victim and Helen is his Persecutor.

Fortified by some bad advice and a lot of liquor, he decides to go home and take command of the situation. This time he smashes through the locked door and threatens Helen. Harry has switched again, this time from Victim to escalated Persecuting behavior and Helen is now the terrorized Victim. She goes to stay with her mother, who is also married to an alcoholic. Her mother doesn't want to take care of her and sides with Harry, arguing that "a woman has to stand by her man." As a result, Helen spends a week in abject depression and insecurity, blaming herself for the entire problem.

Eventually she talks to a counselor who takes her side. She switches from Victim to Persecutor again. She files a restraining order against Harry and gets a divorce lawyer. Harry now switches from Persecutor to Victim, goes to AA, sobers up, apologizes, and begs her to forgive him. Helen feels sorry for him and agrees to move back home with him, thereby switching roles again—this time from Persecutor to the familiar Rescuer.

After a week without a drink, Harry feels squeaky clean and self-righteous. He starts Persecuting Helen for smoking, while he tries to persuade her that she is also an alcoholic and should give up drinking altogether. However, within a week, Harry is drinking again and the process repeats itself; only this time, in a fit of jealous rage over her now-defunct affair, Harry actually strikes Helen.

They circulate in the Rescuer-Persecutor-Victim merry-go-round for a few more years until Harry leaves Helen for another woman who does not mind his drinking and finds him charming. It's Helen's turn to be stunned by the reversal and she goes after Harry for custody of the children. Without some help or intervention, they both will continue to play these games with their family and friends, possibly until they die.

Years ago, Helen should have stopped this process and refused to Rescue, Persecute, or be Victimized. Instead of abruptly switching from Rescuer to Persecutor, she should have gotten support from friends or a self-help group like Al-Anon, then developed a plan of action to take care of her needs and helped Harry decide what do to take care of his.

Then she should have done something that seems all wrong to most people but makes sense from an emotional literacy point of view: She should have apologized to Harry for Rescuing him, and promised not to anymore. After all that was accomplished she might have decided that the relationship was untenable and may decided to leave Harry. If she did it would not have been just another role-switch into Persecution but a genuine script change. On the other hand her refusal to participate in the game and its roles may have helped Harry stop playing as well so that he could give up his script and have a much better life. An example of how to do this follows later in this chapter.

THE VICTIM. As we have just seen, when people Rescue, they eventually get angry. When this happens, the Victim in the game will become aware of the Rescuer's anger and contempt. The Rescued/Victim recipient of the Rescuer's misguided generosity will begin to feel demeaned, treated like a charity case. Few people enjoy being viewed as a Victim, which is why, when people realize they are being Rescued, they feel humiliated and resentful and Persecute their Rescuer.

Helen and Harry's story is a real-life example of the dreary Rescue cycle. Eric Berne used to talk of first, second, and third-degree game playing.[31] You can tell the severity of these roles from the harm eventually done to the Victim. If the Victim is physically abused, as in the case of Helen, we have a case of second-degree Rescue and Persecution. In more common first-degree cases, the harm to the Victim is in the area of humiliation, hurt, and sadness. Third-degree game playing ends up in suicide, murder or mayhem.

Now we come to the touchy subject of the Victim's role and his or her responsibility for what is happening. Clearly, some people are unable to defend themselves against other people's single-minded purpose to persecute and harm them. Examples are plentiful: the relentless victimization of the Jews in World War II, Catholics and Protestants in Ireland, Israelis and Palestinians, African Americans in inner cities, or rape and incest victims.

Yet in some less obvious situations, the Victim contributes to the situation by accepting the Persecution. Certainly, Helen has been cooperating for years with what was happening to her. There is a tendency to blame women who are victims of spousal and child abuse who don't manage to leave the terrible circumstances they fall into. Yet, when a woman is in the grips of a violent situation without the resources to extract herself, it is necessary to consider the possibility of diminished responsibility. In other cases, the Victim must take as much responsibility for the situation as the Rescuer or Persecutor.

Most important to remember is that Rescuing eventually and inevitably causes anger; the Rescuer gets fed up with unfair situations or doing things that he or she does not really want to do, and the Victim gets fed up with being treated as someone who cannot take care of himself. Unavoidably, the Rescuer will Persecute the Victim and/or the Victim will Persecute the Rescuer. Anger will overflow in all directions. When we find that we have been playing any of these three roles, the emotionally literate thing to do is to stop, apologize and rectify the situation.

Summary

THE EMOTIONAL MISTAKES WE MAKE

People need strokes. In human terms, that means they need love and affection. They need to love and be loved and in order to get what they need, people will go to extremes similar to the extremes that people go to when they are hungry for food.

When strokes are not available, people will get them by playing emotional games. Unfortunately, strokes obtained from such games are largely negative and have noxious side effects. People who get their strokes in that way do it in endless succession of games, all of which fit into a life plan. Each different life plan is adopted by the young child early in life and calls for the acceptance of a set of games and roles, each of which generates a different kind of emotionally costly set of emotional mistakes. The roles in these games are the Persecutor, the Rescuer, and the Victim and when people play games they switch from one role to the other in an endless emotional merry-go-round of unhappiness.

CHAPTER 7

Taking Responsibility

There is at the present moment in history a great interest in apologies. From high officials or whole governments who are apologizing to people of their own or other countries, to everyday, garden variety apologies delivered at home, on the street, and at work.

Apologies and atonement are as old as guilt. The Jewish faith establishes a yearly, week-long period of self-examination and atonement. The Catholic religion makes confession, apology to and forgiveness from God a principal aspect of its catechism. Alcoholics Anonymous's recovery program relies heavily on making apologies and amends. Apologies have become the subject of scholarly discussion.[33][34] In too many cases, however, these apologies have become rituals, which though arguably bringing peace of mind to the wrongdoer, seldom have the result of righting the wrongs that people inflict on each other.

The mistakes we make, often swept under the rug, have a growing, lasting, and corrosive effect on our relationships. After years of accumulated emotional damage, many relationships become cold and distant or simply end. To bring about real and lasting change in a relationship that has been allowed to devolve owing to emotional errors, we have to take responsibility for our part in the process. After all, we can become receptive to relationships by opening our hearts and we can learn the outlines of the emotional landscape we live in, but the inevitable emotional damage of any dynamic relationship cannot be repaird between people without an effort to define and admit the faults and errors committed. The problem is that very few people are emotionally skilled enough to apologize sincerely and non-defensively. In short, most people don't know how to say "I am sorry" effectively.

The final emotional literacy skill I teach concerns the fine art of acknowledging one's mistakes and asking, even begging, for forgiveness. The thought of making a deeply felt apology strikes terror in the heart of the average person. Losing face, eating crow—all bring back memories of humiliating school-yard struggles and confrontations with accusing parents. In addition, we have learned to believe that backing down is weak and humiliating. Yet an emotionally mature person will admit mistakes and apologize for any harm his or her actions cause. I can use an example from my own life to illustrate this point.

Personal Case in Point

I had just arrived in Chicago from Paris and gone immediately to the hotel at which I had made reservations. I was exhausted by the flight and ready for a hot bath and a long night's sleep. The clerk, a gentle young woman, looked at her book and after some searching, politely shook her head. "I'm sorry, Dr. Steiner, but we have no reservation for you today. Your reservation is for tomorrow and we have no rooms tonight." I was outraged by this news. "But I specifically called weeks ago!" "Yes, and I see here that we listed you for tomorrow," she insisted. "Well, that was your mistake!" I hissed.

As I carried on loudly, I began to realize in the back of my mind that I was wrong. I had assumed that the reservation would be for the day after I left France, but had forgotten that I would in fact arrive the same day on an east-to-west flight from Europe to the United States. Meanwhile, the clerk had called someone on the phone and was explaining the situation. After a minute she hung up and said, "Dr. Steiner, we will try to get you a room, but…" At that point, I wasn't listening. I had been teaching emotional literacy in Europe and I knew that I had to practice what I preached, even if it meant the possibility of ending up on the street.

"Can I apologize to you?" I asked, feeling the flush of embarrassment in my face.

She looked up, puzzled.

"I just realized that you were right," I continued. "When I called to make my reservation, I was assuming that I would arrive the day after my departure from Paris."

"That's okay," she said. "This happens all the time; people don't realize that there is no time difference when they come back. But people never apologize."

"Well, I owe you an apology for the way I spoke to you before," I insisted. "Will you accept it?"

"Oh, that's all right," she said, looking back down at her book.

"No, no, seriously, will you accept my apology?"

She looked at me and smiled. "Sure, why not? I appreciate it," she said. "People expect us to apologize for our mistakes but rarely apologize for theirs."

As you might guess, this story has a happy ending. She found a room for me and before long I was comfortably asleep. I had practiced what I preached and felt good because of it. I had a room and had enjoyed a refreshingly honest interaction with a gracious young woman. My emotionally literacy skills had paid off.

Obstacles to Taking Responsibility

There are a number of obstacles that must be overcome before we can take responsibility and make a heartfelt apology.

1. Admitting to ourselves that we have made a mistake: Deciding that we have made a mistake is very difficult for most of us because we then become vulnerable to harsh criticism from our Critical Parent. Typical of the criticism you might hear in your mind include some of the following:

- "You fool, what a stupid mistake to make, and then you had to make an even worse fool of yourself by getting into an argument."
- "Right, as usual, you simply don't know better."
- "You have always been crazy, see what you have done now!"

Remember, the goal of the Critical Parent is to make you feel inadequate and not okay, and when you admit a mistake to yourself you give your Critical Parent a perfect opportunity to do just that.

2. Admitting our mistake to others: As if admitting mistakes to ourselves is not enough, admitting to someone else that we have made a mistake makes us vulnerable to *their* anger and disappointment as well as the further scrutiny and wrath of our Critical Parent. This can be a big, humiliating obstacle, but one we must learn to overcome. Admitting our mistakes is a powerful, cleansing experience, one that everyone with any claim to emotional literacy needs to experience.

3. Feeling and conveying true regret: This is where having an open heart will be indispensable, for even if we know and admit to a mistake we have made, we don't necessarily recognize or regret the damage we may have

caused. That is why this phase of emotional literacy training comes last: *It is hard to apologize for emotional damage we don't understand.* A certain level of emotional literacy, especially empathy, has to be developed before we can recognize the pain that we cause others with our actions. Without that recognition, it is hard to assume responsibility. Through the empathy developed in this work, we can see how our actions may have made another person feel sad, ashamed, angry, or afraid. Only when we really see that, will we be inclined to regret our actions.

4. Finally, admitting that amends are needed: Taking responsibility for a mistake usually means making amends. Amends means changing our behavior and even making reparations. When we make amends, we no longer do the things that have hurt others. We stop playing the role we have played in the past. Making amends is an important aspect of obtaining forgiveness. By making amends, we put our money where our mouths are, as it were. In many cases, forgiveness is not be possible without making amends.

By following the advice presented here, you will understand what it means to take responsibility for your actions. You will learn how to admit—to yourself as well as the victim(s) of your mistake—that you have done something wrong and that you wish to do what is necessary to set things right.

Remember, we all make mistakes, including emotional ones. Learning emotional literacy helps us avoid mistakes and to rectify those we do make as quickly as possible.

EMOTIONALLY LITERATE TRANSACTION # 10:
APOLOGIZING FOR OUR RESCUES.

Remedying a Rescue. Tempting though it is to want to do things for others, hard though it may be to say "No," learning not to Rescue is hugely important for anyone who wants to preserve and nurture meaningful relationships. When we find ourselves playing the role of Rescuer in a repetitive cycle of codependency, it is important to rectify our mistake by recognizing it, stopping, and apologizing. Here is how it is done:

"When I (describe action), I Rescued you because:
(1) I did not really want to do it, or
(2) because I believed that I was doing more than my share.
I apologize and will do better next time. Do you accept my apology?"

This needs to be handled with care. Finding out that someone has been Rescuing you can be quite humiliating, and generate much shame and anger especially if you weren't asking to be Rescued. Also, learning that someone close to you no longer wants to do something he or she has been doing for some time can feel like abandonment and generate feelings of fear. It is important to approach this gently and it's very important to be as nurturing as possible when you take proper responsibility for the mistake of Rescuing.

To stop Rescuing, you have to clarify what you want or do not want to do, and what is fair. And of course, you have to decide exactly what action of yours constitutes a Rescue. The best way to do that is to ask yourself questions about what you are doing and whether you should or should not keep doing it. For example, you may need to ask yourself:

- Do I want to continue this conversation?
- Do I want to have sex?
- Do I want to fix the car?
- Do I want to go to the ball game?
- Do I want to spend time with my husband's family?
- Do I want to cook tonight?

Sometimes your Rescue may involve doing more than your share. If that is the case, you have to ask yourself what constitutes a fair share of the effort involved in a relationship. The questions you ask yourself will be similar to these:

- Is it fair for me to do the dishes if Mary cooks, or should I also sweep the floor?
- Is it fair that I always initiate sex?
- Should I always pay for dinner when we go out?
- Is it fair that I always pick up the kids from school?

Sharon has been talking to me about her problems with her sister for months now. Should I let her go on or tell her I am bored with this subject?

I have been trying to be helpful to Tom with his drinking problem but he keeps drinking anyway. Am I more interested in his sobriety than he? Is he trying as hard as I?

In other words, you have to learn to know what you want to do or what you think amounts to a fair distribution of a relationship's responsibilities. Let me clarify by using Harry and Helen's example:

- When Helen cleans up the dishes because Harry says to leave them until next morning, she is doing something she hates, so she is Rescuing.
- When she cooks dinner every night while Harry watches TV, she is doing more than her share—and therefore Rescuing—even if she likes to cook and is willing.
- When she tries to minimize stress in his life so that he won't feel like drinking and he drinks even more, she is doing more than her share in their sobriety enterprise.

When stopping a Rescue, we tend to overcompensate and end up Persecuting. Therefore, while the Rescue must be stopped, it is important to keep a nurturing and loving attitude. To stop Rescuing needs to be a loving act—toward the other and oneself—and there is a fine line between not Rescuing and Persecuting. To the Victim who is no longer being Rescued the difference is like night and day and is devastating, empowering, or both.

EMOTIONALLY LITERATE TRANSACTION # 11:
APOLOGIZING FOR PERSECUTION

The role of Persecutor is more easily recognized and more obvious than the Rescuer role. There is no need to explain why apologies for Persecuting are important; most of us realize that Persecuting people is wrong. There are some people, however, who are sure that it is their duty to correct other people's behavior and thinking, in a harsh manner if needed. Some people are habitual Persecutors, stuck in an angry, blaming role; nothing works, everything is somebody else's fault, and they are constantly angry at something or someone. When we Persecute we are irritable and testy. We may insult, mock, discount, ignore, interrupt, yell, lecture, or constantly contradict others. Or we may lie. These are all power plays, and Persecution is essentially a matter of using power plays to control others.

Persecution can be very obvious or very subtle or somewhere in between. Rather than being deeply stuck in the role of Persecutor, however, most people will switch from normal, reasonable behavior into the Persecutor role for a few transactions which the Persecutor assumes are justified and even beneficial. Then, unaware of the effects of his actions, the Persecutor returns to normal as if nothing had happened. In a game-ridden, script-directed lifestyle, people will absorb these incidents, believe that they have dealt with them, and go on to the next episode of the melodrama; that is what emotional numbing is all about. But if we are to live well-managed emotional lives, we cannot let these injuries pass and we need to set them straight.

The remedying of Persecution follows the same pattern as the Remedying of Rescues. Let me give an example:

Messy & Neat

Beth has just moved in with Richard. Beth is neat and orderly. She is also very concerned about her possessions. For her, all her record albums, every book, her clothes, even her magazines are little treasures she has carefully picked out and preserved through her many moves from apartment to apartment. Richard is an unrepentant creator of chaos. He lives in a pile of papers and boxes of new and old gizmos, with clothing strewn all about.

Richard unwittingly tends to put his stuff on top of Beth's stuff. This makes Beth furious. She is very detail-oriented and always notices where she places her things. She would never throw her coat on top of Richard's shoes or crumple his new magazines. She is also under a lot of stress because of conflicts with her boss and concern over her depressed brother. She finds herself becoming more and more angry at Richard's carelessness.

Because she is not sure how to approach the problem, she often puts on a mockingly furious tone when she complains to Richard: "Oh darling, look whose greasy car manual I found on top of my favorite pumps. Naughty, naughty."

In response, Richard glances in her direction, feeling somewhat guilty and vaguely aware that he's being reprimanded. But the problem continues. Eventually, Beth becomes very angry. "Damn it, Richard, why do you do this? Look at my shoes, they're crushed! I searched for almost an hour for this sweater of mine that you threw in with your laundry! Leave my things alone!"

"They're all over my room," Richard retaliates, defensively.

"Your room? If I can't put my things down on one chair in our living room, then I'm sorry I moved in with you. Maybe I should move out so you can have your room back."

In the back of her mind, Beth is growing uneasy about the harpy-like posture she has drifted into. What went wrong? From an emotionally literate perspective, here is what happened: She should have dealt with her feelings from the beginning in a calm tone, using an action/feeling statement after getting Richard's attention. Instead, she started to complain timidly with a faintly critical joke, which only confused Richard and didn't get the message across. Essentially, she Rescued him, going along with his messiness. Her complaints became hostile when she got fed up with being ignored.

Here is an approach that might work better:

Realizing her mistake, Beth asks Richard when he will be free to talk. He suggests after lunch, and when the time comes, the dialogue proceeds like this:

"Richard, I want to apologize about something."

Richard, who expected her to Persecute him, is surprised. "What?"

"You know how we've been fighting when you do something to my things that I don't like."

Richard raises his eyebrows and makes a "tsk" sound, indicating that he is well aware of the "fights" which to him feel more like blitzkriegs over trivia.

"Well, I believe that I've been persecuting you unfairly. I never really sat down and calmly asked you to do things differently, and I guess I can't expect you to change your ways overnight. I've been really frustrated and upset about my boss and my brother, and I'm probably visiting some of my frustration on you. I'm sorry for being so hostile and impatient."

She waits for Richard's acknowledgment and acceptance of her apology and then says: "I still want you to be careful with what you do with my things. Would you please make an effort?"

With this approach his response might well be, "Okay, I didn't realize how serious you are about your things, I should have listened more closely to you. I'll try to do better. I apologize for calling our living room 'my room.'" This problem may take a while to be solved but it will surely be helped by this apology.

Apologies & Guilt

Apologies are usually associated with guilt, especially if they are apologies for Persecuting, attacking, or directly harming someone. The word "guilt" can refer to a judgment, as in: "The defendant is guilty!" or it can refer to an emotion. However, as an emotion, guilt has come to be seen as relatively useless in that it does not necessarily lead to any positive results. A person's feelings of guilt are not likely to bring important changes or deliver heart-felt amends. The situation between Beth and Richard is not improved by Beth's guilt about being mean or Richard's guilt about his treatment of her things. Guilt may at times inhibit their misbehavior, but it will not generate improvement in theor relationship. Guilt is a self-centered emotion ("I have been bad.") and doesn't necessarily take the other person's experience into consideration.

However, guilt is not the only reason one would apologize. Regret is an emotion akin to sadness rather than guilt, coupled with a realization that we bear responsibility in another person's suffering. Unlike guilt, which causes most people to be defensive and not want to apologize, regret motivates the person in the opposite direction: toward apology and making things right. The most effective apologies are manifestations of sadness and regret experienced by the Child with an Adult program of amends. Beth is sad about the way her anger has hurt Richard and regrets her Rescue of him. Richard, when he finally realizes that Beth's things are very important to her, regrets that he has made her unhappy with his messiness.

Both have felt guilty before to no avail; they are much more likely to make relevant changes under the influence of regret.

The question arises how to help a person replace feelings of guilt with feelings of regret. Regret is based on empathy; being aware of the discomfort or pain that we have caused another person. Beth needed to become aware of how her anger affected Richard and Richard needed to become aware of Beth's feelings about her things. Inviting the person to move their attention from their guilty feelings and toward the feelings of sadness, disappointment, hopelessness, or pain that the other experienced is usually an effective way to accomplish the desired change.

Some have argued that the more enlightened path is to forgive unilaterally, to turn the other cheek without need for an apology. Others may argue that the emphasis on apologies encourages the Victim role and ultimately reinforces game behavior. Both views have their grain of truth. It is true that some are able to forgive unconditionally, but most of us are not quite so ego-less, and when we're hurt we need some sort of justice and redress. It is also true that there are people who gladly occupy and even seek the Victim role in the Drama Triangle and may not be quite deserving of an apology. But these are exceptions; there are people who are true victims of other people's misdeeds and deserve apologies.

To repeat, for most relationships to flourish and move forward, it is essential that we consistently correct the errors we commit. We are fallible and we sometimes give in to our game-playing side; when these errors are not corrected, they add up and can drag down and eventually kill the best of relationships. A complete apology is a transaction that constitutes a corrective experience.

Requirements & Errors of an Apology

The three points that make an apology effective are:

1. BOTH PARTS OF THE APOLOGY TRANSACTION (APOLOGY AND RESPONSE) ARE REQUIRED FOR A COMPLETE APOLOGY.

For an apology transaction to be complete it has to be fully heard, contemplated, and responded to. All too often an apologetic statement is deemed to be sufficient and the assumption is made that once uttered, an apology should and will be accepted by a good-natured, forgiving person. This implies that an apology is a one-sided process, when in fact it is a transactional cycle between two people. When a person hurts another, apologizes in an offhanded way and the other routinely accepts the apology without reflection, the transaction is not healing and can be noxious. If this cycle repeats itself, the participants are locked in the drama triangle, and each apology supports both persons' scripts instead of producing healing results.

In emotionally literate relationships there is no place for a one-sided apology, no matter how well delivered. If there is no response, the apology is incomplete in the transactional sense. A one-sided apology may be better than none, in some cases, but that is not the issue here. I am discussing an apology transaction which effectively rectifies an emotional mistake when completed.

2. TO BE EFFECTIVE, AN APOLOGY HAS TO DESCRIBE THE OFFENSE.

An injury can be described in terms of the actions that caused the injury. In order to work, the apology has to specify an act the victim perceived as injurious, even if it was not intended to injure.

Sometimes, people apologize for an action that was not problematic, overlooking the action that was. John, at a staff meeting repeatedly ignores Mary's statements. Eventually, he offers coffee or tea to everyone except Mary. Later she complains bitterly to him about his behavior.

John: "I'm sorry, Mary."

Mary: "What are you I apologizing for?"

John: "For not offering you coffee. Will you forgive me?"

Mary: "Actually, I don't particularly care about the coffee. I need you to apologize for the way you kept ignoring the suggestions I made at the meeting."

With this, Mary has described John's offending actions. Now John knows what to apologize for if he wants to deal with Mary in an effective way.

3. In addition to a description of the offending behavior, the apology needs to include a recognition of its magnitude.

John: "Did I really? I don't think that it was that bad but I am sorry."

Mary: "It was that bad and has been a lot worse than you seem to think. I need you to recognize that."

At this point John needs to examine the situation a bit more seriously. He wants to deliver an apology about coffee and cookies. Mary has a larger offense in mind. Can he accept that he has been seriously discounting and thereby causing Mary feelings of anger, sadness, shame, and hopelessness? If he does, he will acknowledge the magnitude of his discount. If he demurs, he may fail to satisfy Mary.

In addition, we need to keep in mind the following two possible errors:

Apology Error # 1:
Giving Lip Service

Lately the importance of apology seems to have gained well-deserved recognition. Alcoholics Anonymous long ago included apologizing and making amends as two of the twelve steps of its program. Recently, numerous articles and books have been written about apologies.

People who are in frequent contact with the public, such as telephone operators, flight attendants and bank clerks, are taught to apologize as a way to quiet angry customers when necessary. These superficial apologies may mollify temporarily, but in time they feel hollow and fail to satisfy. The fact is that a phone operator cannot apologize for the management misdeeds of a credit card or mail order company.

People apologize all the time, but that does not necessarily mean that they are asking for anything or expecting a response. Very often the apology is a ritual, basically:

"Sorry"

and the response:

"No problem"

For the most banal offenses, such a bumping into someone or occasionally interrupting while somebody is speaking, this kind of a transaction suffices to remedy the offense by the exchange of a couple of strokes to avoid any appearance of rudeness.

But beyond that type of extremely minor example, when someone does something to injure another, more will be needed to restore harmony and bring the relationship back to a cooperative, healthy footing.

Apologies and asking for forgiveness can be attempted through a variety of non-productive attitudes:

▧ An unemotional, even legalistic appraisal of one's wrongdoing. It sounds good but may fail to satisfy. For example:

Bill: (in a serious tone) "I showed lack of judgment. I may have misled you and for that I apologize."

▧ Another example: a guilt-laden self-rebuke in response to Critical Parent which somehow manages to avoid responsibility:

John: (weeping) "I was weak, and gave in to the Devil, I deserve eternal damnation. I am, oh so sorry!"

▧ An apology can also be hypocritical and manage to make light of the injury it has caused.

Mark: (smiling) "I know, I know, I am so terrible. I am sorry."

Each one of these transactions reflects a different attitude (rational, self-hating, smug). These attitudes have their source in a defensive Child ego state. Again, the attitude and coherent emotional content required for an effective apology are heartfelt, empathic, emotional responses to the harm or pain that one's behavior has caused.

Harry, for instance, apologized with self-hate, often and profusely to Helen. However, he barely realized what he was saying and certainly was only minimally sincere. He knew it pacified Helen, so he went ahead and apologized whenever he got in trouble with her. She would accept his apology but within days—maybe hours—she felt as if she had been cheated. An apology has to be heartfelt and has to be for specific behavior, or it is meaningless and ultimately ineffective. Words alone do not change things or soothe the aggrieved party. And, of course, an apology that is not followed by a change of behavior will quickly prove meaningless.

APOLOGY ERROR #2:
BLAMING THE VICTIM

When we discover that we have been Rescuing someone, it is easy to get mad at him or her. Helen is an example: After much Rescuing, she was furious at Harry. Attacking another person because we are angry is rarely the right response and is certainly the wrong choice when you decide to stop a Rescuing. Getting angry can hurt your relationship with the person you have been Rescuing, which is why it is important to stop before your anger builds up. Do this with a gentle and nurturing explanation rather than an abrupt withdrawal. Above all, do not blame the Victim for your mistake. Don't forget, Rescuing is definitely a mistake on your part and not necessarily on the part of the Rescued/Victim-who may not even know that you are Rescuing and may not want to be Rescued.

EMOTIONALLY LITERATE TRANSACTION #12: APOLOGIZING FOR PLAYING THE VICTIM ROLE

Last, but certainly not least in this catalogue of corrective procedures is the Remedying of Victim behavior.

One way to get strokes and regain some power when we feel completely defeated and powerless is to play games in the role of the Victim. One of the first games that Eric Berne discovered and which illustrates that principle beautifully is "Why don't you? Yes, but."

In this game, a person in the Victim role hooks one or more people into giving advice on a problem that he considers hopeless. For example, Bruce hates his job and his boss and is sure that his coworkers hate him. What is he to do? He describes the situation to a number of his friends. They try to help:

Ted: "Why don't you quit and find another job?"

Bruce: "Yes that's a good idea, but there are no jobs that pay as well as this one."

Ned: "Why don't you get a union mediator and work it out with your boss?"

Bruce: "Yes, I thought of that, but the union mediator right now is a woman and she doesn't understand these kinds of problems."

Fred: "Why don't you go to a meditation weekend and develop a white light around you that protects you from harm?"

Bruce: "Yeah sure, have you seen how much those weekends cost?"

Ted: "I guess you're right; it's a pretty hopeless situation. If I was in your place I'd want to kill myself."

Bruce: "I know there's no use. I guess you guys can't help me. It's really up to me, isn't it? Let's get drunk."

At this point everybody is depressed. Bruce is gloating over his power to bring down a roomful of drinking buddies and his gloomy view of the world is vindicated. The next day, Bruce buys the book *Achieving Emotional Literacy* and reads about the Victim role. He realizes his tendency to be depressed and feel hopeless and that the best way to get out of this role is to apologize. The next time he gets together with his buddies, he startles everybody by saying:

"Listen guys, I want to apologize about something." Everyone is stunned into silence, but listening. "I feel that when I start complaining about my job and not taking the advice that is offered, that I am really acting like a powerless victim and I realize it must be a bummer. I apologize. I'm not going to do that anymore."

Ted: "What is this, twelve-step amends or something?"

Bruce: "Something like that. I am serious though, and I want you guys to accept my apology. Will you?"

EMOTIONALLY LITERATE TRANSACTION #13:
ACCEPTING AN APOLOGY.

After hearing an apology and after thoughtful soul-searching, we can do one of the following:
- Grant forgiveness
- Postpone, pending additional amends
- Deny it

To be forgiven is a gift that cannot always be granted. Forgiveness depends entirely on whether our hearts respond in a forgiving manner to the apology, and it is not possible or advisable to force the heart in matters of love, hate, or forgiveness. Consequently, it is as important in emotionally literate relationships that we properly grant or decline forgiveness as that we ask for it.

There is obviously a great deal of skill involved in making a heartfelt apology. Few people realize, however, that there is an equally important skill involved in accepting, or rejecting, an apology once it is given.

In the case of Mary and John and the staff meeting, John's initial apology (about coffee and cookies) does not work. How does Mary handle her coworker's apology without accepting it just yet?

ACCEPTING APOLOGY ERROR #1: FORGIVING TOO EASILY

Mary might say, "No problem, that's okay." Doing this is probably a means of trying to avoid the humiliation of feeling patronized. Or she may even be trying to Rescue John from his responsibility to be civil.

It is best not to do that. An apology doesn't accomplish much emotional healing if it is accepted without reflection. If someone gives you a perfunctory apology and you say, "No problem," you will probably feel just as bad as before. You probably accepted the apology because you have learned what's socially expected of you. Even if the apology is heartfelt and sincere, you can render it useless by accepting it in a perfunctory way. The emotionally appropriate response is always to think about the apology and decide whether you want to accept it or not. If the apology doesn't work, it is important to decline it.

ACCEPTING APOLOGY ERROR #2: BASHING THE RIGHTEOUS

Another error is what I call "Bashing the Righteous." Let's continue discussing Mary and John. Let's say that John earnestly apologizes to Mary for discounting her at meetings. Mary now sees an opportunity to get even, to hurt him the way that she has been hurt.

"Well, it's about time you apologized," she might say. "I resent it and I am very angry with you. You are such a bastard sometimes!"

If you are trying to develop emotional literacy, this type of response won't do, either. If Mary is angry, she can use an action/feeling statement to deal with his reaction. She might say, for instance, "It makes me angry that you spoke to me the way you did. I also feel embarrassed. But I appreciate your apology. Please don't do it again."

Acceptance of Apology with Conditions

If the injured person hears the apologetic statement and her heart does not open, perhaps something more is needed.

Mary: "I am sorry but you don't seem to really understand how difficult your behavior is for me. I am afraid that I can't accept your apology. I need more than just words to feel better." Thinking further, she says: "I would appreciate it if you apologized to me in the meeting and asked the other people to remind you if they see you do it again. Can you do that?"

EMOTIONALLY LITERATE TRANSACTION #14:
REJECTION OF AN APOLOGY:

Sometimes apologies simply don't work:

- Diana's heart was broken when her fiancé called off their engagement. She was devastated and humiliated. Days later, he came to apologize but she was much too angry and sad to accept. It was only months later, after several long discussions about his decision to break off their engagement, that she was finally able to accept the apology she needed.

- A victim of his wife's long string of large impulsive purchases, Peter is unable to forgive her. He needs a much more extensive apology for the years of financial worries she has caused him and some concrete assurances of her intention to change her ways. There may be nothing she can do to remedy her mistakes.

- Andres apologizes to Clyde for accepting an invitation to a dinner party on his behalf, without asking him. Clyde is beginning to feel that Andres is ignoring his distaste for social outings with new people. He always thinks each party is an exception. He refuses the apology because Andres does not seem to care that he always puts Clyde in awkward situations.

Sometimes an apology does not work because the injury was too large to be dispelled by a simple apology. Perhaps the Victim needs an explanation or some form of amends. For example, Peter, the man who has been financially damaged by his wife, needs her to explain how she has changed and that she will get a job to bring them back into solvency. Clyde needs Andres to admit that he has accepted invitations for Clyde hoping to break him of his shyness. He promises to stop doing that and to check with Clyde about every social event that involves both of them. It is important to keep in mind that the ultimate purpose of an apology is to give the victim a chance to feel better about the way he or she has been hurt.

The above examples illustrate that it would be an error to accept an apology that doesn't truly make you feel better. You should explain to the person apologizing why it falls short, if you can. Then the person can try to apologize in a way that acknowledges the true nature of the mistake. But if the effort fails, the apology should be gently declined in favor of a renewed effort to make it work.

Case Study: Both Sides of Apology

Here is an example of a properly delivered and accepted apology: Laura frequently found herself having unwanted sex with her husband, Brian. He would tell her that he had a tough day at work and needed her, or that he was all wound up and could not get to sleep if she did not have sex with him. If she refused him, he would become angry or pout. At that point, no matter how Laura felt, she would give in.

Laura consulted me to change her relationship with Brian. She loved him, she said, but felt as though he was taking advantage of her. Lately she had started resenting him and getting angry at irrelevant little things. She thought that some emotional literacy training might be helpful and she came to me for the tools. After talking to her for a while, I could see that Laura was a habitual Rescuer, not just with Brian, but in all sorts of situations.

With Brian, her worse Rescue was that even when she did not want to have sex with him, she did it anyway. Now she was feeling used and wanted to Persecute him to the point of considering leaving him. I explained to her the importance of taking responsibility for her actions and explained how to frame an apology for being a Rescuer. I told her that she needed to stop rescuing in all sorts of places but that it would be a good idea to start with Brian.

Here is what happened next: Friday evening, Laura told Brian that she would like to talk about something very important. Brian seemed wary and somewhat alarmed.

"I want to talk about something I've been thinking about," said Laura. "I'll make an early dinner and we can have a relaxed conversation."

Following Saturday evening's dinner, Laura took a deep breath and began. "Brian, I have been feeling bad about something between us, may I tell you about it?"

Brian shrugged. Although he smiled, he was scared. "Well, that seems to be why we're here," he said warily.

"Okay," Laura began, "I am worried that you are going to be upset about what I am going to say. Here it goes," she gulped. "I feel bad that I've been making love with you lately and some of the times I didn't really feel like it." She eyed Brian nervously, trying to gauge his response. Seeing nothing in his face she continued, "Maybe I didn't make it clear enough that I didn't want to. I guess I gave you mixed messages, and I'm sorry."

Brian erupted. "What are you trying to say? You don't want to sleep with me?"

"No, I'm not saying I never want to have sex, I just mean that I feel that we have sex when you are in the mood, not when I am, and I don't want to go on making love when I'm not in the mood. I'm not blaming you for what I've done up until now, going along with your wishes and ignoring mine. I am trying to take responsibility for that, but I also want to change things."

"Well, it sounds like you're not attracted to me, as if I'm your sexual charity case."

"Sometimes I'm tired or preoccupied or just not feeling sexual. I just don't feel like having sex."

"Well, are you ever in the mood? It seems to me that if I didn't start things, you never would."

"It's true I don't usually think to initiate sex, but sometimes when you do I really like it. Other times I'm tired and not really interested. I don't want to continue having sex like that, when I don't really feel like it. It makes me ashamed of myself and sometimes even angry at you. Maybe if we didn't have sex when I'm not in the mood, I might be in the mood more often."

Brian listened quietly as Laura continued.

"The point is that it's not your fault. I take responsibility for my decisions to go along. But I want to do things differently from now on. I just want things to be good between us, as good as they can be, because I love you."

Brian looked at her warily. "Well, I'm just going to leave you alone. I don't want to be your sexual charity project. If you want to make love, you can let me know."

With that, he walked over to the couch and turned on the baseball game. Laura was very upset, though I had warned her that Brian might be quite defensive at first. I also told her that once the initial shock subsided, he would probably relax and accept her feelings and proposal. She went to the bedroom, where she knew she wouldn't be heard, and called her sister up to unburden herself about the upsetting situation. Then she read a novel in bed. She decided to let the dishes wait until morning. When Brian came to bed, she pretended to be asleep to avoid a confrontation. He got into bed without touching her at all, and after lying awake awhile, fell asleep. Once she heard his regular breathing pattern, Laura moved over and held him close until she fell asleep. She was worried but kept reminding herself that things would get better.

In the morning, Brian, who had noticed that Laura cuddled with him throughout the night, was aloof, reading the paper and drinking coffee. Then he unexpectedly left, announcing last-minute Sunday plans with some male friends. When Brian came home that evening, he handed Laura a small, scraggly bunch of wildflowers he had picked at the last minute on the way home. She kissed him appreciatively. For a moment Brian wanted to grab Laura and kiss her passionately. At that point he stopped himself, feeling vaguely humiliated.

She sensed his turmoil and went into the kitchen to fix some tea. Brian sat on the couch, wrestling with his stormy feelings. After all, he thought, she's not blaming me. He remembered a few times early in the relationship when she had wanted to have sex and he was too tired. He decided to try not to take the situation personally. "Let's eat out tonight," he announced impulsively.

At dinner, Brian said, "Can I tell you how I feel?" Laura agreed eagerly. "When you told me about the unwanted sex last night, I felt angry at first, and then scared that you weren't attracted to me anymore. Then I became sad that we have been having sex without you enjoying it." (Brian had been reading this book, you see.)

Laura nodded. Brian continued. "I accept your apology for going along. Let's see if we can have sex only when we both want it." That night, after dinner, they kissed in bed. Brian decided not to push for intercourse, and Laura fell asleep in his arms. He felt sexually needy and lay awake for a while, but it was reassuring to feel Laura nuzzle against him in her sleep. Eventually, when he could not fall asleep, he moved to the living room and read until he fell asleep on the couch. The next morning, he made an effort to keep a loving attitude as he explained why he had left their bed. It took a few months before the tensions between Laura and Brian subsided. Gradually, however, he accepted her sexual rhythm and got over his feelings of embarrassment and abandonment. For her part, Laura made an effort to take a sexual initiative, especially on the weekend, when she had more energy. Through conversations and compromise, they got out of the destructive Rescue pattern that was secretly threatening their sex life and ultimately, their marriage. Their sex life improved.

EMOTIONALLY LITERATE TRANSACTION# 15:
BEGGING FORGIVENESS—AN EMOTIONALLY LITERATE WAY OF APOLOGIZING FOR AN ACTION THAT HAS DEEPLY HURT ANOTHER PERSON

Garden-variety emotional errors occur frequently. It is therefore a part of emotional housekeeping to keep track of them and clean them up when needed. Sometimes, however, we make hurtful mistakes that can cause long-term damage. When that happens, it is important to make a major apology, and if necessary, beg for forgiveness.

Case Study: Begging Forgiveness

A dramatic example of begging for forgiveness is the story of Rose and Edgar, two 60-somethings who were about to celebrate their 40th wedding anniversary when they attended one of my emotional literacy workshops. After we discussed the power of apologies, Edgar declared that he needed to do some emotional work with Rose.

After getting her agreement, he explained why: Thirty-five years ago, on the evening of the birth of their son, he'd had sex with another woman. It happened right after he saw the baby and visited Rose in the recovery room. He left the hospital late at night but was too excited to go directly home. Instead, strangely energized, he went into a neighborhood bar to have a drink. As he sat enjoying a double whisky, he noticed a young woman coworker. He told her about his new son and offered to buy her a drink. One drink led to another and before he knew it, they were in her apartment having sex.

When he left the next morning, Edgar was overcome with guilt. He felt terrible that he had cheated on his wife and impulsively told Rose what he had done. Rose was devastated by the news. Even though he assured his wife that he had been stupidly drunk and never wanted to see the woman again, Rose was inconsolable and unforgiving. For the next 35 years, virtually every argument between them contained references to the incident. Every time Rose felt Edgar was taking her for granted or did not give her the attention she should have, she would bring up the dreaded incident. They were both very distressed about this. After all these years the incident was still like a thorn in both of their sides, a thorn they had pretty much given up trying to remove.

On this occasion, Edgar thought that he needed to do something he had never done: take full responsibility for his infidelity and beg Rose for forgiveness. He did this in the most touching way. In front of the entire group, Edgar got on his knees and grasped Rose's hand. With tears in his eyes, he began to speak. "Rose," he asked, "may I speak to you about something?"

"Yes," she agreed.

"Rose, I know that I have apologized a hundred times about this and I have complained that it doesn't seem to work."

She nodded.

"I realize from this discussion that even though I apologized, my apologies have been hollow, and I am not surprised that they haven't worked."

Again, she nodded.

"I understand why. It is because I have not really acknowledged how much I hurt you. I really didn't want to accept that I had hurt you so much. So I made excuses and never stopped to experience your pain." He wiped his eyes and asked, "May I apologize now?"

At this point there wasn't a dry eye in the room, including Rose's. She nodded again, this time warmly, covering his hands with hers.

"Rose, after all these years, I realize how much what I did hurt you. I am so sorry that I did it and so sorry that it took me so long to realize the extent of your pain. Would you please forgive me?"

Rose took a long time to think. Finally, she broke into a tearful smile and agreed. "Yes, I will, and I must say that I believe now that I have been harsh in my anger. I have always thought, in the back of my mind, that you did it because you felt potent and manly after we had our first son. But I see that you finally understand how much that hurt me. I forgive you." They hugged, surrounded by a smiling group of fellow emotional literacy enthusiasts.

One year later, I happened to meet Edgar. I asked him how things were. He told me that they had just had a wonderful anniversary celebration, with many friends and family. "By the way," he added, "Rose has never brought up that incident again."

One That Didn't Work

Sadly, it may at times happen that forgiveness will not be granted under any circumstances.

Karla spent five years recovering from the devastating heartbreak of an extremely acrimonious divorce. Bill, her husband, had abruptly left her for his secret lover of six months and then tried to prevent her from receiving a proper division of their assets. Her pain lasted a full five years, but eventually she overcame her distress, met another man, and remarried happily.

Even today, Karla's eyes tear when she talks about the events of the past. Very soon after the divorce, Bill's relationship fell apart and he attempted to reconnect with Karla to be friends. Karla was completely unwilling even to speak to Bill, but over the years, through common friends who liked them both and for the sake of their teenage son, she began to speak to him on the phone occasionally.

She had long ago concluded that their marriage had been very flawed and that terminating it had been good. But she could not forget or forgive the lies that Bill had told and the financial maneuvers she had had to fight.

Through friends, she let it be known that no relationship was possible without an apology. Bill, eager to reestablish the friendship, wrote her a note:

Dear Karla,

I want to apologize for my part in hurting your feelings. I am sorry,

Bill

When Karla received that note, she was furious. Was she supposed to take this hastily written note as an apology? She didn't even bother to respond. Eventually, Bill called her. After some polite preliminaries, he asked:

"Did you get my note?"

"Yes."

"Well?"

"Well, what?"

"Do you forgive me?"

"For what?"

"What do you mean, for what? I thought you wanted an apology!"

"Oh, I see. Well, I guess I don't forgive you."

"Why not?"

"You haven't really apologized."

"What about my note?"

"Your note was okay as a start. What are you apologizing for?"

"For hurting you."

"I need an apology for what you did."

"What do you mean?"

"You lied, you were cruel, you tried to cheat me."

"I don't know about that. That's a matter of opinion."

"Well, what are you apologizing for then? It's not enough to say that you had a part in hurting me. What part did you have? Unless you can acknowledge what you did to hurt me, I am not really interested in an apology."

There the conversation ended. Several years later, Bill again wanted to make things right. He wrote another note:

Dear Karla,

I thought about what we talked about and I agree that I lied to you, but it was because I thought you would be more upset if you knew the truth, and financially I was afraid that you would rip me off. I am sorry if I hurt your feelings and I apologize.

Bill

Again, Karla was less than satisfied. Bill had acknowledged that he had lied, but his rationalizations for what he now admitted doing detracted from the apology enough that her heart did not open, and she could see no reason to let Bill back into her life. There seemed to be no acknowledgment of how badly he had hurt her. She wrote him back the following note:

Bill,

I got your letter and I see that you are making an effort to make things right. However, you are spending more words in giving excuses for what you did than in acknowledging what a brutal and painful experience I went through. We both made mistakes that we are paying for. I was not perfect. But if you want us to be friends, I will have to be convinced that you realize how you hurt me, how much of the pain I suffered was caused by your actions. And then you have to feel and communicate some sorrow or regret or guilt to me. I need to experience that kind of feeling from you, and until then, I feel and believe it's best for me that we keep our distance.

Karla

There the matter was left. Bill may eventually recognize what he needs to do or he may decide he can't or won't, but Karla is taking care of herself emotionally by refusing to grant forgiveness prematurely. If she had softened and let Bill off the hook without feeling the healing satisfaction that comes from a heartfelt apology, she would never really open to Bill and their "friendship" would have been a painful sham. The process of apology and forgiveness is extremely important in an emotionally literate life and is worth pursuing—sometimes to excruciating extremes.

This brings us to the end of the fifteen emotionally literate transactions that constitute emotional literacy training. These emotionally literate transactions lose their initial awkwardness as people become skilled in using them. They become part of everyday emotional housekeeping, like raking leaves, walking the dog, or flossing teeth. Once assimilated into everyday life and language, these fifteen transactions contribute to a well-ordered emotional existence in which feelings are acknowledged and given their proper place as a source of power and well-being. But the rewards of emotional literacy are more than just a tidy emotional house. When our emotions are clear and fully expressed and other people's feelings matter as much to us as our own, life becomes powerfully moving and at times truly joyous. It is then that the rewards of an emotionally literate existence show their full promise.

Summary

TAKING RESPONSIBILITY

You'll find that the hardest part of becoming emotionally literate is to own up to the mistakes you've made in your relationships.

First, you admit to yourself that you have made a mistake. Then you have to admit your mistake to others. Next, you must feel true regret and convey that to the person you have hurt. Finally, you should agree to make some real, relevant changes in yourself, and you may have to make amends.

We make emotional mistakes when we let ourselves be drawn into one of three roles: Rescuer, Persecutor, or Victim. As a Rescuer, you do things for people that you don't want to do and that they should do for themselves. As a Persecutor, you become angry and self-righteously attack other people, often the very people you have Rescued. As a Victim, you either allow yourself to be taken care of by a Rescuer or attacked by a Persecutor, all the while acting as if you can't do anything about the situation.

If you have acted as a Rescuer, Persecutor, or Victim or have otherwise abused another person, emotional literacy requires that you apologize to the people you have hurt or created problems for and that you resolve to act like a responsible adult in the future. If you have been hurt, you need to learn to ask for apologies. If an apology is forthcoming, it is important to learn the proper way to grant, postpone, or deny forgiveness.

CHAPTER 8

Emotional Literacy with Couples & Children

Learning emotional literacy requires a group of people; it can't be learned alone. A very good small group is a new couple or friendship. The agreements that are required to make emotional learning possible can more easily be made between two people, especially two like-minded people who have no history of unresolved interpersonal issues with each other.

Finding a partner is difficult enough. Finding a partner who is willing to make a commitment and be completely honest and equal increases the difficulty. Many people have discovered that the old system of domination/submission, where one person leads and the other follows, is largely obsolete. Still, people who sincerely believe in equality often fall back into traditional patterns of inequality. In relationships between men and women, men still tend to dominate, while women find it hard to assert themselves. The same patterns seem to surface in same-gender couples, as well. There always seems to be a "top" and a "bottom" in each couple. Therefore, men and women need to be vigilant and work continuously to maintain the goals of partnership, in which emotional needs are met equally.

People are genuinely confused about how to make the modern style of relationships work. In the old patriarchal system, the man's emotional needs took priority while the woman's priorities were usually not even perceived and if perceived they were ridiculed as childish, and overlooked. Consequently, after a few years of marriage (about seven, on average) many women could no longer tolerate the neglect and rebelled furiously or went mad with frustration. The modern system of equality brings new problems. One major problem is that when dominance/submission is given up, it is replaced by competition between the partners. Instead of one person leading and the other following, they compete and argue over every point.

It's no wonder that more and more people are simply giving up and living alone.[35] An alternative is a cooperative relationship, as defined in this book, based upon:

- a conviction that both partners have equal rights in the relationship,
- an agreement not to power play each other, and
- a commitment to honesty.

Equality & Honesty in Intimate Relationships

My recommendation for those who want an emotionally literate relationship is to quickly establish a cooperative contract based on equality and honesty. In a cooperative relationship:

- neither person tries to manipulate the other with power plays, and
- neither does anything he or she doesn't want to do, and

168

- they both gently and lovingly ask for everything they want, while
- listening empathically to what the other needs.

These ground rules will require that you overcome the old established patterns of power playing, Rescuing, and lying. These changes are not easy and will not come overnight, but you will find that the energy and optimism released in this process will invigorate any relationship, new or old. When mistakes are made from time to time, apologies and amends keep the relationship on a positive, cooperative course.

EQUALITY

Equality is based on the idea that both people need to have equal rights and should make an equal contribution toward the relationship's success. Equality doesn't mean that people can't differ from each other. Especially between men and women, who are in important ways different from each other—for cultural and genetic reasons—it simply means that those differences don't give one person privilege over the other.

Equal contribution does not mean that both partners have to work and earn the same or that expenses and housework are shared fifty-fifty. Equality in an emotionally literate relationship means that both partners make an equal effort to contribute what they have to offer in such a way that both feel satisfied. If they become dissatisfied with the other's contribution, they must feel free to say so with the assurance that their partner will work toward a fair compromise.

HONESTY

Honesty is the most important agreement in a relationship between equals. No one enters into a serious relationship expecting to be lied to. In fact, it is assumed that two people in love should not lie to each other at all. Many relationships are consecrated in ceremonies in which vows are made: "For richer or for poorer, in sickness or health, to honor, love, and cherish." These vows don't normally include a vow to be completely honest. Small wonder since by that time, in most relationships, at least one of the participants has already lied about something. Sometimes both have.

Even in the most honest of relationships, a few things have been swept under the rug. Maybe he has always longed for more strokes about his looks, but felt too embarrassed to ask for them. Or perhaps she has not been honest about her dissatisfaction with their lovemaking. Even the smallest lie or secret has a damaging effect on an intimate relationship because it can be the seed for further and bigger dishonesty.

When a long-term couple tries to clean the slate of lies and secrets, there may be dark secrets that could truly upset the other person. Maybe there has been a one-night stand or even a full-blown affair. Or maybe one partner has recklessly spent money from the joint account without telling the other. Maybe there is some long-term unhappiness or deep dissatisfaction with the other's looks, intelligence, sense of humor, or sexual style. If that is the case, it may be a good idea to reveal these secrets with the help of a third person: a trusted friend, a therapist, or a minister.

Lies of omission—usually about sex, money, or appearance—cannot be allowed to remain secret in an emotionally literate relationship. They must be revealed. If a partner with a secret does not reveal it and the other partner finds out, it is my experience that the lie hurts more than the misdeed itself. How long the secret has been kept, how many others know about it, and all the ramifications of the lie are often so devastating that they can permanently damage or wreck the relationship. It is difficult to forgive missteps, but far more difficult to forgive the lies that surround them.

Even people who claim they would rather not know if their partner has strayed will likely find the truth extremely humiliating and hurtful. When we condone secrets and say "I'd rather not know," "Don't ask, don't tell," we have probably not anticipated how terrible it would feel to unwittingly discover such a secret. That is why lying is so damaging and why it needs to be removed from any emotionally literate relationship.

To summarize:

Equality takes two: Keep in mind that an emotionally literate relationship requires both partners to work at it as equals. To do this, you must grant each other equal rights and expect equal responsibilities.

Cooperation is the key: Agree with your partner to have a relationship of equality free of power plays, especially lies and Rescues. Make it clear that you want a relationship in which both of you ask for everything you want and don't do anything that you don't want to do. If you are getting involved in a new relationship, begin talking about this notion as soon as you feel that the relationship has long-term potential. Start talking about a cooperative relationship right away. This is especially important if you are in love, when everything is seen through a radiant mist. Just talking frankly about issues will bring clarity and reality to your budding rapport.

Pre-nuptial Emotional Agreements

Fran and John are in love. They are lying in the grass, warmed by the spring sunshine on their day off. Both have agreed that they would like to get married. She has been married before with bad results and wants to do better this time.

Fran: "John, can I bring up something that I would like us to talk about before we get married?"

John: "Sure, what is it?"

Fran: "I have been reading a book about how to have an emotionally literate relationship."

John: "What kind of a relationship?"

Fran: "It's a relationship in which you are emotionally involved and aware. A cooperative relationship where both people agree ahead of time about some things."

John: "What things?"

Fran: "Well, this book talks about an honest relationship between equals and I really liked what it says; the idea is that we agree to always say what we want and to make sure that we never get pressured into doing things we don't want to do."

John: "I like that. But it seems like we already do it. Don't you think?"

Fran: "I know we both want to, but sometimes I think we don't, actually."

John: "Like when?"

Fran: "I think we both lie about what we want and go along with the other person sometimes. Like this morning when we went to the Blue Barn for breakfast. I really wanted to go to the Brick Shack, but I lied because I wanted to please you."

John: "Lied? Isn't that what being generous is all about?"

Fran: "In emotional literacy it's called Rescuing, and it's not good because after a while the person who Rescues gets angry. Usually it's me who goes along with you."

John: "I know you do and I love that about you; you spoil me. Does that mean you are going to get mad at me later?"

Fran: "Could be, that's what happened in my previous marriage, and I really don't want that again. And maybe there is stuff you are going along with that I don't know about. Is there?"

John: "Well a couple of things, but I don't mind."

Fran: "Well, I think Steiner is right; it would be better if we were completely honest about that kind of a thing. What are you going along with?"

John: "Why do you want me to look for things to complain about? I love you!"

Fran: "I just want us to learn to have a cooperative, honest relationship."

John: "I'll try." He thinks for a moment. "Okay. The truth is, I would rather not meet all your girlfriends and hang out with them the way we do."

Fran: "Really."

John: "It's just not something I'm into. It's not very interesting. I mean, I want to meet them, but I don't want to make a special point to spend time with each of them. I don't have the time to get to know every one of your friends, you know. I'm sorry, is this too hard on you?"

Fran: "A little, but it's okay, let's go ahead. Thanks for asking."

John: "Okay, if you're sure." With a concerned look he continues. "There is one other thing, I'm really glad you introduced me to your parents. But I'm not that much into family things, like your aunt's Thanksgiving dinner. That was a bit much for me, meeting all these people who don't seem that important to us."

Fran: "Okay," she answers in a subdued voice. Once I mean, I'm disappointed and embarrassed now to think that I introduced you to everyone so enthusiastically and you were wishing you were somewhere else."

John: "It wasn't that bad, I'd just rather pass."

Fran: "Well. I really do like spending time with my family. I have ever since I was a kid. But if you don't want to come along I'll just go by myself."

A thoughtful silence ensues. John begins again. "I'll tell you what, why don't you tell me which events are really important to you and I'll go with you to those. Maybe you can go early and I'll meet you a little later, so I don't have to stay as long. That would be interesting to me."

Fran: "That sounds fair."

They hold each other tightly. They both have a bit to think about, but Fran was proud of herself for initiating an emotionally literate dialogue, and John was relieved to have gotten out of some unwanted social obligations.

You may wonder why two happy young lovers should start discussing the small dissatisfactions that seem wholly unimportant compared to the wonderful love they feel for each other. But these are the things that, when the bright lights of new love begin to soften and reality returns, often drive apart couples who once thought nothing could ever come between them. Fran learned this the hard way with her first marriage. She is right to take the initiative and start a dialogue about ground rules that establish a level of honesty and awareness that later will be very important to avoid another emotional disaster.

Honesty Is the Best Policy

Does your partner know enough about you to have an unclouded view of who you are? If not, be brave and fill in the picture. Honesty is frightening, but it pays off when it builds a stronger, more intimate relationship.

If you have information that you are keeping secret, plan to tell your partner as soon as possible. Hoping for a better time to bring it up usually doesn't work, because that better time rarely comes. Instead of waiting, just do it now.

Realize that honesty includes saying what you want, talking about how you feel, and asking for apologies when you can't let go of a partner's misdeed.

Sloan and Carol have been married for a couple of years. Theirs is a good relationship that dates back to high school, where they were voted cutest couple by their senior class. In a romantic moment Carol tells Sloan how good it feels to her that they haven't had sex with anyone but each other.

Sloan swallows hard. It turns out that three years ago, during a six-month separation in which they reassessed their relationship, he had a one-night stand with an acquaintance of Carol's. He did not tell Carol, reasoning that it was not part of their agreement to do so. Now, however, he feels that he must speak up:

"Carol, how do you feel about the idea that if we are going to have a long-term relationship there should be no secrets or lies between us?"

Carol looks alarmed. "Why, have you been lying to me about something?!"

"No, Carol, I don't think so, and I don't want to start now. Let's sit down. There is something that I never realized until now that I need to tell you. Can I tell you?"

"What is it, for God's sake!"

Sloan walks Carol over to the couch. Looking in Carol' eyes he asks, "Do you remember the time we were separated back in college?"

"Yes," she answers, beginning to realize what he's about to say.

"Well, I never stopped thinking about you during those months, but I also thought you might decide that you didn't want to be with me anymore. I was trying to get used to whatever might happen, and I was very depressed. One night, I went on a date with Suzie Green."

"My old friend Susan?" she said, a shrill sound in her voice. She had always felt a little insecure beside the beautiful and popular Susan.

"Yeah. I think I should tell you about that date."

"Oh God, Sloan!"

"I'm sorry. I didn't think I would have to tell you. But after what you said about never having other lovers I realize now that I have to. Anyway, I want you to know everything about me."

As he looks at her and sees her expression, he gets scared. Determined to go on, he asks, "Can I tell you?"

"Go ahead, tell me," she says, crying.

"I spent the night with Suzie; we made love."

She begins to cry more loudly.

"It was nothing to write home about, but it happened."

Carol looks up at him. Her eyes full of tears, she puts her head against Sloan's shoulder. He tries to pull her into his arms, but she won't let him.

"Why didn't you tell me before?" she pleads.

"Even though we had agreed that we would be free to see other people, I knew it would bother you. I know it would have bothered me. I felt guilty and I told myself that we both probably slept with other people during that time, and I felt then that I didn't want to hear about your other lovers. I figured you would feel the same.

"I'm so happy to find out that I'm the only man in your life. You're the only woman I've ever loved and that's the truth, Carol. When you said before that neither of us had ever been with anyone, I felt so bad. I didn't want to lie to you when you were being so loving with me. I didn't want to confuse you and I decided that you deserve the whole truth. Now that you know, I don't have to worry about hiding anything ever again."

Carol was very upset. She said she was not so much upset with the actual deed but with the idea that he had been keeping a secret from her for so long. She felt foolish to think that she had been under a false impression about her husband, the closest person in her life. She feared that this revelation would spoil her love for him. But what hurt Carol more than Sloan's one-night stand was the loss of trust caused by this long-held secret.

That night, they held each other tighter than ever. It was a night to remember and it went a long way to help Carol get over her hurt feelings. Later, she even felt flattered that Sloan had preferred her over the universally sought-after Suzie. She understood why he had not told her and decided that, though it was hard to accept at first, she could live with this new information. In the future, when she momentarily found herself wondering if Sloan might be keeping any secrets from her, she was reassured by the thought that if he could tell her about that night, he would probably never lie to her about anything. She felt profoundly safe with him and her fear that this revelation would spoil their relationship did not materialize.

People will vehemently argue that this kind of honesty is unnecessary, or worse, an act of irresponsible, sadistic cruelty. They may argue further that a person in Sloan's position, having made a hurtful mistake, should bear the burden of legitimate remorse and keep the painful information away from his wife. These arguments ignore some important facts: the damaging effect of even the smallest lie—how it can proliferate into further and bigger lies and how keeping secrets from a partner undermines the intuitive and empathic process between them. Most important, they ignore the far greater pain that people feel when they find out that they have been repeatedly lied to (if only by omission) over a long time. Imagine how Carol would feel if after five or six years of occasionally meeting Susan Green socially, she found out, through a casual remark by Susan's husband, that Sloan and Susan had been lovers.

HOUSEKEEPING REQUIRED

Do put time aside for emotional housekeeping. My good friend David Geisinger points out that a relationship is only as good as its dialogue. If the dialogue is thoughtful, honest, and affectionate, so will the relationship be. Tell each other about your suspicions, hunches, or paranoid fantasies. Listen carefully. Take the opportunity to apologize for hurts. And most of all, find time to give each other strokes.

Don't take care of emotional business during television commercials or when you are too tired to talk about them: Set aside quality time for conversation. Addressing emotional issues during a walk is a recommendation I frequently make. Another possibility is to have regular dates during which you air emotional questions.

REVIEW, REVIEW, REVIEW

Make sure that you review agreements regularly. In this era of rapid change, agreements that made sense six months ago may no longer make sense.

Talk frequently about issues like sex, money and time, especially where and how each of them should be spent.

Just because you have done things a certain way for a long time doesn't mean that it is acceptable to your partner now. This is especially true when it comes to sex, which can become routine and acceptable to one person and cease to be acceptable to the other.

Be flexible, be willing to change your agreements, even after you have negotiated them extensively. Accept change and new points of view. After all, the goal is for both of you to work together in cooperation and produce feelings of affection and hope rather than resentment and despair.

A WALK IN THE WOODS

William and Hillary are both very busy people. They have no children and they work very hard. When they finally get together in the evenings, they rush through dinner and barely have enough energy for a few chores and a little television in bed. They cuddle while watching TV and usually fall asleep before the set turns itself off.

Without talking about it, they seem to have agreed to avoid difficult emotional issues. Hillary has been feeling that she is not getting enough intimate discussion time to process some of the problems they have been sweeping under the rug.

One morning as they are getting ready to go to work, Hillary suggests that they take Saturday morning off, drive to the hiking trail, and talk over some subjects. William balks at first because he has a golf date, but Hillary insists that he cancel it and he eventually agrees. On Saturday, as they start on their hike in the woods, Hillary says:

"I'm worried that we are drifting apart. Even though we seem to get along and love each other, I am afraid that things are building up between us that feel bad, to me anyway."

"Well, I am feeling okay about things," William says. "Is there something you are unhappy about?"

"See, that could be a problem right there. You don't seem to notice that we have these little disagreements which usually end up in one of us, mostly me, going along with you in order to avoid trouble. I keep thinking I am too tired or we'll deal with it tomorrow or that maybe I am being petty, but I'm beginning to feel bad."

William interrupted, "I realize we are having these little problems but I thought we were dealing with them as we go. I feel okay about them."

"Maybe that is the first problem to talk about, because I am not feeling so good. When you say that you think that these problems are being solved, can I tell you how I feel?"

William nods.

"Actually," Hillary says, "I feel very angry."

William nods again, but he is shaken. Hillary goes on.

"Can I tell you what I am guessing? I suspect that when we disagree, you don't realize that most of the time I am going along with you just to keep a good feeling going."

William, somewhat annoyed, says, "I had no idea. I assumed that we are coming to our agreements honestly. This is upsetting, really."

For the next half hour Hillary recalled a number of incidents where somehow things had gone William's way. Some of the incidents were admittedly minor, like the fact that on a crowded sidewalk William always walks ahead, or that he almost always drives when they are together, or that he won't make suggestions about restaurants when they go out, or that he is often distracted when they speak. Nevertheless, they were important to her and needed to be acknowledged.

All of this is building some anger in Hillary. He points out that because she does not complain, he didn't realize she was upset. In fact, he is annoyed at her for going along with him against her better judgment. She agrees, but says that she is often just too worn out to struggle about these things, and that she would like him to be more aware of these subtle tensions between them. The conversation becomes argumentative and heated. They both realize—Hillary is first to point it out—that they need to cool down. After some minutes, they apologize to each other: Hillary for Rescuing him, William for subtly power playing her.

They resume their conversation and it seems that the most serious problem was that they didn't have enough time with each other to make Hillary happy.

William was content to sit together and watch TV, sleep together, make love in the mornings or on weekends, and have a few meals out, and for a while Hillary was okay with this, too.

"I don't want to have sex in the mornings anymore," she blurted out.

"Well, when then? You say yourself that we are too tired in the evenings, we are both morning people."

"Well, I guess I want us to take time in the evenings, take a whole evening off after dinner, go out for a drink, talk, get reacquainted with each other's changing lives."

William was alarmed by this proposal. He had been happy with their arrangements and he feared that this would take too much time out of their precisely timed lives. He hesitated, and Hillary felt irritated. Their tempers flared and just as they were about to change the subject, Hillary said,

"See, this is the way it always goes. We don't deal with our disagreements, and if I let this go, we would be back where we started. Let's stay with this, please."

They talked for another hour and arrived at some new decisions. William realized he hadn't been making his wife a priority. He was willing to try Hillary's unsettling proposal. They also agreed to have one of these "housekeeping walks" once a month.

In the end, things did not go exactly as planned, but they did take off one evening a week, television-free, to just be with each other. Their walks sometimes only happened every three months. But all in all, this discussion had a very beneficial effect. They were flexible in reviewing their agreements and they established a way for their relationship to continue on an emotionally literate basis.

Emotional Literacy & Children

Emotional literacy can be learned at any point in life, but it is best developed in childhood. Daniel Goleman[3] describes a "window of opportunity" during which learning emotional skills is very different from learning them later in life. Reading, for example, is easily learned in our youth. Yet an illiterate adult can have a very difficult time learning to read. The same is true of other skills, such as playing sports, learning foreign languages, music, and, yes, emotional literacy.

It is during this critical learning period in which children learn by the example set by their parents that children establish their various lifelong attitudes. They begin to visualize themselves as good or bad, skillful or clumsy, happy or unhappy. They may even think of themselves as fantasy characters. Some children, for instance, will identify with Snow White or one of the Seven Dwarfs. Others will see themselves as Superman or Lois Lane, the Pied Piper or Little Red Riding Hood, even Jesus Christ or the Devil. They will also adopt the emotional habits that fit their view of themselves: grumpy, sweet, imperturbable, impatient, scheming, saintly, or wicked. And once children start acting a certain way, they will be seen by others in that way and will get labeled bad or good, happy or unhappy, gentle or violent.

For the most part, children learn their emotional ways from parents and others around them. Once adopted, these habits become narratives or scripts about what life is and what it will be like. Unless something is done to change them, these scripts can last a lifetime:

- The child that is habitually sad and afraid may become an adult who is depressed and suicidal.
- The child that learns to suppress his tears may become hard-hearted.
- The child that can't control her tantrums may become prone to addictive behaviors as an adult.

THE WRONG WAY & THE RIGHT WAY

As an example of how emotional patterns are established by parents, let's look at a typical household "mini-tragedy" and two ways it might be handled by parents.

First, the emotionally illiterate way:

Matthew, a five-year-old, has just fallen from a chair while trying to sneak some cookies. He is crying loudly. Not only does his knee hurt from where he struck it on the floor, but he is ashamed to be caught raiding the cookie jar. He feels angry, guilty, and frightened at the same time. His father reaches the kitchen and realizes what his son has been doing.

"What happened? Did you hurt yourself?" the father asks angrily. "Stop crying!"

How is Matthew to interpret this? Is he supposed to stop feeling pain? How about his fear and guilt? Is he supposed to keep feeling these things but not cry? Angry and confused, he screams louder. If his father was emotionally literate, he would let well enough alone. Instead, he sees this as an opportunity to teach Matthew a lesson about life.

"Come on, Matthew, stop being such a crybaby," he says. "You're worse than your sister." Now Matthew gets the idea that crying is bad and that girls can cry but boys cannot. He tries to suppress his crying, but he can't. Frustrated, he cries even louder.

Suppose now that his father becomes even more upset and decides to continue his lesson. "Matthew, that's enough! You know better than this." Knowing full well the answer, he asks, "What were you doing on the kitchen counter anyway? You are being—a sissy."

Matthew has heard about sissies and boys who act like girls from the other kids at school. Now he decides to stop crying at all costs. He clenches his teeth together and quiets down.

"That's a good boy," says his father.

Many parents feel that it is not proper masculine behavior for boys to cry. Boys who are raised not to cry become grown men who are ashamed to cry. When such a man becomes sad enough to cry, he will hide it by lying about how he feels. Eventually, he will become so unaware of his own sadness that he will deny it even to himself. He will deny other feelings of vulnerability, too, such as shame or longing. At that point he will only recognize the strongest of his emotions, such as furious anger or mad love.

Girls are treated differently. When they cry, it is often considered sweet or touching. Almost never are girls made to feel that it is not feminine or ladylike to cry. This may be one reason women are generally more emotional than men.

A Better Approach

Now let's look at a more emotionally literate response to the cookie incident. When Matthew's father finds him crying on the floor of the kitchen, he picks him up and says: "Boy, are you upset! Did you hurt yourself?"

Instead of answering, Matthew lets out a loud scream. He is feeling physical hurt from the fall and guilt from getting caught stealing a cookie. "Sounds like you are mad at me," says his father, wiping away his son's tears. "Yeaaaa," says Matthew.

"Why? I'm trying to help you here," says his father. "Can I kiss your boo-boo?" He rocks Matthew until the boy begins to calm down. "Were you trying to get some cookies?"

Matthew begins to cry again.

"Are you feeling guilty? Are you worried I'll get mad?" Matthew doesn't answer but he is quieting down. "Well, you know I don't like you to eat so many sweets between meals, but I'm sorry you hurt yourself," says Father. "Next time, don't try to get any cookies on your own, okay?"

Instead of trying to stop Matthew's crying, he has helped him understand why he was so upset. He has shown empathy while giving his son the physical strokes of hugs and kisses. After Matthew calms down, his father will have a conversation with him about what happened, how he felt, and some facts about cookies and cookie jars. Matthew will have learned that his feelings of guilt, anger and fear are valued and that he can safely express them.

Emotional Literacy Guidelines for Children

Children can begin to learn emotional literacy as soon as you show it to them. Eventually, you can talk to them about their feelings, usually as soon as they can form a sentence. Between the ages of two and three, children begin to feel guilt and are able to empathize with others so they can apologize for the hurt they caused. The same rules of cooperation that apply to adult relationships should be applied to those between children and adults. Equality, honesty, and the avoidance of power plays are just as important with children, though they may need to be customized to fit the situation. That usually means that you should give children as much power as possible and be as open as you can, avoiding lies in every way possible. Here are some guidelines that will teach your child emotional literacy.

KEEP THE HEART OPEN

Kiss and hug your children often and tell them that you love them. Like all of us, they crave and enjoy affection. If you show them love through physical strokes when they are young, they will be openhearted as they grow up.

DON'T POWER PLAY YOUR CHILDREN

Don't hit your children. When you use power plays to get what you want from children, they will learn to be motivated by fear. If you do power play your children (as we all do at one time or another), make sure to apologize and explain how you felt. Offer not to do that kind of thing again. Then, with the child and perhaps other family members, work out a better method of getting them to mind you.

Example: Three-year-old Sarah is fond of pushing buttons and turning dials wherever she can find them. Many times she has turned off fax machines, readjusted the settings on stereos and TVs, redialed phone calls, and lately has been seen wanting to turn on the gas stove. Her mother, Jane, is very frightened of a gas leak and has told Sarah "No!" many times, but Sarah seems to be devilishly focused on the gas stove. One time, Jane surprised Sarah when she was turning a gas knob. Jane lost control. Yelling at her, she gave Sarah a strong whack on her bottom. Sarah was petrified, screaming and crying loudly for a few minutes. After Sarah calmed down, the following conversation took place:

"Sarah, are you still upset?"

Sarah nods.

"Well, I got very angry and I am sorry I hit you. You are not allowed to play with the stove."

"Yes I am."

"No. The stove is hot and it will burn you. If you do it again, you'll go to your room for time out."

"No I won't, Mama."

"Well, if you promise to stop pushing and turning buttons I promise not to scare you any more. Do you promise to stop?"

Sarah nods imperceptibly.

"Is that a yes?" Sarah nods again. "Okay, if you promise, I won't yell at you again, and you won't go to time out. And I am sorry I scared you."

Sarah starts crying again, and hugs her mother, who hugs her back. "It's okay, honey, I love you, you are a good girl."

Be sensitive to what children want, regardless of how silly it might seem. Listen empathically to them. Try to be understanding when they don't want something because it scares them, embarrasses them, or offends their sense of esthetics or taste. Be flexible when making demands.

Be Honest

Being truthful with your children is important, second only to not abusing them with power plays. Explain to them how you feel and what you want from them. Never tell them bald-faced lies, and keep your lies of omission to a minimum, making sure to be truthful as soon as possible. If you want them to be truthful, you must first be truthful with them. After all, children sense when secrets are kept from them and will learn to keep secrets from you.

If you have been honest with your children, you should assume that they will be truthful with you. Given how commonplace lying is, however, you should look out for lies from children as vigilantly as you eventually will have to look out for drug use. Sooner or later, your child will tell a major lie and I believe that to be an extremely important opportunity to practice what you have learned here.

An example: Sally, 13, has just come home from school and has gone to her room. She is staying in there longer than usual. Checking, you find her in her room reading.

"Hi, Sally. Back from school?" She looks up and seems to be covering what she is reading with a book.

"What are you reading?"

"Nothing."

"It looks like a magazine."

"I said, nothing."

By now, you can tell something is fishy. You remind yourself to stay calm, in your Adult.

"It's a magazine, isn't it?"

"Yeah, Mom," she says morosely, rolling her eyes.

"Whose is it?"

"Kathy's, she lent it to me."

By now Sally looks scared. Meanwhile, you have gone over to her and picked up the magazine.

"This seems brand new to me. Where did you get it?"

"I told you!"

You sit down next to her, look at her averted eyes, and speaking from the heart as kindly as possible you say: "Sally, are you telling me the truth? Please don't lie to me. You know how I feel about lying. However you got this is not as important to me as you telling the truth. Just tell me and we'll work it out."

"I bought it."

"Oh good, I was afraid that maybe you stole it. I know some kids think it's cool to steal from 7-Eleven."

"Mother, I wouldn't steal. You know that!"

"Good. So how did you get the money to buy it? Just last night you told me you had spent al your allowance. Tell the truth."

Sally is clearly upset. She looks down. She clams up. You wait. After a minute of silence she says: "I took the money from your wallet."

"Sally, did you really?"

"Yes."

Silence again. You search your feelings. You are scared by what Sally has done and you are sad that she lied to you. You are angry because she has been rebellious lately. You want to tell her that taking money from you is just as bad as stealing from 7-Eleven.

TIME FOR AN ACTION/FEELING STATEMENT

"Sally, can I tell you how I feel about this?"

Sally shrugs and then nods. Keeping a loving tone, from the heart you say:

"When you take money from my wallet to buy a magazine, and then try to lie about it to me, it makes me feel scared and very sad and also angry. Can you understand that?"

She is listening and agrees. You now have an opportunity to find out why she feels she had to steal to buy a trashy magazine. She tells you that you would not buy it for her or let her use her allowance. She tells you the magazine has interesting stories in it. You pick it up and look at the table of contents. Definitely junk.

"Well, Sally, I definitely don't like it, but on the other hand I realize that I can't stop you from being interested in it. But you are not allowed to take money from my wallet and I would like you to apologize for that. More important, I want you to agree not to lie to me. Your lying is what scares me and makes me sad. Because if you start lying, we won't be able to talk the way we are used to. And that would be too bad, don't you think?"

Sally agrees.

Make truthfulness between you and your child the most important bond between you.

LET GO OF CONTROL

Give your children power by letting them take charge in games. Wrestle with them, let them hit you lightly in play, briefly pretend to cry or get sad. This kind of behavior shows them that you are not always in control. By the same token, tell them about your feelings. If they want to know why you feel the way you do, explain it to them in short and simple sentences.

UNDERSTAND YOUR CHILDREN'S DEMONS

Be aware of your children's fears and accept them. Learn to recognize when they are afraid and why. Spiders, snakes, dogs, the dark, the boogie man, whatever frightens them is real to them and needs to be taken seriously. Talk about their fears, validate them, and help them avoid the situations that cause them. On the other hand, if you are out of control with your own emotions, shield them from this experience, since it can frighten them badly.

ENCOURAGE EMOTIONALLY LITERATE MEDIA

Read emotionally literate books to your children. Take them to emotionally literate films and plays. Avoid stories containing violence and cruelty, unless they make a clear moral statement about anger and how to deal with it in a good way. The same is true of love and sex: Make sure the message is emotionally literate. Read them "The Warm Fuzzy Tale", about "warm fuzzies" and "cold pricklies."[29]

TEACH EMOTIONAL SELF-DEFENSE

Teach children how to defend their boundaries and reject behavior they don't want by saying, "I don't like that," or "Please stop it," or "Leave me alone." These are all acceptable and effective ways of deflecting unwanted behavior. Role play such situations and teach them how to respond to different scenarios.

BE PATIENT

Educating children takes time, but once they've learned a lesson, it will stick. Repeat your lessons over and over in a consistent manner and be sure to live what you preach. Remember: An apple doesn't fall far from the tree.

CHAPTER 9

Emotional Literacy in the Workplace

So far, I have shown how I teach emotional literacy in controlled situations in which mutual agreements of cooperation and honesty can be made: training groups, couples, and parents and children. But in the real world we have to make do without the safety of such agreements. The workplace is such a situation. There is no guarantee that your work mates have even the slightest interest in emotional literacy. Introducing emotional literacy in the workplace is an experimental undertaking and worthy of a whole book. I can only hope to give some basic hints here.

Again, emotional literacy is best learned when we have an agreement with people to conduct a cooperative relationship that is free of power plays and where Rescues and lies are consciously avoided. Work environments are usually just the opposite. It is in the workplace that we are most likely to find power plays, wholesale lying, and keeping of secrets. In fact, most work settings actually encourage emotionally illiterate behavior. It is not uncommon to hear about managers who threaten workers with losing their jobs if they step out of line, or to hear about workers who are sexually harassed. Even though workers may have the law on their side, the law has no teeth without a union or an expensive lawyer to back it up and most workers have little recourse.

There are some companies which endeavor to provide an emotionally literate and safe work environment. But most workers are not that fortunate. Secrets about salaries, promotions, and firings are routine. In addition subtle power plays abound, not just from bosses and management but among workers. Pecking orders develop and with them come subtle insults, secrets, gossip, lies, and hurtful humor. Even though most people realize what is going on, there is no agreement or company policy to stop these actions or to prevent them. Consequently, the workplace can be a minefield of emotionally illiterate, toxic transactions.

How can a person create an emotionally literate workplace? It isn't easy. Even in work environments that pride themselves on easygoing friendliness, a great deal of deeply entrenched emotionally illiterate behavior can be taking place.

Basically, you are proposing to replace an emotionally illiterate culture with a different one, in which power plays are not used and emotions are considered worthy of attention and respect. You can start the process of change by finding at least one person inside the organization who has the same interest in emotional literacy as you do. Then find others. You can build interest by showing this book to people or by posting a copy of the Emotional Literacy Commandments, which can be found at the end of this chapter.

Everything I have tried to teach in this book can be tried in the workplace, though it may be more difficult. Emotional literacy at work is more risky because it has to be practiced without a cooperative contract to protect you from power plays. Be prepared for people to refuse to cooperate, or even have a hostile reaction.

For instance, Mark, a coworker on your team, regularly makes supposedly funny comments about your colorful ties and clothes. You suspect that he feels competitive with you because you have some advanced computer skills that he lacks. In any case, you want to tell him that the way he keeps kidding you makes you angry, but you have no idea of how to approach this touchy subject.

You wind up feeling depressed and hopeless about working with him. You realize that you have contributed to the problem by going along with the joke so far. Maybe you are now being oversensitive but you would like him to stop. All the basic rules apply: You should first obtain permission from him to talk about your irritation. But in this case, people are not used to being asked, and if asked may agree without thinking. So you must be extra careful to have "informed consent" from him, instead of just agreement.

"Hey, Mark, when you have a minute I'd like to pick a bone with you. Is that okay?"

Mark: (perplexed) "Yeah, sure."

"Well it's sort of a complaint, are you sure you want to hear it?"

Mark: (looking genuinely alarmed) "What did I do wrong?"

"It's not that bad, but I want to make sure that you want to hear."

Mark: "Sure. How about now?"

"Now? Later might be better, when we have a little time."

"How about after work?"

"That's good."

"Don't worry about it, it's just something that has been troubling me. But I'm sure we'll work it out just fine. Let's meet at the Hut."

You can see that what would take one transaction in a contractual, cooperative relationship can take several minutes of conversation in the real world. And of course it may not work out as neatly as I suggest. But that does not mean that it can't be done. In all probability, given a skillful, open-hearted approach, Mark will be primed and ready to hear your feedback and you'll be able to establish an understanding so that he will stop kidding you about your clothes.

You can give strokes, ask for strokes, accept and reject strokes in the "real world" just as I have explained; but again, every one of these transactions will require more preparation. Each will be more complicated and lengthy and have more risk of backfiring.

You can deliver action/feeling statements and intuitive hunches and you can hope that you will get an emotionally literate response. Or you can try to extract a better response, but that may be more difficult.

For instance, you might feel that you have worked long and hard on a project for your boss and haven't gotten enough praise for it. You are feeling bad about yourself and you need strokes. Instead of just asking for permission and then simply asking for some strokes from your boss, you have to approach the matter much more diplomatically.

"Helen, do you have a minute? I would like to ask you something."

"I'm busy now." Helen is not a woman of many words. You sense that she likes you, but this will not be easy.

"How about later?" you ask.

"Okay," she says, without looking up from her work. Not unfriendly, just busy.

"What's a convenient time for you?"

"I'll call you in your office as soon as I'm done here. About a half an hour."

Great. Now comes the hard part.

Helen phones you in your office. "You wanted to talk?"

You are scared, your mouth is dry, and at this point it feels safer to drop the matter, but you are determined and you press on: "Yes, can I come over to your office?"

"You don't want to speak on the phone?"

"I would rather speak face to face if you don't mind." There is a split second of silence.

Helen is getting the idea that this conversation is special. "Okay, come right over."

Seconds later, when you get to Helen's office, she looks up from her desk and beckons you in. She is clearly curious. She signals you to sit down. "So what's on your mind?"

"Helen, I am a bit nervous doing this, but I wanted to ask you a question. May I?"

"Sure, go ahead."

"You know that we just finished a very large project and that I worked long and hard hours on it."

"Yes."

"Well, I am not clear on whether you liked the job I did."

"I thought I told you that I appreciated how hard you worked on it, didn't I?"

"Yes, you did, but you know, I don't get any feeling that you appreciated anything but how hard I worked. I mean, working hard is no guarantee of quality. Did you find the work I did particularly good?"

Yes of course, that goes without saying."

"If you don't mind, if there is something specific you can say about it I would really appreciate hearing it. I am feeling under appreciated these days, not particularly by you, but in general. Would you mind?"

"Actually, I thought the work was quite exceptional, really."

"I hate to press you on this, but could you say how so?"

"It was very creative and also very precise. I thought you knew that."

"I guess I do, but it's good to hear it from you. Thanks for indulging me. I hope this wasn't a bother for you."

"Not at all, I am sorry that you have been feeling under appreciated. I am very glad that you are working for me."

Of course, this is a very positive scenario. Helen could have chided you for fishing for praise or being childish. Or she could have refused to elaborate on her praise. In an emotionally illiterate environment, that would not be too unusual. Had this happened, you would have had to discreetly excuse yourself and leave the matter there, or use the information to improve your work. But most people, even in emotionally illiterate situations, want to be good to others, and the likely outcome in most of these situations will be positive.

Practice What You Preach

If you are in a position to supervise people, you will be in a better position to put some of these principles into practice. Discreetly ask permission whenever you bring up emotionally loaded material. You can give strokes and ask for strokes. You can gladly accept strokes you want and politely reject strokes you don't want. You can even give yourself strokes. Practice telling people how their actions make you feel and get them to hear you without being defensive. Listen to their feelings. State your intuitive hunches and attempt to extract validation for them. If you do this in an openhearted and flexible manner, most people will be receptive, since you are in a position to protect them from power plays.

If you are the boss, however, you will be responsible for making sure that you are not forcing these ideas on powerless and unwilling people who have to go along with you.

As an example, let's assume that you are a line supervisor in a factory with 25 workers under you. You enjoy being friendly with your workers and you like to be treated in a friendly way. One of your best workers seems to be unhappy at work. She does not greet you in her usual friendly fashion and she seems withdrawn from other workers. Your intuition tells you that there is something wrong and you decide to investigate in an emotionally literate fashion. You approach Paula on her break.

"How are you today, Paula?"

"Fine."

"May I ask you a question?"

She nods. You must make sure that Paula is genuinely willing. "Are you sure? I don't want to intrude." The tone of your voice will have everything to do with her feeling that she has a choice. You must really mean that she is free to decline your question.

Let's say you gain her permission. "Well, I have noticed that you seem quiet. I have a hunch that something is upsetting you."

"Oh no, everything is okay," she says unconvincingly. Normally, in a cooperative situation, it would be perfectly permissible to insist on more of an answer. But in this instance, if you insist you could be abusing your power; she may not want to tell you what's wrong or talk to you at all.

"That's good, I'm glad. Can I tell you how I feel?"

Again, she nods.

"When you are so quiet I get worried that something is wrong. And I would be sad if there is something I could help with, and you didn't ask."

She looks at you dubiously.

"Do you believe me?"

She nods again.

"Okay, well, please keep in mind that I am here to be helpful if I can. Let me know if there is anything you want me to do."

With that, you best leave the situation alone. You may feel sad or even angered by Paula's unwillingness to talk to you. You may be mistaken that there is anything wrong.

In any case, you have laid a foundation for future emotionally literate conversations with Paula. If you behave in this manner reliably, you will acquire a good reputation with your workers and with your superiors. You may actually be able to demonstrate that this approach improves morale and productivity with your workers and even succeed in having other supervisors try it.

For a person in a position of power, apologizing is a good way of demonstrating that you really mean to be emotionally literate. You will, obviously, make mistakes, and in the traditional workplace these mistakes are usually not acknowledged. It will be truly impressive to your workers if you seem cognizant of your errors, admit them, apologize, and make amends to those you may have affected badly with them.

Start an Emotional Literacy Study & Support Group

Notice who in your workplace is able to accept and even enjoy the steps of this program and stroke them for it. They are the ones who will most likely be interested in joining a support group. The ideal size of such a support group is eight to 12 people. With a group this size, you can begin to institute real change. For example, a lunchtime group of this size would have a noticeable presence in most organizations and would certainly grow. You could even organize a training weekend. Possibly, the group could convince your boss to finance a weekend retreat by showing him how it would improve the mood and productivity of the workplace.

At work, as well as in the world at large, you will have to be creative if you want to use these ideas. Try little experiments and observe the results. The basic ideas of emotional literacy, which I have put into the Ten Commandments at the end of this chapter, are:

- EQUALITY IS THE PREMISE
- LOVE IS THE ENERGY
- HONESTY IS THE METHOD

Why should these efforts create a positive result at all? Because people want love, desire good strokes, and need to safely be able to express how they feel—whether they believe in emotional literacy training or not. If provided with the opportunity to give and receive what emotional literacy provides, they will be happier and more productive. And if you develop a set of good techniques and learn to apply them, after five years or so, maybe you will be able to write a definitive book about emotional literacy in the workplace!

The Ten Commandments of Emotional Literacy

I. PLACE LOVE AT THE CENTER OF YOUR EMOTIONAL LIFE

Heart-centered emotional intelligence empowers everyone it touches.

II. EMOTIONAL LITERACY REQUIRES THAT YOU NOT LIE BY OMISSION OR COMMISSION

Except where your safety or the safety of others is concerned, do not lie.

III. STAND UP FOR HOW YOU FEEL AND WHAT YOU WANT

If you don't, it is not likely that anyone else will.

IV. EMOTIONAL LITERACY REQUIRES THAT YOU DO NOT POWER PLAY OTHERS

Gently but firmly ask for what you want until you are satisfied.

V. DO NOT ALLOW YOURSELF TO BE POWER PLAYED

Gently but firmly refuse to do anything you are not willing to do of your own free will.

VI. RESPECT THE IDEAS, FEELINGS, AND WISHES OF OTHERS AS MUCH AS YOU DO YOUR OWN

Respecting ideas does not mean that you have to submit to them.

VII. APOLOGIZE AND MAKE AMENDS FOR YOUR MISTAKES

Nothing will grow you faster.

VIII. DO NOT ACCEPT FALSE APOLOGIES

They are worth less than no apologies at all.

IX. LOVE YOURSELF, OTHERS, AND TRUTH IN EQUAL PARTS

Never sacrifice one to the other.

X. FOLLOW THESE COMMANDMENTS ACCORDING TO YOUR BEST JUDGMENT

After all, they are not written in stone.

BOOK THREE

The
Emotional
Warrior

CHAPTER 10

The Emotional Warrior

In this book, I have shown you a series of powerful techniques to increase your heart-centered emotional intelligence. These techniques will help you improve your relationships in all areas of your life. They will also increase your level of personal power.

Some people have been so impressed by the results of emotional literacy training that they want to involve their friends, family, and lovers with these ideas. Some of them even believe that these ideas should become part of a moral code. Over the years, I have met a number of people who have seen emotional literacy training as a tool for social change and want to apply it beyond their own personal lives. These people belong in a worldwide team of activists that I call "Emotional Warriors."

The Ancient Regime

Throughout history, people in power have used any and all methods available to dominate people and stay in control. These methods can be physical or psychological, but intimidating threats of violence are always in the background to back them up. In this system of domination, people are placed on a pyramid of power, one-up to some and one-down to others, with every level controlling the level below.

This system of domination is part of the basic structure of our society known as patriarchy. In classic patriarchy, a father heads a clan or tribe, and his authority is passed down through the male line. In today's patriarchies, the father figure passes power down according to his whim—usually to one or more of his male followers, but sometimes, also, to carefully selected women.

Riane Eisler, in *The Chalice and the Blade*[37] describes patriarchy as:

"…a male-dominated and generally hierarchic social structure [that] has historically been reflected and maintained by a male-dominated religious pantheon and by religious doctrines in which the subordination of women is said to be divinely ordained."

The system is kept in place by domination, whether in government, the workplace, or in families. Domination is exercised through person-to-person transactions or power plays. The sergeant who reports a soldier for not saluting properly, the boss who expects a greeting from his secretary but who doesn't himself bother to respond to the greeting, the husband who demands but does not provide sexual satisfaction, the father who lectures his daughter and smiles dismissively whenever she wants to be heard—these are all dominating power transactions.

Understanding the Power of Control

We hardly notice how domination works, because we are immersed in it from birth. The value of transactional analysis as a tool to understand relationships can be clearly seen here. Domination is put into effect through interpersonal transactions. With transactional analysis, you can observe power relations, analyze them and once you understand them, figure out how to avoid them in yourself and others.

After spending our childhood at the mercy of other people's whims, we accept as natural that we should be either Victimizers or Victims, one-up to some and one-down to others, leader or follower, dominator or dominated. The slapped child becomes the parent who slaps, the child who is dominated and controlled becomes the parent who dominates and controls. We accept abuse and control power as the way of the world.

If we want to fight unreasonable control and power abuse effectively, we need to fully understand how power plays work. There are two main forms of control power: physical and psychological. Each can be expressed either subtly or crudely. There are four types of power plays:

I   CRUDE PHYSICAL
III SUBTLE PHYSICAL
II CRUDE PSYCHOLOGICAL
IV SUBTLE PSYCHOLOGICAL

A power play is a transaction in which one person tries to force another person to do something against his or her will.

I CRUDE PHYSICAL POWER plays are obvious to the naked eye and include hitting, shoving, throwing things, banging doors, or worse, kidnapping, imprisoning, torture, rape and murder.

CRUDE

I Crude, Physical
murder
rape
imprisonment
torture
beating
shoving
banging doors

II Crude, Psychological
insults
menacing tones
interrupting
sulking
ignoring
blatant lying
interrupting

PHYSICAL   PSYCHOLOGICAL

touching
looming
space invasion
leading by the arm
making someone stand or sit
patting on the head

false logic
sarcastic humor
discounting
"attitude"
lies of omission
advertising
propaganda

III Subtle, Physical   IV Subtle, Psychological

SUBTLE

Power Plays

III SUBTLE PHYSICAL POWER plays are not as easily visible, although if you are a victim of them you may become aware that you are being power-played after a while. Still, you may have no idea how power plays work or how to stop them. Subtle physical power plays include such things as towering over people or standing close to them so that you invade their personal space, leading them by the elbow or hand or walking ahead of them, making people stand or sit, or blocking their path.

These power plays are often used by men on women, some of whom accept them as a matter of normal male behavior.

Psychological power plays work because people are trained to obey from early childhood. Without using physical force, I can intimidate you with threats or with the tone of my voice. I can push you to action by making you feel guilty. I can seduce you with a smile or a promise, or persuade you that what I want is the right thing to do. I can trick you, con you, or sell you a preposterous lie. If I can overcome your resistance without using physical force, I have used a psychological power play.

Psychological power plays are all around us in daily life. Some are crude, some are subtle.

II CRUDE PSYCHOLOGICAL POWER plays include menacing tones and looks, insults, bald-faced lies and blatant sulking. Also: interrupting, ignoring, making faces, rolling your eyes, tapping your fingers, and humming while others talk.

IV SUBTLE PSYCHOLOGICAL POWER plays include clever lies, lies of omission, subtle sulking, sarcastic humor, gossip, false logic, ignoring what people say, and at a mass level, advertising and propaganda. In every case, a power play is a transaction designed to cause or prevent an action by another person against that person's better judgment or free will.

Examples of physical power abuse are more shocking than those of psychological abuse, and they are less widespread. Even in the most violent environments, such as prisons or battlefields, people do not suffer primarily from direct physical oppression. Instead, their minds are controlled by the threat of violence. In our society, this is especially true in homes where women and children are physically abused and battered.

Avenues to Power

There are two widely different ways of becoming powerful in this world: power plays and power literacy. The first requires being a person with no feeling for others and therefore no limits to his grasping needs. Chronic power players feel little empathy for another person; such people need to be cold to their victims' pain and will do whatever is necessary to keep control.

I have been speaking and teaching about an important source of personal power in this book, the power of emotional literacy. To become an Emotional Warrior, however, you need "power literacy" in addition to emotional literacy. In other words, you need to understand how power operates, how it is accumulated, how to take power, how to share it, and, at times, how to give it up.

The problem is that in a domination-based system such as ours, power is often inaccurately defined as "the capacity to control other people." Unfortunately, most thinking about power runs along these lines. Power theorists ignore other important forms of power, such as the power of communication, knowledge, or love.

To be passionate, centered, or spiritually aware is to be powerful. Take, for example, Nelson Mandela, who completely changed the political direction of South Africa from his prison cell and eventually became President of that nation. And what historical figure was more powerful than Jesus of Nazareth? He was a poor carpenter who changed the world with his message of love deserved by all.

Knowledge is another example of power that rivals control. That is why authoritarian governments have always done what they could to prevent people from being educated or from gathering freely to learn from each other.

One reason the totalitarian, Soviet bloc governments of Eastern Europe collapsed in the 1980s was that improved communications across their borders destroyed their ability to control the flow of information and neutralized their propaganda. This is an example of how control is ultimately an impotent approach to power; it's a validation of the saying "The pen is mightier than the sword."

Some people renounce power because they see it used only for dominance or control; they confuse being powerful with being power hungry and abusing power. They think that to be powerful, you can't love people and be truly concerned about their fate. Because of this, rejecting power is seen as a good and necessary thing. But equating powerlessness with virtue is a form of power illiteracy. In fact, personal power—no different from power in the physical sense—is simply the capacity to bring about change, to make things happen. People should strive to be as powerful as they can be, without taking power away from others.

The Many Faces of Personal Power

Personal power goes far beyond being able to manipulate or control people. You have power when you can bring about what you seek and prevent what you don't want. On the other hand, you are powerless when you can't bring about what you want or can't stop things you wish to avoid. The enormously powerful and wealthy president of a global corporation who manipulates politicians and workers may be powerless to get the love of his wife and children. All his control power is useless to get him a happy personal life; he can't even get a sweet caress or loving glance from the ones he loves.

Most of us don't have the kinds of problems associated with wealth and control. Ordinary people are powerless when they can't control what they eat, drink, or put in their bodies; when they can't sleep or stay awake; when they can't think clearly or control their emotions. We are especially powerless, and feel this keenly, when we can't curb other people's controlling and oppressive behavior. If you are able to cope with these problems, your life will likely develop satisfactorily. If you can't muster the energy and skills to overcome them, your life will be joyless and filled with turmoil and depression, psychosis, and addiction.

Our Inner Enemy—The Critical Parent

One important reason we become powerless is that many of us have an internal foe that constantly weakens us from within.

When people are systematically abused, most of them will, in time, abuse other people and themselves. In this way, they become their own and each other's abusers. Dramatic examples abound in which oppressed people turned on each other and treated each other as viciously as their oppressors did. An example of this happened in Nazi concentration camps where Jewish inmate "capos," appointed by the wardens to guard their fellow Jews, adopted their captors' cruel ways.

This process also works when people are subjected to less dramatic, subtle psychological abuse. Such abuse is hidden and unacknowledged and tends to be forgotten. But it is taken in and eventually becomes internalized. I use the label Critical Parent for that internalized self-abuse which keeps people in line and punishes them for every thought or act that breaks its oppressive rules. When traditionally powerless people like children, introverts, women, people of color, workers, lesbians, gay men, disabled, old, poor, or "ugly" folk are mistreated, they can feel so powerless that they come to accept the mistreatment and believe that it is deserved.

Eventually, the powerless abuse themselves, physically and psychologically, as they follow the dictates of the Critical Parent in scores of self-destructive, self-loathing ways. In this way, they have absorbed society's patriarchal scheme, which says it is all right for some people to dominate and for others to be beaten down. In this scheme, those who are beaten down are somehow "wrong." It labels the poor as "lazy," or women as "irrational," or minorities as intellectually or morally "inferior."

In this book, I have explained how the Critical Parent operates. Self-persecution is the work of the Critical Parent, called variously the "harsh superego," the "Pig Parent," "the destructive critic," "catastrophic ideation," "stinking thinking," "low self-esteem," the "enemy," and so on, depending on the theory or system of thought that recognizes its destructive influence. Whatever it is called, it is a voice or an image in the mind saying that the person is bad, stupid, ugly, crazy, sick, or doomed—in short, not okay. What's more, these attributions can be passed down from parents to children, and become part of a family's script through the generations.

In emotional literacy training we have vowed to remove the Critical Parent from our lives: a hard but worthwhile task. But fighting our own Critical Parent is not enough. In fact, it is a hopeless task unless we also become aware of and resist the controlling patriarchal influences that surround us.

No one needs to fight this battle alone. People everywhere are struggling to run their own lives and are eager to join others in the fight for self-determination. To succeed, we need to develop a new form of personal non-abusive power known as "charisma."

Seven Sources of Power

Let me describe seven sources of non-abusive power. Students of Eastern religions will recognize their source in the ancient theory of the chakras of Kundalini yoga: Earth, Sex, Power, Heart, Throat, Third Eye, and Cosmos.[36]

I have renamed these seven power sources Balance, Passion, Control, Love, Communication, Information, and Transcendence.

Not any one of these powers should be valued over another. Instead, they should be used together, for each has its own unique capacity to bring about change. When you use them in combination, you will find that this rainbow of options is much more powerful than the blunt, often brutal forms of control power that dominate so many of us.

BALANCE

or *grounding,* is the capacity to be rooted and comfortable while sitting, standing, climbing, walking, or running. When you have a well-developed capacity for balance, you "know where you stand" and you are able to "stand your ground." Because you know where you stand, you will not be easily pushed out of your physical or personal position. Your body will be firmly planted, and your mind will be steady.

Balance is a particularly valuable power source for women. Patriarchy discourages women from attaining a strong sense of physical balance. Women's fashions, designed to please men—tight clothes, miniskirts, high heels—interfere with physical stability. So do the requirements of modesty—limited and careful motion—for women of "breeding."

Men, on the other hand, are free to be as physically comfortable as they desire, wear roomy clothing and shoes, and have minimal requirements for grooming and modesty.

In the Western World, as women move slowly toward equal status with men, they are casting aside many of the dictates of dress and grooming that have been required for them. As a result, they are feeling more powerful—more rooted, grounded, and balanced. That, in spite of the fact that some of the gains accomplished along these lines are being nullified by increased pressure to look younger and thinner, diet, wear skimpier clothes, and engage in plastic surgery which, though aimed at both sexes, affects women more powerfully.

As with all the other power sources, you should try to reach a "happy medium" in regard to Balance. If you are deficient in Balance, you will be too obedient, easily frightened, and timid. But if you overdevelop Balance, you will be stubborn, stony, dense, unmovable, and dull, and you will not be able to tolerate or handle being thrown off your equilibrium.

PASSION

The power of passion can invigorate like nothing else can. Passion can create or destroy. Passion brings opposites together, forces confrontation and change.

In the absence of sexual passion, there would be no Romeo and Juliet, few marriages, no unrequited love. But passion is not only sexual. It also fuels missionary zeal, quixotic quests, revolution.

If your passion is underdeveloped, you will be tepid, boring, and gutless. If your passion is excessive, it can get out of control and become destructive.

CONTROL

has been badly used but is an essential form of power. Control allows you to manipulate your environment and the objects, machines, animals, and people in it.

Control, which can be both physical and psychological, also gives you power over yourself. Control is especially important when, in the form of self-discipline, it lets you regulate your other powers such as passion, information, communication, and very importantly, your emotions. This control is vital when events around you run amok and threaten your survival. Emotional literacy is partially a matter of controlling emotions: expressing them or holding them back for a powerful personal approach.

If you lack in control power, you can be victimized by emotional turmoil and become addicted, depressed, sleepless, and slothful. Or you may be victimized by the outer world, becoming unemployed, homeless, battered, persecuted, mentally ill, or sickened by pollution. You will be seen as lacking discipline, unable to control what you feel, say, and do, and what you put in your mouth, up your nose, or into your veins. On the opposite end of the spectrum, when obsessed by control, you become preoccupied with absolute control of every living soul.

LOVE

Everyone wants to love and to be loved, knowing how good it feels when it actually happens. But few people look beyond love's obvious pleasures to see its power. Fewer yet fully develop that power.

Love is more than just Valentine's Day cards, the thrill that you get when you see or touch your beloved, or the warm hug of a mother's child. Love has the power to bind people together, enabling them to work tirelessly side by side on the hardest tasks, instilling hope that can propel them out of the most hellish situations: floods, famines, wars, plane wrecks.

If your power of love is underdeveloped, you will be cold, lacking in warmth or empathy for other people, unable to nurture or to be nurtured, unable even to love yourself. If this power is overdeveloped, you will be a habitual Rescuer, driven to excessive sacrifices for others while neglecting yourself.

A loving attitude guides the Emotional Warrior. This attitude applies to three elementary realms: love of self, love of others, and love of truth. These three qualities provide the vision necessary for a heart-centered approach to living:

1. LOVE OF SELF—bedrock individuality. When we love ourselves we will stand our ground in defense of our

personal uniqueness. Individuality keeps us firmly focused on what we want and makes us capable of deciding what will contribute to or detract from our personal path. Only a passionate love of self will give one the strength to persevere in our decisions when everyone loses faith in who we are or what we are doing.

2. LOVE OF OTHERS—steadfast loyalty. By being loyal we are aware of our involvement in the lives of other human beings and as passionate about others as we are about ourselves. Love of self without love of others is selfishness. Love of others without love of self, turns us into Rescuers ready to give everything away. Love of self and others can only be sustained by keeping in touch with our own true feelings on the one hand and the feelings of others on the other hand.

3. LOVE OF TRUTH—conscious truthfulness. Love of self and others is intimately dependent on the love of truth. Truthfulness is especially important in the Information Age, where we can be "well-informed" and at the same time under the influence of false and deceitful information. Love of truth is the attribute that keeps a person actively involved in pursuing valid information: information that reflects the realities of the world. "Radical truth-telling," explored in the "Notes for Philosophers" at the end of this book, is the application of the love of truth to relationships.

COMMUNICATION

The power of communication depends on the capacity to reproduce one's thoughts and feelings in others. But communication will not work without the willing ear of its recipient. Two operations are involved: sending and receiving, speaking and listening. Two-way communication is needed to transmit knowledge, to solve problems with others, to build satisfying relationships—in short, to achieve emotional literacy.

If you are lacking in communication power, you will be unable to learn or teach much. If you stress communication too much, you could become a compulsive, careless talker, paying too little attention to what you are saying or its effect on others.

All the sources of power work with each other. A very powerful combination of powers, used by great teachers is made of communication, information, and love. Their communication is inspired by the love of truth and the love of people. They do not browbeat or use control to persuade. Instead they explain, and if they are not understood, try to understand why; their students are free to compare what they are learning with what they already know, thus forming their own well-grounded opinions.

INFORMATION

The power of information is that it reduces your uncertainty so you can make effective decisions. When you have information, you can anticipate events and you can make things happen or prevent them from happening.

If you are lacking in the power of information, you suffer from ignorance. If this power is overdeveloped, you tend to rely excessively on science and technology, becoming hyper-intellectual and lacking heart.

Information comes in four forms: science, intuition, history, and vision.

1. SCIENCE gathers facts methodically, by taking a careful look at things and noting how they work. Science is like a camera taking focused and sharp pictures of reality. It is a powerful source of certainty.

2. INTUITION is fuzzy, not exact like science, but it is a powerful guide toward what is probably true. Intuition grasps the flow of things. It produces "educated guesses" about the way things are. Because it directs the investigator's attention to certain areas of inquiry, intuition is often vital in the early stages of important scientific discoveries.

3. HISTORICAL KNOWLEDGE comes from knowledge of past events, either through personal experience or through

the study of history. Historical perspective can be a powerful tool to help you forecast and understand events.

4. VISION is the ability to see what lies ahead directly, through dreams and visions. We all have visions of the future but it takes great self-confidence to be a visionary. Vision, when recognized, is a highly valued form of information.

Ordinarily, our society considers science the only valid source of knowledge; history is for old people, intuition for women, and vision for lunatics. Still, each of these forms of information has validity and when effectively used, can add to your charisma.

Information has been badly misused over the ages. It has been used in the service of control, to wage war, to seize land, and to impose political and religious views. Today, in the Information Age, the misuse of information comes in the form of disinformation, false advertising, negative political ads, and other forms of modern propaganda. It is used to manipulate millions of people through television and other mass media and to persuade people to live certain lifestyles and buy the products that go with them.

Information in the service of love would be starkly different. It would be freely available and used to build people's power: their health through medical and psychological knowledge, their wisdom through education, their relationships through emotional literacy.

TRANSCENDENCE

When viewed as a source of power, transcendence is the power of equanimity, of letting events take their course without getting upset or letting your ego get involved. It lets you find calm and see things as they are, even in the midst of earthshaking events. We find transcendence by realizing how insignificant we are in the universe, how brief life is, how ephemeral our successes and failures. The power of transcendence gives one hope and faith that there is a meaning to life even if one's limited intelligence can't grasp it. With it, we can "rise above" a particular situation and trust and feel our power in spite of material conditions.

If your capacity for transcendence is underdeveloped, you will see yourself at the very center of things and cling desperately to your beliefs and desires, aversions and cravings, successes and failures, no matter the cost. You will fail to see the effect that you have on other human beings and the environment, because all that matters to you, is you. On the other hand, if transcendence becomes an overused method of coping, you will become detached from earthly matters, so that you will "float away" oblivious of events around you, unwilling and unable to touch the ground.

My knowledge about these sources of power varies; I understand some (control, communication) better than others (transcendence, vision). I invite you, dear reader, to add what you know about these subjects by communicating with me by mail or through the web page given at the end of this book.

A Shift for the Millennium

At its worst, Western culture today is an engine of absolute control. The six other sources of power have been diminished and put at the service of control's purpose:

Transcendence has been distorted into patriarchal religions worshiping wrathful gods and headed by corrupt religious leaders whose self-aggrandizing aim is the accumulation of money and/or power.

Information is becoming an increasingly expensive commodity developed by science to serve war and police technology and to manufacture and sell goods. Valid information is becoming indistinguishable from disinformation, propaganda, and "infotainment."

Communication has become a one-way process to manipulate people through the media.

Love has been reduced to a parody of itself, laden with jealousy and obsession, heralded in popular songs and films but unavailable and ignored in real life.

Passion has been limited to lust and violence as portrayed in the media. The passionate love of truth, fairness, and equality has become an unpopular concern of an increasingly distressed minority.

Balance, as people become increasingly inactive and overweight, has become the realm of athletic super-heroes.

At its best, Western culture could be an environment that empowers people. As pioneered by Riane Eisler in *The Chalice and the Blade*,[37] we can shift away from patriarchy and control in the direction of democracy, partnership, and love. Together, as Emotional Warriors, we can use our love-centered powers to make these changes happen.

You can enlist in this effort by developing your individual powers and charisma in its many forms. You need:

- Balance to stand your ground.
- Passion to energize you.
- Control to keep a steady course.
- Communication to effectively interact with others.
- Information to make accurate predictions.
- Transcendence to keep perspective.
- Love to harmonize and give all these capacities a powerful forward thrust.

Emotional literacy training speaks directly to the heart, calling for people everywhere to practice three interconnected virtues: love of self, love of others, and love of truth. This is the path of the Emotional Warrior.

Summary

THE EMOTIONAL WARRIOR

You don't have to go along with a world in which human power is expressed through power plays or violence. You can link up with others to struggle for a world in which power is expressed through love: of self, others, and truth. You can do this by becoming emotionally literate and teaching emotional literacy techniques to others. To be passionate, balanced, and spiritually aware is to be powerful. There are seven nonviolent sources of power you can draw on: Balance, Passion, Control, Love, Communication, Information, and Transcendence.

By making an earnest pledge of radical honesty and leading with your heart you can join me and others around the world in our purpose of learning and teaching emotional literacy. If you do, you will become an Emotional Warrior.

CHAPTER 11

One Last Word

Love is a word often used in this book, a word gener-ally overused and easily abused and yet, love, I think most would agree, makes the world go 'round. What love is, exactly, is not clear, but certainly it goes beyond the well-known passion between lovers or the adoration of our offspring. It is the deep instinct that makes us enjoy being with each other, taking care of one another, and doing things together. When we give it full expression, it helps us survive and prosper.

Of the many things I have said in this book, I want to reemphasize one: Love is at the very center of emotional literacy. Any emotional intelligence that we may accu-mulate apart from the loving emotion is like a paint-by-the-numbers canvas that may look good upon casual gaze but is not the real thing. If you begin by giving and taking strokes, you will open up your heart and access the only lasting basis for an emotionally literate life.

Very likely, you will wonder how the practice of a few transactional exercises could possibly produce such a powerful source of energy and power. Isn't that claim of simple-minded alchemy to turn psychological lead into gold? But I am not promising to *create* a loving heart. What I am assuring is that these transactions, practiced honestly with another willing and sympathetic person, will *unleash* your heart's power. Giving and receiving strokes will force open the gates that imprison your heart. The rest is up to that irresistible power of nature: Love. It may not seem so to some, but Love is ready to surge forth and do battle with our dark side, if we will let it and if we can find ways to make it safe and nurture it as it grows.

Eventually, whether or not you develop your emotional literacy will depend on a number of factors: your desire, whether you can find people to practice with, the opportunities afforded you in this cruel world, and how successful you are in avoiding its dark side. In these last words I want to make sure, dear reader, you understand that this book's message has everything to do with Love—of self, of others, and of truth.

Claude Steiner
BERKELEY, CALIFORNIA
AUGUST 2003

Notes for Philosophers

With these notes I am following the example set by Eric Berne. In his writings, he provided his readers with the historical and philosophical background for his views. These notes are the result of conversations with Jude Hall about the philosophical controversies surrounding the issues raised in this book.

LOVE AS A FUNDAMENTAL GOOD

The idea of love as a basic good, to be universally pursued with all other human beings, is a markedly Christian notion. It was first espoused in the West by Jesus Christ and in China by Mo Di, a contemporary of Confucius' disciple Mencius. The most influential critic of Christianity's concept of love is Friedrich Nietzsche.[38] He held that the universal love espoused by Christians is disingenuous, hypocritical, neurotic, and leads to depressive nihilism (what he called passive nihilism) and to the degeneracy of society and the arts. He maintained that the universal love and altruism to which Christians aspire necessitates an egalitarian leveling which prevents society from producing excellence by assigning privilege evenly among a people, when it should go to the especially gifted. These special individuals should be allowed to secure the power they need to achieve their vision.

Nietzsche's idols were Napoleon, Julius Caesar, Augustus Caesar, and early Roman emperors, strong men after the fashion of his human ideal, the superman. While this may sound bizarre to the average reader, Nietzsche (who died in 1900) is considered one of the most influential figures in 20th-century thought, and his critique of the hidden psychological roots of altruism is accepted by thinkers as diverse as Max Horkheimer, Theodore Adorno and Michael Foucault. Some aspects of Nietzschian thought have even influenced as egalitarian a thinker as Herbert Marcuse. Thus, as deviant as Nietzsche's ideas may seem to the uninitiated, they cannot be dismissed. Students of contemporary politics may recognize the traces of the Nietzschian point of view in the theories of conservative politicians today. The belief that social services and government subsidies to help the disadvantaged are undesirable is the permissible manifestation of a far more extreme elitist conviction which permeates the corridors of conservatism throughout the world.

Paradoxically, though the love-centered views of this book originate in the teachings of Jesus of Nazareth, they are likely to be classified as secular humanism, anathema to fundamentalist Christians and despised by conservatives.

LYING & HONESTY

The idea that lying is a universal evil was recorded in one of the ten commandments brought down from Mt. Sinai by Moses: "Thou shall not bear false witness." Though it is a fundamental Judeo-Christian dictum, there is very little attention paid to just what, precisely, obeying the rule would imply. When speaking of truth in this book, I am applying the well-known criteria followed in the courts, namely that in order not to lie one needs to tell "the whole truth [no lies of omission] and nothing but the truth [no lies of commission]." According to this definition, a lie is a conscious act, so that a person cannot lie without being aware of it. The truth here is simply the truth as the speaker knows it—subjective truth—and different from and only vaguely related to the abstract and unattainable concept of "the truth" (See notes on The Truth, below). St. Augustine[39] was the foremost proponent of absolute truthfulness. He believed that "God forbids all lies." The notion that one should never lie was taken to its political extreme by Immanuel Kant,[40] who argued that it would be a moral crime to lie to a murderer about the whereabouts of a potential victim. Benjamin Constant[41] countered that "No one has the right to a truth that injures others."

In this book, while arguing that being truthful is a requirement of emotional literacy, I recognize that the imperative of truth-telling is secondary to the imperative of safety. Thus, any person aspiring to be radically truthful has to keep in mind that truth-telling can, on occasion, be harmful and needs to be evaluated according to circumstances. This may seem to open the door for all manner of lies to preserve people's safety. But there are, in everyday life, very few situations that warrant lying on the basis of safety and certainly no justification whatsoever for the constant dishonesty accepted as normal. Most of the lies people tell have nothing to do with protecting others or oneself from harm, and everything to do with manipulating people to one's advantage, often under the guise of attempting to shield each other from "needless" pain.

According to Dr. Bella de Paulo,[42] "everyday lies are part of the fabric of social life," and in a study of people lying she found that people lie in one-fifth of their social interactions and that 70 percent of those who lie would tell the lies again. Sixty percent of the lies were outright deceptions, a tenth of the lies were exaggerations, and the rest were subtle lies, often lies of omission.

In her book, *Lying,* Sissela Bok,[43] the acknowledged expert on the issue, classifies all manner of lies and secrets and acknowledges the harm that chronic lying causes us. Yet she does not go as far as to recommend that people should not lie at all, mostly, it seems, because of her apprehension that radical honesty can lend itself to sadistic misuse.

In his book *Radical Honesty*, Brad Blanton,[44] asserts that "We all lie like hell. It wears us out. It is the major source of all human stress. Lying kills people." Yet, he also falls short of recommending that we not lie at all. He fails to endorse a radical policy of truth-telling (in spite of the title of his book) because part of our chronic lying, as he sees it, are lies we tell ourselves, something not so easily defined and even less easily stopped. I avoid the self-lying conundrum by defining a lie as a conscious act. Given this definition, lying to ourselves is impossible.

THE TRUTH

By writing about the truth and love of truth, I am opening myself for a huge philosophical debate which has frozen in their tracks greater and infinitely more meticulous minds than mine. The idea that truth is something to be discovered with the mind rather than accepted from religion was first recorded in the 4th century BC. It was a result of a new interest in the workings of the physical universe.

Socrates and Plato extended their exploration of truth into the realms of ethics, aesthetics, politics, and psychology. (Aristotle shifted the emphasis back to empirical inquiry, in defiance of his teacher, Plato, who favored speculation and logic with little empirical grounding.) It was the Greek sophists, Plato's contemporaries and intellectual antagonists, who first began to argue that emotion and prejudice are as important as reason in the pursuit of truth. Plato argued for absolute truth, discoverable through a dialogic process which he called dialectic; the sophists believed that opinion, or "doxa," is truth and that truth is wholly relative. Hence Protagoras' famous dictum "Man is the measure of all things."[45] The dominance of religious truth returned with the Middle Ages, but in the Enlightenment the debate resumed. The Rationalists echoed Plato in arguing that reason is the best guide to truth; the Empiricists, like Aristotle, preferred to rely on the physical facts; the Romantics inadvertently came to parallel the sophists by asserting the importance of emotion and the irrational. (It should be noted that while the sophists were often disingenuous hustlers, the Romantics were earnest seekers rebelling against the excesses of rationalism and industrialization.)

Though Nietzsche was the inheritor of the Romantic tradition from his early idol, Schopenhauer, he was one of the least dewy-eyed thinkers who ever lived. He argued that language (and even thought) are inherently deceptive and that no society can survive without mutually agreed upon falsehoods: to be truthful means to employ the usual metaphors. Thus, to express it morally, there is the duty to lie according to a fixed convention, to lie with the herd and in a manner binding upon everyone."[46] Today, those familiar with the work of Nietzsche's inheritors, the structuralist and post-structuralist philosophers, such as Derrida and Foucault, may sneer at the notion that the concept of truth has any meaning or that it can be discovered.

To my mind, there is nothing that can be called "the truth." The truth changes with time. There are several sometimes seemingly contradictory truths and there is no way to contain the hugely complex facts of nature in any one set of words. But I believe that some statements are truer than others. This book does not propose to have a monopoly on universal moral truths. Instead, it offers a paradigm which, within our culture, has the potential to make our lives happier and richer. What I can say with certainty is that to reap the benefits of practicing emotional literacy, one must take "love of truth" seriously and seriously strive to be truthful. Love of truth implies, as George Sand is believed to have said: "We must accept truth even if it changes our point of view." We need to be particularly vigilant within the context of loving, cooperative relationships, where lies often seem necessary to prevent harm but so often create much more harm than they avert.

VIOLENCE & THE DARK SIDE

People have, deep in their hearts, a real need and desire to bond, to be open, loving, and respectful of other's feelings. One of the first tenets of Transactional Analysis is that everyone is born Okay.[47] This idea probably filtered down to Eric Berne from the 19th century philosopher, Jean Jacques Rousseau, who maintained that people are born good and it is social ills that make them bad. Philosopher Herbert Marcuse, and initially, Sigmund Freud, have called this original goodness the "inborn social instinct" Eros, and the energy that drives it, "libido." Freud originally believed that our ability to live harmoniously and lovingly with each other comes from this "Eros principle," while violence and exploitation come from the "ego principle," the side of human nature that is concerned with self-preservation and therefore strives to become as powerful (and therefore safe) as possible and is willing to harm others to achieve its ends.

There are others, like Francis Fukuyama,[48] who have suggested that this Rousseauian conviction that people are intrinsically good while all negativity comes from bad social conditions is a naive, liberal notion. Freud himself in the later part of his life, after witnessing the horrors of WWII, decided that there was, in addition to libido, the life principle, another innate human tendency, an inborn antisocial instinct which he called "thanatos," the Death instinct.

In addition to the positive, cooperative side of people, there is a dark side of human nature that we have to reckon with. Beyond the simple lessons of this book, we will be confronted with hard situations, and as Emotional Warriors, we should not be taken by surprise if our efforts are met with hard—if not nasty—resistance.

The pursuit of emotional literacy presupposes that people are born with an innate tendency toward goodness, cooperation, and love: that is, a tendency to exercise ethical power. Without that tendency, we would be fighting a constant, exhausting, uphill battle. But we also have forces within that are profoundly unethical, which are not just implanted by a bad culture but are probably innate. These forces involve aggression, greed, and unethical manifestations of sexuality. They stem from primitive, irrepressible, and even vital and valuable survival instincts.

The moral philosophers of the Enlightenment generally defined evil as error. In the terms of this book, error is equivalent to emotional illiteracy, or a lack of a sense of enlightened self-interest that would make it evident to us that our evil deeds will eventually hurt us by leaving us isolated from the tribe. But the root of evil may not be only error, but the result of deep, instinctive, unchecked survival impulses.

To be an effective Emotional Warrior you must be able to admit your own aggression, selfishness, and greed, your own inborn urge to survive at all costs. You must also be aware of and accept these impulses in others. An Emotional Warrior knows that we all have selfish and aggressive instincts and that managing those instincts in an ethical way is one of the primary aims of emotional wisdom.

Fyodor Dostoyevsky acknowledged this irreducible selfishness in human nature when he wrote:

> "To love another as oneself according to Christ's commandment is impossible. Only Christ was able to do this, but Christ is a perpetual and eternal ideal towards which man strives."[49]

There is a dark side, not only to human nature, but also to the human condition. All human beings live every day with the possibility of loss, tragedy, and even disaster.

In the modern world, with technology, we have protected ourselves from many types of tragedy. However, we may have paved the way for a greater collective tragedy— a worldwide catastrophe—for that same technology, if left unchecked, may destroy the biosphere.

The awareness of tragedy is relevant to the pursuit of emotional literacy, especially for the Emotional Warrior. Some survivors of tragedy feel that they no longer have the resources to worry about the rights and needs of others. They may fall into a nihilistic attitude of "After all I've been through, I deserve to be happy, by any means necessary" or "I've suffered, why shouldn't others suffer, too?" An Emotional Warrior must understand this temptation to succumb to the dark side of our nature in response to tragedy, and must be able to resist this temptation. She must understand that she may not be rewarded materially for her efforts and may even suffer tragedy in spite of her valor. Sometimes, virtue is not only its own reward, but along with knowledge and meaning, its only reward. A warrior must be prepared for that possibility.

An Emotional Warrior is aware of the dark side, both the dark side of human nature (innate greed and aggression) and the dark side of the human condition (tragedy) and strives to practice honorable ethical power even when one or both of these twin facets of the dark side threaten to wreak havoc.

VIOLENCE & ABUSE

The connection between childhood abuse and violent adult behavior, mediated by emotional numbing, is a strongly established one. The relationship is not perfect. For instance, there are certain neurological determinants of violent behavior strongly associated with trauma to the brain. That is to say, youngsters who experience head injuries, whether accidental or from abuse, exhibit a certain lack of inhibitory capacity which can result in and is correlated with uncontrolled violent behavior. On the other hand, childhood abuse is also highly correlated with violent adult behavior. In fact, abuse is more strongly correlated with adult violence than brain injury. This underscores the urgent need to stop domestic violence.

The most dangerous mixture of violence determinants is the combination of both abuse and neurological damage.

Using time spent in jail as a rough measure of violent behavior, the results of a study of 95 male juveniles are startling:[50]

No neurological determinants, no abuse

NO JAIL TIME

Neurological determinants, no abuse

360 DAYS JAIL TIME

No neurological determinants and abuse

562 DAYS JAIL TIME

Neurological determinants and abuse

1,214 DAYS JAIL TIME

Children with brain injuries almost always incur them from neglect or abuse. Child abuse, especially child abuse that involves blows to the head, is a serious determinant of violent adult behavior. And the trauma of neglect and abuse causes the kind of emotional numbing that makes one capable of abusing or neglecting a child. Intervention and emotional literacy training are desperately needed. By teaching empathy, emotional literacy training stops the vicious cycle of abuse and neglect.

THE CRITICAL PARENT

Critical thinkers will question the concept of the Critical Parent. Some argue that it is too much like a *homunculus,* a little person inside of our heads. However, the Critical Parent is just a way to visualize and make accessible a method for taking away psychic energy from a set of recurrent, debilitating, prejudiced, and deprecatory thoughts. These self-abusive, self-limiting thoughts are not based on the facts of current reality. They are prejudices which distract, de-motivate, and demoralize us.

Some people hear the Critical Parent as derogatory, insulting, or doom-ridden "voices in the head." This makes the process of decathecting and disconnecting from the Critical Parent easier. It is easier because you can speak to, disagree with, and evict a voice in your head, whereas it is more difficult to respond to and resist a doom-ridden image or amorphous feelings of inadequacy.

This discussion leads to questions of the validity of the concept of ego states. Are there really three and only three completely distinct states of the ego which manifest themselves in sequence and which operate in three distinctly different ways? The value of these concepts is that they help us to better understand human social behavior. They are metaphors useful for representing human beings in their social transactions. When transactional analysts draw two people with their three ego states on the chalkboard, we know that these are not complete representations of these people any more than a street map is a complete representation of a city. They are approximations of human behavior and structure, based on observation and the application of evolutionary and neuroscience information. Basically, ego states are highly useful; as useful as a street map for getting around in the human situation.

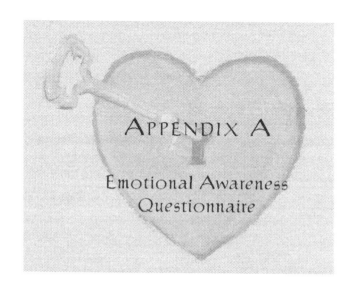

Appendix A

Emotional Awareness Questionnaire

Although there is no scientifically valid emotional intelligence or literacy test, the questionnaire below can give you a good idea of your level of emotional awareness, which is an essential part of emotional literacy.

Please answer these questions as honestly as possible. The point is not to look good, but to find out for yourself where you stand in terms of emotional awareness. If you can't decide whether your answer is Yes or No, answer Not Sure.

1A. I have noticed that sometimes when I find myself with a person who is very emotional, I am surprisingly calm and without feeling.

      Yes   No   Not Sure

1B. At times when I am about to interact with people I don't know well, I feel sensations like heart palpitations, stomach cramps, a lump or dryness in the throat, or a shortness of breath, but I don't know why this is happening.

     YES   NO   NOT SURE

1C.   Sometimes I am flooded by emotions that disorganize and confuse me.

     YES   NO   NOT SURE

1D.   From time to time, I am aware of having feelings of anger, from slight irritation to rage.

     YES   NO   NOT SURE

1E.   If another person is emotional, I am usually able to tell what emotion they feel, such as fear, happiness, sadness, hope, or anger.

     YES   NO   NOT SURE

1F.   I enjoy situations in which people are having strong positive emotions of love, hope, and joy, like at weddings or in church services.

     YES   NO   NOT SURE

2A.   Sometimes after a difficult time with another person, I feel as if parts of my body are numb.

     YES   NO   NOT SURE

2B.   I take one or more over-the-counter drugs to deal with headaches, stomach and digestive symptoms, or body pains that my doctor can't explain.

     YES   NO   NOT SURE

2C.   I know I have very strong feelings, but I am frequently unable to talk about them with other people.

     YES   NO   NOT SURE

2D. I am aware of having feelings of fear, from apprehension to terror.

       YES   NO   NOT SURE

2E. Sometimes I can feel other people's feelings in my body.

       YES   NO   NOT SURE

2F. I am appreciated by other people because I know how to cool down emotional situations.

       YES   NO   NOT SURE

※ ※ ※

3A. I can easily kill a small animal like a snake or chicken without feeling anything in particular.

       YES   NO   NOT SURE

3B. I am often jumpy and irritable, and I can't help it.

       YES   NO   NOT SURE

3C. I find myself lying about my feelings because I am embarrassed to speak about them.

       YES   NO   NOT SURE

3D. I am aware of having strong feelings of love and joy.

       YES   NO   NOT SURE

3E. I often do things for other people because I sympathize with them and can't say no to people.

       YES   NO   NOT SURE

3F. I am good at helping people sort out their emotions because I usually understand why they are feeling them.

       YES   NO   NOT SURE

4A. I can be around people who are suffering physical pain without getting upset about it.

        Yes   No   Not Sure

4B. I get sweaty palms around people I don't know.

        Yes   No   Not Sure

4C. I know I have strong feelings, but most of the time I don't know what those feelings are.

        Yes   No   Not Sure

4D. I am pretty good at knowing what I feel and why.

        Yes   No   Not Sure

4E. Sometimes other people's feelings are very clear to me, and that can be a problem.

        Yes   No   Not Sure

4F. I can usually handle people who have strong feelings and unload them on me.

        Yes   No   Not Sure

5A. I am almost always a rational person and have no problems with my emotions.

        Yes   No   Not Sure

5B. I have been in love and suddenly, inexplicably lost that feeling completely.

        Yes   No   Not Sure

5C. I am overwhelmed by bad mood sometimes.

        Yes   No   Not Sure

5D. When I have to make an important decision, I usually know how I feel about it, whether it be scared, excited, angry, or some other combination of emotions.

YES   NO   NOT SURE

5E. In a competitive situation in which I am winning or clearly superior, I feel bad for the other person.

YES   NO   NOT SURE

5F. When I am in a room full of people, I can tell how the group is feeling—excited, angry, bored, or scared.

YES   NO   NOT SURE

6A. I very, very rarely cry.

YES   NO   NOT SURE

6B. Sometimes when I watch a TV commercial, tears come to my eyes, and I don't really understand why.

YES   NO   NOT SURE

6C. Sometimes when I am feeling bad, I can't tell if I am scared or angry.

YES   NO   NOT SURE

6D. I am a person who at times feels shame and guilt.

YES   NO   NOT SURE

6E. I have had the opportunity to shoot an animal like a bird, rabbit, or deer, and was not able to do it because I felt bad for the animal.

YES   NO   NOT SURE

6F. I often change the way I act toward another person because I figure it will make things easier between us.

YES   NO   NOT SURE

Now that you have answered all the questions, you can score the questionnaire.

Count up the number of "Yes" responses on all questions marked A. Write that number (from 1 to 6) in the space marked "A" below. Repeat that process with B, C, D, E, and F questions.

A _____   D _____

B _____   E _____

C _____   F _____

There now should be a number (from 1 to 6) next to each letter above. Later you will be able to use these numbers to create a bar chart and determine your emotional awareness profile.

Your Emotional Awareness Profile

Let's get back to the bar chart that you generated with the questionnaire about yourself. First of all, I want to reemphasize that this profile is not a measurement of your emotional literacy but an examination of awareness, which is only an aspect (though a very important one) of emotional literacy.

Create a blank bar chart similar to the ones below on a separate piece of paper and fill in the boxes based on your scores. For example, if you answered "Yes" to six D questions, fill in the D column all the way up through the number 6 row. If you answered "Yes" to two B questions, fill in the B column through the number 2 row. Shade your remaining scores. When you have finished, you will have a bar chart similar to the example below based on the emotional awareness scale.

The A questions examine emotional numbness (EN); B questions test for physical symptoms (PS); C questions refer to chaotic primal experience (CE); D questions test for differentiation (DF); E questions for empathy (EM); and F for interactivity (IA). The profile you generated will help you see what kind of work you need to do to improve your emotional literacy. The three most common profiles are:

Low awareness profile:

	EN	PS	CE	DF	EM	IA
6						
5						
4	XX					
3	XX	XX				
2	XX	XX	XX	XX		
1	XX	XX	XX	XX	XX	

EN	PS	CE	DF	EM	IA
(A)	(B)	(C)	(D)	(E)	(F)

If your profile looks like this, you are a person who hasn't paid much attention to your feelings and tends to be puzzled by the feelings of others. Most of the time, you are not aware of feeling any emotions at all; they're not part of your normal life as far as you can tell. On the occasions that you have a strong emotional response, you feel anger or fear and you do everything you can to overcome that unwelcome state. You will profit from working on your emotional literacy.

High awareness profile:

	EN	PS	CE	DF	EM	IA
6						
5						
4						XX
3				XX	XX	XX
2				XX	XX	XX
1		XX	XX	XX	XX	XX

EN	PS	CE	DF	EM	IA
(A)	(B)	(C)	(D)	(E)	(F)

If your profile looks like this, your emotions are part of your everyday life awareness. You know how you feel, why, and how strongly most of the time. You feel comfortable talking about emotional subjects and understand other people's emotions, but you may find that your awareness is a problem. If you talk about your emotions, you may create problems for yourself, and if you don't, you may feel like a stranger in a strange land where no one sees what you see. You are in a very good position to develop a high level of emotional literacy.

The average awareness profile:

6					
5					
4		XX			
3		XX	XX		
2		XX	XX	XX	
1	XX	XX	XX	XX	XX	XX

EN	PS	CE	DF	EM	IA
(A)	(B)	(C)	(D)	(E)	(F)

If your profile looks like this, you are aware of your feelings but don't always know what to do about them. You understand some of your emotions but are puzzled by others. You are able to empathize at times but at times you are left cold by other people's feelings. Most of the time, when in an emotional state, your feelings are a bothersome, chaotic jumble which you try to get away from by ignoring them. When you try to talk about them to other people, the results are mixed. Sometimes feelings are resolved, sometimes they are made worse. You are the person most likely to profit from this book.

APPENDIX B

Emotional Literacy Worksheets

For use in emotional literacy training

These forms can be obtained in MS Word format from www.claudesteiner.com

Contracts

> **Contracts are made to protect the participants from the fearsome possibilities of emotional work; being coerced into opening up, being judged, attacked, ridiculed or deceived, being made responsible for other people's actions, being gossiped about or shunned from the group. Safety facilitates honest and free communication essential for emotional literacy.**

In Transactional Analysis we use three types of contracts:

1. Confidentiality Contract

We have two options:

Confidentiality Contract; Type I:

- Nothing transpiring in the meeting will be discussed outside of the meeting.

Confidentiality Contract; Type II:

- When discussing the events of the meeting outside of the meeting the person will take responsibility to make sure that the identities of the people discussed cannot be recognized.
- Anyone can impose a partial or total ban on being discussed outside of the meeting by just requesting it.

2. Treatment or Teaching Contract

As in the case of any legal contract a treatment or teaching contract is mutual agreement between consenting adult individuals in which a certain service is performed by the therapist or teacher for the student or client for consideration. Contracts can be long term (as in curing depression) or short term (as in learning how to give or take strokes.)

3. COOPERATIVE CONTRACT

> **A cooperative contract is a mutual agreement to abstain from power plays.**

A power play is any maneuver designed to get another person to do (or stop from doing) something that she/he would not do of his/her free will. Power plays range from the gross, physical to the subtle, psychological.

Two types of subtle, psychological power plays are especially important in human relationships and should be especially avoided:

LIES Bold-face lies or lies by omission; including
a) lies about what we want or don't want for ourselves and
b) lies about how we feel.

RESCUES A Rescue occurs when a person either:
a) does something he/she does not want to do or
b) he/she does more than her/his fair share in a situation.

> **Instead we will ask for what we want, while not doing what we don't want to do, and negotiate to a mutually satisfying, cooperative consensus.**

Asking Permission

> **We agree to precede every emotional communication with a request for permission to proceed. This gives the person addressed the choice to engage or decline a potentially difficult transaction.**

ABOUT STROKES

> **Strokes are units of interpersonal recognition.**

1. Strokes are essential for emotional and physical health and survival.

2. Strokes Can be Positive or Negative:
- Positive, good strokes (AKA*: Warm Fuzzies) are wholly positive, heartfelt and truthful recognition transactions.
- Negative, bad strokes (AKA*: Cold Pricklies) are toxic recognition transactions.
    1.) Overt devaluation and insults.
    2.) Covert devaluation and insults.
        a. Comparisons.
        b. Insincere strokes (AKA*: Plastic Fuzzies.)

   * AKA: also known as

3. Strokes Can be Wanted or Unwanted:
A person may not necessarily want a stroke even though it may be positive in nature.

4. Strokes Can be Physical, Verbal or Non-verbal (Action Strokes):
- Physical strokes can be simple touch, hugs, kisses, caresses, back rubs, being held, holding hands.
- Verbal strokes can be about a person's clothing, intelligence, generosity, creativity, elegance, wisdom, dignity, leadership ability, tact, warmth, energy, taste, honesty, looks or any attribute a person possesses.
- Action strokes are non-verbal forms of recognition like listening empathizing, or visibly liking or loving someone.

5. Strokes Have Power:

They have the power to soothe or agitate, to create good or bad feelings, to make people feel OK or Not OK about themselves, to heal or cause physical and mental illness. Some strokes are more powerful than others depending on how much they are wanted, who is giving them and how strongly they are worded or delivered. Stroke starvation can lead to physical and mental and emotional illness. Depression is most often the result of stroke deficit. Stroke satisfaction "opens the heart."

6. Strokes Involve Risk:

The risk of giving or asking for strokes depends on how much they are wanted and the likelihood of rejection or how much the critical Parent opposes them. When risky, stroking exchanges takes courage.

The Critical Parent

> **Q: People need positive strokes. So why don't people exchange them freely?**
>
> **A: Because of the Stroke Economy rules enforced by the Critical Parent**

The Critical Parent: AKA (also known as) the Pig Parent, Enemy, internalized oppressor, prison guard, harsh superego, low self esteem, electrode, negative self talk, cognitive traps, catastrophic expectations, stinking thinking, etc.

The Critical Parent is a coherent, learned set of critical and controlling points of view which are often, but not always, heard as an internal, parental voice. It can also operate as a set of anxiety provoking expectations,

THE BASIC MESSAGE OF THE CRITICAL PARENT IS:

> ## You Are Not OK
>
> Specifically:
>
> You are **bad** (sinful, lazy, wicked, etc.)
>
> You are **ugly** (ugly face, ugly body, etc.)
>
> You are **crazy** (mentally, emotionally, irrational, out of control, etc.)
>
> You are **stupid** (retarded, can't think straight, confused, etc.)
>
> You are **doomed** (ill, hopeless, self destructive, etc.)
>
> YOU WILL NOT BE LOVED &
> YOU WILL BE EXCLUDED FROM THE TRIBE.

The Critical Parent's role in relation to strokes is to enforce the rules of the Stroke Economy. The Stroke Economy is a set of rules that regulates the exchange of human affection.

The Stroke Economy

> **The Stroke Economy is a set of rules that regulates the exchange of human affection.**

THE STROKE ECONOMY'S RULES OF THE CRITICAL PARENT ARE:

> **Don't give strokes:** If you have a stroke you want to give don't give it.
> **Don't ask for strokes:** If there is a stroke you want don't ask for it.
> **Don't accept strokes:** Don't accept a stroke you want.
> **Don't reject strokes:** Don't reject a stroke you don't want.
> **Don't give yourself strokes.**

When most people follow some or all of these rules, the eventual outcome is that there will be a steady and dramatic decrease in the strokes exchanged between people. An endemic population-wide state of stroke hunger results.

Any stroke is better than no strokes at all. People who are stroke starved become willing or even eager to accept negative, toxic strokes. People get used to surviving on a reduced diet of strokes, often negative strokes. The result is that we don't enjoy our loving feelings and, as predicted by the Critical Parent, we can't love and we are not loved by others.

Opening The Heart

> **Opening the Heart** is an exercise for the free exchange of strokes. We begin emotional literacy training with Opening the Heart because the heart is the gateway to our emotions and it is there that we can begin to explore feelings in relative safety.

WE OPEN THE HEART BY DISMANTLING THE STROKE ECONOMY WHEN WE:

A. GIVE STROKES
- Overcoming Critical Parent prohibitions against giving strokes
- (Strokes must be truthful, not manufactured or exaggerated.
- Poetry is allowed, however.)

B. ASK FOR STROKES
- Overcoming Critical Parent prohibitions against asking for strokes.
- (When asking for strokes, depending on the risk we want to take, we can ask for a specific verbal or physical stroke from a specific person or for any kind of a stroke from any person.)

C. ACCEPT/REJECT STROKES
- Overcoming Critical Parent prohibitions against taking strokes we want.
- Overcoming Critical Parent prohibitions against rejecting strokes we don't want
- Errors we commit:
  - i. Rejecting positive strokes we want
  - ii. Accepting toxic strokes (negative strokes disguised as positive strokes, or "plastic fuzzies.")
  - iii. Accepting positive strokes we don't want.

D. GIVING ONESELF STROKES

Overcoming Critical Parent prohibitions against giving oneself strokes.

> The practice of this exercise has the effect of increasing the exchange of positive strokes, resulting in an expansion of positive feelings—opening the heart—between participants.

Three Stages &
Ten Steps to Emotional Literacy

0. Asking for Permission:
Preparing for an emotionally literate communication.

STAGE ONE:
OPENING THE HEART*
1. Giving Strokes: Making wholly positive, truthful, non-comparative statements of recognition.
2. Taking Strokes: Asking for, accepting and giving oneself strokes. Rejecting strokes we don't want.

STAGE TWO:
SURVEYING THE EMOTIONAL LANDSCAPE
    Part I, Action/Feeling Statement.
3. Action/Feeling Statement: "When you (describe action) I felt (name feeling)" No judgments, accusations or theories.
4. **Accepting an A/F statement**: Non-defensive acceptance of the emotional information being given.
    Part II. Intuition,
5. **Revealing Intuitions, Empathic Perceptions or Paranoid Fantasies**: Tentative presentation of an intuitive perception about another person's feelings actions or intentions.
6. **Validation of a Paranoid Fantasy or Intuition**: Searching, without defensiveness, for the validating truth, however small (grain of truth) which accounts for the above intuitive impression.

STAGE THREE:
TAKING RESPONSIBILITY: RECTIFICATION & APOLOGY
7. **Rectifying lies, Rescue, Persecution or Victim Behavior**: "When I (describe action,) I:
a.) "I lied or did not tell you the whole truth."

250

b.) "I Rescued you because, (i) I did not want to do it, or (ii) I was, in my opinion, doing more than my share."

c.) "I Persecuted you because I addressed you with anger that did not fairly belong to you."

d.) "I acted as a Victim because I expected or demanded that you Rescue me. I apologize and I will endeavor to change my behavior. Do you accept my apology?"

8. **Accepting Rectification**: Non defensive acceptance of the emotional information being given, followed by acceptance or rejection of the apology. When rejected, an apology may need to be rephrased, postponed or withdrawn.

9. **Apology and Begging for Forgiveness**: "I apologize for (action): it was wrong and I regret having hurt you. Will you forgive me?"

10. **Accepting Apology and Granting or Denying Forgiveness**: Hearing the apology and after thoughtful soul-searching, either a) granting forgiveness or, b) postponing forgiveness, pending rephrasing or additional amends.

This set of emotionally literate transactions is arranged in order of difficulty. "Asking for Permission" should be used every time an emotionally literate communication is initiated. The other ten transactions are to be used when appropriate.

THE EMOTIONAL AWARENESS SCALE

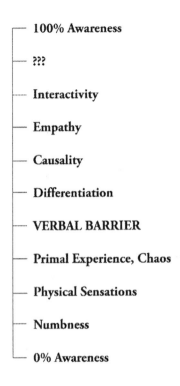

— 100% Awareness

— ???

— Interactivity

— Empathy

— Causality

— Differentiation

— VERBAL BARRIER

— Primal Experience, Chaos

— Physical Sensations

— Numbness

— 0% Awareness

NUMBNESS People in this state are not aware of anything they call feelings even if they are under the influence of strong emotions.

PHYSICAL SENSATIONS At this level of emotional awareness, the physical sensations that accompany emotions are experienced but not the emotions themselves. A person might feel his quickened heartbeat but is not aware that he is afraid. He might experience a hot flash, a knot in his stomach, tingling sensations or shooting pains. He may feel all of these sensations of the emotion, but not be aware of the emotion itself.

EMOTIONAL CHAOS OR PRIMAL EXPERIENCE In this stage, people are conscious of emotions, but they cannot put them into words. Primal, because it is similar to the emotional experience of babies and lower mammals who clearly experience emotions but would not be able to name them.

THE VERBAL BARRIER Awareness of emotions depends on the ability to speak about what we feel and why. Crossing this linguistic barrier requires an environment with people that are friendly to emotional discourse. Once a person is able to talk about his emotions with fellow human beings he can develop an increasing awareness of his emotions.

DIFFERENTIATION As we discuss our emotions with others we begin to recognizing different emotions and their intensity as well as learning how to speak about them to others. At this stage we become aware of the differences between basic emotions like anger, love, shame, joy, or hatred. We also realize that any feeling can occur at various intensities. Fear can vary from apprehension to terror. Anger can range from irritation to hatred. Love can be felt at many levels from affection to passion.

CAUSALITY As we become aware of our emotions we can also understand their causes.

EMPATHY As we learn about our emotions we begin to perceive and intuit similar texture and subtlety in the emotions of those around us. Empathy is a form of intuition specifically about emotions. Empathy, like all intuition, is imprecise and of little value until we develop ways of objectively confirming the accuracy of our perceptions.

INTERACTIVITY Knowing how others feel does not necessarily mean we know what to do about it. Emotional interactivity requires knowing how people will respond to each other's emotions and when that interaction might escalate for better or for worse.

??? This category indicates the possibility of as yet unknown level of emotional awareness.

Surveying the Emotional Landscape

> **Surveying the Emotional Landscape is an exercise about emotional awareness, emotional honesty and empathy and about people's emotional interconnections.**

Part I an exercise that teaches to effectively show others how their actions affect our feelings and that shows how to accept that sort of information without defensiveness

1. Making an Action/Feeling Statement:

The A/F transaction is a reciprocal exchange of information about how one person's action has affected another person's feelings.

When delivering an A/F statement we simply inform another person, as follows: "When you (describe action) I felt (name feeling)"

When speaking of an action it is important to characterize it in strict descriptive, behavioral terms; what the person did. No judgments, accusations or theories.

When describing a feeling it is important to specify the feeling (angry, happy, hurt, etc.) and its intensity (furious, annoyed, irritated, etc.) Again, no judgments, accusations or theories.

2. When accepting an A/F statement we acknowledge that a certain action of ours caused a certain feeling in another person.

"I understand; when I (describe action,) you felt (name feeling.)"

No defensiveness or attempts to explain or justify our actions.

With the action/feeling transaction we learn about the feelings we cause in people, the feelings they cause in us, and their intensity. We also learn to control our need to argue and be defensive when confronted with the consequences of our actions. Surveying the Emotional

Part 2 Validating Intuition, is an exercise in which we develop our intuitive skills and learn to be emotionally honest.

VALIDATING INTUITION, EMPATHIC PERCEPTION OR PARANOID FANTASY.

Intuition is a powerful tool for the acquisition of knowledge. Intuition can express itself as a hunch, an empathic perception or a paranoid fantasy. Intuitive knowledge, to be properly used must be checked out. Validating intuition is a reciprocal exchange of information about the accuracy of our intuitive perceptions.

1. When attempting to validate an intuition we ask the following kind of a question : "I have a hunch about how you are feeling. Can I tell you about it ?
    After permission is given:
    "I have the hunch that you are feeling (explain)" or
    "I have a paranoid fantasy that (explain.)"

2. When responding to an intuitive perception we endeavor to validate (instead of discounting) how much of it is correct, even if just a "grain of truth."

With this transactional exchange we learn to become aware of our intuitive perceptions, to word them and to respectfully question others about their validity. When faced with another person's perceptions we learn to honestly validate, instead of discounting their accuracy.

Taking Responsibility

> **Taking Responsibility concerns the emotional damage we cause each other and how to take sincere, open-hearted liability, apologize and make amends.**

Rectification of Emotional Damage

Most of the emotional damage done in relationships is done while lying and power playing in one of the three basic game roles: Rescuer, Persecutor or Victim. When we discover that we have been relating to others in one of these three roles it is important, as a way of rectifying the situation, to take responsibility and apologize:

RESCUE: "When I (action,) I Rescued you because:
a. "I was doing something I did not want to do" and/or
b. "In my opinion, I was doing more than my fair share."

PERSECUTION: "When I (action,) I Persecuted you because I addressed you with anger which did not fairly belong to you."

VICTIM: "When I (action,) I acted as a Victim; I expected (or demanded) that you Rescue me. I apologize, and I will endeavor to change my behavior. Will you accept my apology?"

An apology to be complete has to be accepted. The injured person has to experience the desire to forgive and grant forgiveness. This requires that:
▪ the apology is delivered with the proper emotional tone of sadness, sorrow, shame or regret and devoid of anger, pride or self pity.

- the apology clearly states the injurious actions committed and the injured person agrees that those were the actions requiring an apology, and
- the apology assumes that forgiveness may not be forthcoming and accepts that outcome if it occurs.

APOLOGY & BEGGING FORGIVENESS FOR SEVERE EMOTIONAL DAMAGE

Apologies vary from minor, everyday apologies to major begging for forgiveness. On occasion we commit acts which are so injurious that even when such actions are forgotten and their effects swept under the rug, they leave indelible scars in their victims which can only be repaired through a major apology and offer of amends and time to heal. If, after thoughtful soul searching, the apology is accepted and forgiveness is granted, there may be psychic healing possible. However it is important that the injured party be free not to forgive, to postpone or to set conditions for forgiveness and reconsideration.

The Ten Commandments of Emotional Literacy

I. Place love at the center of your emotional life. Heart-centered emotional intelligence empowers everyone it touches.

II. Emotional Literacy requires that you not lie by omission or commission. Except where your safety or the safety of others is concerned, do not lie.

III. Stand up for how you feel and what you want. If you don't, it is not likely that anyone else will.

IV. Emotional Literacy requires that you do not power play others. Gently but firmly ask instead for what you want, until you are satisfied.

V. Do not allow yourself to be power played. Gently but firmly refuse to do , or stop doing, anything against your free will.

VI. Respect and try to understand the ideas, feelings and wishes of others as much as you do your own. Respecting ideas does not mean that you have to submit to them.

VII. Apologize and make amends for your mistakes. Nothing will make you grow faster.

VIII. Do not accept false apologies. They are worth less than no apologies at all.

IX. Love yourself and others equally. Love truth above all.

X. Follow these commandments according to your best judgment. After all, they are not written in stone.

Adult: the rational ego state. Also known as the "neopsyche" because it is thought to be located in the neocortex of the brain.

Berne, Eric: the father of Transactional Analysis.

Charisma: the sum total of an individual's personal power.

Child: the creative, aware, spontaneous, intimate ego state. The locus of our emotions.

Contract: a mutual agreement between consenting individuals.

Cooperation: a social system that shuns power plays and pursues equality.

Critical Parent: a negatively prejudiced Parent ego state. Often heard as a voice that tells us we are not okay; bad, stupid, ugly, crazy, sick or doomed. The internal and external enforcer of patriarchal values.

Ego State: one of three separate, coherent ways in which people behave; Parent, Adult or Child.

Emotions: biochemically based bodily states that motivate and affect our behavior.

Emotional awareness: awareness of feelings as opposed to emotional literacy, a far more complicated skill.

Emotional Intelligence: Sophistication about emotions. Understanding our own and other people's emotions.

Emotional Literacy: a skill that involves emotional intelligence as well as knowing how our emotions are best utilized for the enhancement of ethical, personal and social power to benefit ourselves and others. Intelligence of the Heart.

Emotional Numbing: the drastic suppression of the awareness of emotions due, usually, to severe trauma.

Emotional Tone Deafness: the inability to feel certain specific emotions. Similar to color blindness.

Emotional Warrior: an individual who struggles against patriarchal domination with the aim of replacing it with Emotional Literacy in his or her personal life and in society.

Empath: a person who is keenly aware of his or her emotions as well as the emotions of others. An empath when not emotionally literate can suffer greatly from his or her heightened awareness. The opposite of an unpath.

Empathy: an intuitive capacity to understand emotions.

Existential Payoff: the satisfaction that people get from playing a game because the negative payoff confirms an existential position held as part of a script, usually since childhood.

Feelings: the awareness of emotional states.

Game: a series of transactions which fails to accomplish the purpose of acquiring positive strokes, producing negative strokes instead.

Intuition: a human faculty with which we can sense reality without having to study it.

Limbic brain: In the triune brain theory, the portion of the brain that evolved after the reptilian brain and which had as a function protecting the offspring and is the source of love, sadness and guilt and other bonding emotions. Sympathy.

Love: the master emotion that causes people to play together, be together and work together. The pleasurable feeling of nurturing and cooperation.

Love of Truth: the eminently human desire that finds pleasure in the understanding of reality. It implies a willingness to abandon one's beliefs in the face of contradictory information.

Lying: the conscious hiding of the truth. We lie by commission when saying something that we believe to be false, or by omission, when failing to say something that we believe another person is entitled to know.

Negative Stroke: a stroke delivered with a hateful feeling. A stroke that feels bad.

Neocortical brain: The uniquely human portion of the brain that evolved after the limbic and reptilian brains. The locus of language and symbolic thinking.

Nurturing Parent: a positively prejudiced Parent ego state.

Paranoia: from the Greek meaning "knowledge on the side." A valid intuitive notion which is usually not completely correct.

Paranoid Fantasy: what happens to paranoid hunches when they are discounted and invalidated. Usually, ideas of being persecuted when we are in the dark about what is going on.

Parent: the prejudging, traditional ego state. The Nurturing Parent is positively prejudiced, the Critical Parent is negatively prejudiced.

Persecutor: an angry, resentful person who vents his or her feelings on other people.

Positive Stroke: a stroke delivered with a loving feeling. A stroke that feels good.

Psychopath: an antiquated term for an antisocial personality. A person who lacks empathy and is unable to feel emotion.

Reptilian brain: The most primitive portion of the brain that has as a function reproduction and the acquisition and defense of territory and mates and is the source of anger, fear and lust and other territorial emotions.

Rescuer (capitalized): a person who does things he doesn't want to do for other people or who does more than his or her share in any given situation. As opposed to a rescuer (lower case) who helps people in need.

Responsibility: The awareness and accounting of the effect of our actions on the emotions of other people.

Stroke: an act of social recognition that satisfies an innate, biological need for contact. (See also positive and negative stroke.)

Stroke City: a group exercise also known as Opening the Heart designed to undermine the stroke economy and teach people how to love.

Stroke Economy: a system of prohibitions about stroking which, when enacted, curtails the availability of strokes and leads to generalized stroke hunger.

Stroke Hunger: The consequence of stroke deprivation.

Script: a life plan decided upon, usually but not always, early in childhood as a way of coping with the prevailing conditions we live in at the time.

Sympathy: the mental aspect of empathy. The kindly disposed understanding of other people's emotions without an accompanying emotion of one's own.

Transaction: a social exchange of information or strokes.

Transactional Analysis: a system of psychology and psychotherapy that analyzes transactions and stroking patterns to understand people and help them change.

Triune brain: a system of brain organization that postulates three distinct, philogenetically consecutive portions of the brain: reptilian, limbic, and neo-cortical.

Truth: an elusive concept. Truth does not exist but it can be approximated. Truth is a belief and we approximate truth when our beliefs reflect the realities of the world. The best approach to truth is the consensus of large numbers of free thinking people operating in their Adult ego state.

Truthfulness: speaking what one believes to be the truth. (see Lying)

Unpath: The opposite of an empath. A person with very little empathy.

Victim (capitalized): a person who will not help himself. As opposed to victim (lower case) who is a casualty of bad circumstances.

Window of Opportunity: an optimal period, in early life, in which to learn a certain skill.

About the Author

Dr. Claude Steiner, Ph.D., was born in Paris, France in 1935. His family subsequently moved to Spain and from there, Mexico. Dr. Steiner came to the United States to study physics, and eventually, psychology. He is a clinical psychologist with a doctorate from the University of Michigan, Ann Arbor. Dr. Steiner was a disciple, and later, friend and colleague, of Eric Berne, the psychiatrist author of *Games People Play*, and with him, a founding member of The Transactional Analysis Association. After Berne's death in 1971, Dr. Steiner went on to develop the theory and practice of Heart-Centered Emotional Literacy. His books include *Games Alcoholics Play, Scripts People Live, Healing Alcoholism, The Other Side of Power,* and *When a Man Loves a Woman*. He was also editor of two anthologies: *Beyond Games and Scripts* and *Readings in Radical Psychiatry*, as well as the author of the ubiquitous fable of *The Warm Fuzzy Tale*.

Steiner's books have been translated into seven languages and he has a worldwide lecturing and teaching audience. He has three grown children and lives and practices in Berkeley and on his ranch in Mendocino County, California.

If you want to read and/or download Dr Steiner's other writings or want to learn about emotional literacy training activities around the world, please visit:

www.claudesteiner.com

or write Dr. Steiner at
csteiner@claudesteiner.com

REFERENCES

[1] Steiner, Claude. *Achieving Emotional Literacy; A Personal Program to Increase Your Emotional Intelligence.* Avon Books 1997.

[2] Grossman, D.C., Neckerman, H.J., Koepsell, T.D., Liu, P.Y., Asher, K. N., Beland, K., Frey, K., & Rivara, F.P. Effectiveness of a violence prevention curriculum among children in elementary school: A randomized controlled trial (1997). *Journal of the American Medical Association,* 277:1605-1611.

[3] Goleman, Daniel. *Emotional Intelligence.* New York: Bantam Books 1996.

[4] Berne, Eric. *Transactional Analysis in Psychotherapy.* New York: Grove Press 1961.

[5] Stewart, Ian and Joines, Vann. *TA Today A New Introduction to Transactional Analysis.* Chapel Hill, Lifespace Publishing 1987.

[6] Steiner, Claude. *Scripts People Live.* New York: Grove Press 1974.

[7] Steiner, Claude. *Readings in Radical Psychiatry.* New York: Grove Press 1975.

[8] Laing Ronald D. *The Politics of the Family.* New York: Pantheon Books 1971.

[9] Sternberg, Robert. *Why smart people can be so stupid.* Yale University Press: Princeton 2002.

[10] Gilligan, James. *Violence; Reflections on a national epidemic.* New York: Vintage 1997.

[11] Kline, Paul. *Intelligence: The Psychometric View.* London: Routledge 1991.

[12] Salovey, Peter and Mayer John D. "Emotional Intelligence" *Imagination Cognition and Personality* 1989-90: vf.9, #31: 185.

[13] Steiner, Claude. *Healing Alcoholism.* New York: Grove Press 1979.

[14] Darwin, Charles. *The Expression of the Emotions in Man and Animals.* University of Chicago Press 1985.

[15] Gladwell, Malcolm. "The Naked Face," *The New Yorker.* Aug 5, 2002.

[16] Le Doux, Joseph. *The Emotional Brain; The Mysterious Underpinning of Emotional Life.* New York: Touchstone 1996.

[17] Chomsky, Noam and Mitsou Ronat. *On Language; Chomsky's Classic Works.* New York: New Press 1998

[18] Pinker, Steven *How the Mind Works.* New York: Norton 1998

[19] MacLean, Paul. "The Triune Brain, Emotion and Scientific Bias," *The Neurosciences: The Second Study Program,* ed. F.O. Schmitt. New York: Rockefeller University Press 1970.

[20] Ardrey, Robert. *The Territorial Imperative.* New York: Kodansha International 1966.

[21] Lewis, Thomas et al. *A General Theory of Love.* New York: Vintage 2001.

[22] Damasio, Antonio. *Descartes' Error: Emotion, Reason, and the Human Brain.* New York: Grosset/Putnam Press 1994.

[23] Damasio Antonio. *The Feelings of What Happens; Body, Emotion and the Making of Consciousness.* London: Vintage 1999.

[24] Carolyn Zahn-Waxler, Pamela M. Cole, and Karen Caplovitz Barrett. "Guilt and empathy: Sex differences and implications for the development of depression," *The development of emotion regulation and dysregulation.* New York: Cambridge, 1991: 243-272.

[25] Janoff-Bulman, R. Rebuilding shattered assumptions after traumatic events: Coping processes and outcomes. In C.R. Snyder (ed.), *Coping: The psychology of what works.* New York: Oxford University Press 1999.

[26] Wyckoff, Hogie. "The Stroke Economy in Women's Scripts," *Transactional Analysis Journal I,3* (1971): pp. 16-30.

[27] Fischer, Anton. Sex differences in emotionality: Fact or stereotype. *Feminism and Psychology,* (1993): 3, 303-318.

[28] Ornish, Dean. *Love and Survival. The Scientific Basis for the Healing Power of Intimacy.* New York: Harper Collins 1997.

[29] Steiner, Claude. *The Warm Fuzzy Tale.* Sacramento: Jalmar Press *1977.*

[30] Berne, Eric. *Intuition and Ego States; The Origins of Transactional Analysis,* Paul McCormick, ed. San Francisco: Harper and Row 1977.

[31] Berne, Eric. *Games People Play.* Grove Press 1964.

[32] Karpman, Steven. Fairy Tales and Script Drama Analysis. *TA Bulletin v 7.# 26* April 1968.

[33] Engel, Beverly. "Making Amends," *Psychology Today* August 2002.

[34] Luskin, Fred. *Forgive for Good; A proven prescription for health and happiness.* San Francisco: Harper 2001.

[35] Putnam, Robert D. *Bowling Alone; The collapse and revival of American community.* New York: Touchstone 2000.

[36] Judith, Anodea. *Eastern Body Western Mind; Psychology and the Chacra System.* Berkeley: Ten Speed Press 1996.

[37] Eisler,Raine. *The Chalice and the Blade.* New York: Harper-Collins 1988.

[38] Nietzshe, Friedrich. *On The Genealogy of Morals.* New York: Random House 1967.

39 St. Augustine. "Lying," *Treatise on Various Subjects, vol. 14,* ed. R. J. Deferrari, Fathers of the Church. Catholic University of America Press, 1952.

40 Kant, Immanuel. Critique of Practical Reason and Other Writings in *Moral Philosophy.* Chicago: University of Chicago Press 1949.

41 Constant, Benjamin. in *Lying* by Sissela Bok New York: Vintage 1978.

42 De Paulo, Bella M., et al. "Lying in Everyday Life." *Journal of Personality and Social Psychology.* May 1996, v. 70, no. 5.

43 Bok, Sissela. *Lying* New York: Vintage 1978.

44 Blanton, Brad. *Radical Honesty.* New York: Dell 1996.

45 *The Encyclopedia of Philosophy.* New York: Macmillan Publishing Co., Inc. 1967.

46 Nietzsche, Friedrich. *Philosophy and Truth: Selections from Nietzsche's Notebooks of the early 1870s.* Translated and edited, with an introduction and notes, by Daniel Breazeale. Foreword by Walter Kaufmann. New Jersey: Humanities Press 1979.

47 Berne, Eric. *What Do You Say After You Say Hello?* New York: Grove Press 1976.

48 Fukuyama, Francis. *The End of History and the Last Man.* New York: The Free Press 1992.

49 Dostoyevsky, Fyodor, from his personal diary, April 16, 1864, quoted in *Fyodor Dostoyevsky, A Writer's Life,* Geir Kjetsaa, 1987.

50 Gladwell, Malcolm. "Damaged," *The New Yorker Magazine,* Feb. 24, 1997.

INDEX

A

A General Theory of Love 26
abuse, abusing 13, 188, 199, 207, 209-212, 232, 233
Achieving Emotional Literacy 154
action strokes 84
action/feeling case study 90
action/feeling error 91, 95
action/feeling exchanges 90
action/feeling formula 96
action/feeling statement(s) 54, 89-93, 96-101, 113, 116, 117, 120, 146, 155, 190, 196
action/feeling transaction that worked 100
action strokes 61
Adult 24, 102, 103, 147, 183
Adult to Adult 103
alchemy of emotions 36
Alcoholics Anonymous 137, 150
alexithymia 29
anger 4, 6, 34, 50, 68, 85, 88, 91, 95, 119, 134, 136, 142, 150, 182, 186
anxiety disorders 44
apology(ies), apologize(ing) 121, 136, 137, 140-144, 146-157, 161-162, 164-167, 176, 179, 182, 187, 200
apology error 150, 152, 155
Apology with Conditions 156
archeopsyche 24
Avenues to Power 210

B

balance 214, 221, 222
Bashing the Righteous 155
Eric Berne 24, 64, 103, 121, 128, 135, 153, 225, 230
Brad Blanton 227
Sissela Bok 227
brain 24-26, 33, 44, 126, 128, 232, 233

C

causality 35, 45
Chalice and the Blade 206, 221
chaos, chaotic experience 10, 45, 88
Child(ren) 24, 79, 103, 147, 152, 183-191, 207, 233

childhood 11, 183, 232
children's demons 191
Noam Chomsky 25
clarifying an action/feeling statement 96
codependence (dency) 129, 131, 142
communication 217, 220-222
compassion 14
compliance 17
Benjamin Constant 227
control 47, 144, 190, 207, 210-211, 215-216, 218-222
Dean Cornish, MD 59-60
Critical Parent 64, 66, 70-78, 81, 83-85, 140, 212-213, 233
Crude physical power 207
crude psychological power 209

D

Antonio Damasio 27, 33
Charles Darwin 16
Bella de Paulo 227
defense mechanisms 9
depression 17, 30, 212
destructive critic 213
differentiation 34, 45
discounting intuition 107
dominance, domination 206-207, 211
Drama Triangle 148-149
drugs 13, 31

E

ego state(s) 24, 102, 152, 234
ego state theory 25
Riane Eisler 206, 221
emotional awareness 14, 24, 27, 30-32, 40-45, 88
Emotional Awareness Scale 27
Emotional Brain 44
Emotional Brain; The Mysterious Underpinnings
  of Emotional Life 18
emotional chaos 31, 47, 113, 124
emotional conflict 90
emotional damage 10, 19, 137, 138, 141
emotional discount 108
emotional experience(s) 13, 22, 95
emotional expression(s) 17, 97

emotional healing 155

emotional housekeeping 179

emotional illiteracy 2, 30, 36, 48, 87, 231

Emotional Intelligence 15, 18, 40, 205, 223

emotional interactivity 19, 20, 41

emotional landscape 43, 49, 50-55, 59, 85, 88, 94, 114, 116, 120, 138

emotional literacy 1, 7-8, 16, 21-22, 32-33, 37-39, 44, 52-55, 59, 67-70, 84, 112, 120, 125, 138-140, 155, 161, 163, 167, 169, 183, 186, 193, 200-201, 210, 217, 219, 222-224, 227, 229

emotional literacy guidelines for children 186

emotional literacy training 2, 17, 18, 22, 50, 53, 59, 80, 102, 111, 121, 157, 201, 205, 213, 221, 233

emotional mistakes 2, 4, 6, 121, 136, 167

emotional numbing, numbness 47, 49, 144, 233

emotional patterns 184

emotional quotient 15

emotional self-defense. 191

emotional trauma 9, 10, 22, 47

Emotional Warrior(s) 48, 205, 210, 216, 221-222, 230-232

emotionally illiterate 32, 184, 193-194, 198

emotionally literate 2, 7, 86, 97-101, 111, 120, 136, 146, 183-185, 194, 196, 199-200, 222-223

emotionally literate dialogue 109, 110, 113, 176

emotionally literate media 191

emotionally literate relationship(s) 90, 149, 170-173

emotionally literate transaction 68-70, 74-76, 79, 82, 89, 98, 102, 109, 141, 144, 153-156, 161, 166

emotions 1, 2, 12, 19, 26-27, 32-33, 40-41, 51-52, 63, 74, 85-89, 94-95, 98, 102, 119, 120, 166, 194, 211

empath(s), (ic) 14, 37, 40, 43, 179

empathic awareness 37

empathic intuitions 39

empathy(ize) 7, 14, 18, 32, 36-40, 45, 51, 84, 107, 114, 141, 148, 210, 216

enabling 129

energizing process 51

EQ & IQ 15, 17

equality 171-173, 186, 201

evolutionary psychology 25

exchange of strokes 64
existential advantage 123
existential statements 123
Expression of the Emotions in Man and Animals 16

F

fantasy characters 183
fear 2, 68, 85, 88, 93-95, 113, 130, 142, 186
Feeling of What Happens; Body, Emotion and the Making of Consciousness 33
feelings 1, 2, 8, 18, 23, 34, 50-52, 86-92, 95, 97-101, 107, 110-113, 116-122, 142, 148, 166, 178-180, 190-191, 198, 217
first, second, and third-degree game playing 135
flashbacks 9
forgiveness 154, 161-162, 166, 167
Francis Fukuyama 230

G

game(s) 122, 128, 135-136, 144, 148
Games People Play 122
genetic commonality 17
Gestalt Prayer 86
James Gilligan 13
Daniel Goleman 15, 18, 183
guilt(y) 13, 23, 91, 94, 98-99, 113, 137, 147-148, 162, 184-186

H

Jude Hall 225
hatred 13, 34
Healing Alcoholism 16
hereditary 124
history 218
honesty 70, 170-171, 176, 179, 186, 193, 201, 226
hope 9, 34, 41, 50, 88, 94-95, 219
hopelessness 94, 148, 150
How the Mind Works 25
hunches 179
hypersensitivity 10

I

Information 222
Inner Child 103

insecurity 4
interactivity 40, 43, 45
intimacy 12, 60
intimidate(ing) 17, 11, 2062
intuition 36-37, 70, 102-114, 118, 120, 199, 218
intuition in action, a case study 106
intuitive, intuitive hunch(es) 54, 102, 113, 120, 179, 196-198

J

jealous(y) 4, 6, 94, 106, 221
joy 9, 34, 41, 50, 88, 95

K

Immanuel Kant 226
Stephen Karpman 126
kindness 14, 119

L

lack of emotion 8
Joseph LeDoux 18, 44
lies of commission 226
lies of omission 172, 188, 226
love 9, 22, 34, 41, 49, 60, 88, 95, 113, 116, 119-121, 136, 185, 201, 216, 221-223
Love and Survival: The Scientific Basis for the Healing Power of Intimacy 60
love of truth 228, 229
lying, *Lying* 226, 227

M

Paul MacLean 25
John Mayer 16
melancholy 94
mistakes 4
motional literacy 187

N

National Institute of Mental Health 25
negative emotions 19, 85, 88, 93
negative strokes 62-63, 66-67, 122
neopsyche 24
nformation 221
Friedrich Nietzsche 225
nightmares 9, 47

non-defensive reception of emotional information 98
numbness 9, 10, 13, 27, 45, 88
Nurturing Parent 83-84
O

Opening the Heart 51, 68, 84, 113
P

paranoia 108
paranoid fantasies 105-106, 179
Parent 24, 207
Parent to Child 103
passion 12, 95, 119, 215, 221-222
patriarchy 206, 221
patterns 169, 171
Fritz Perls 86
permission 68-69, 77, 110, 196-199
Persecute(ing) 143-147, 158
Persecutor 125-128, 131-136, 144, 167
Persecutor script 124
personal power 4, 7, 44, 205, 211
physical strokes 60, 84
Pig Parent 213
Steve Pinker 25
poetry of strokes 74
positive emotions 85, 93
positive strokes 84, 123
post-traumatic stress 10
power 190, 200, 206-207, 211, 216, 219-220, 224
power literacy 210
power of control 207
power of information 218
power of strokes 59
power plays 144, 173, 186-187, 193-194, 198, 206-210, 222
power transactions 206
pre-nuptial emotional agreements 173
primal awareness 32
primary & secondary emotions 93
primary emotions 93-95, 116-118
Protagoras 228
R

Radical Honesty 227

relationship(s) 1, 3, 6, 12, 37, 43, 110-120, 131, 134, 137, 138, 143, 147-148, 164, 167-173, 176, 179, 183, 196, 205-207, 217-219, 232

remedying a rescue 141

Remedying of Rescues 144

Remedying of Victim 153

Requirements & Errors of an Apology 149

rescue(s)(ing) 142-147, 152, 161, 171-173, 182

Rescuer 125, 129-136, 142, 158, 167, 216-217

Rescuer-Persecutor-Victim merry-go-round 129, 134

responsibility, taking responsibility 4, 49-55, 59, 80, 98, 114, 129, 135, 140-142, 159, 162, 167

ritual(s) 137, 151

role switching 132

S

sadness 7, 11, 30, 34, 95, 147-150, 185

Peter Salovey 16

science 218

script 123-125, 128, 134, 144

script payoff 123

secondary emotions 95

self-destructive games 122

selfishness 119, 131, 217

self-protective 12

Seven Sources of Power 213

sexual strokes 79

shame 6, 34, 85, 88, 116, 142, 150

somatization 30

St. Augustine3 226

strategies of emotional literacy 52

stroke economy 49, 66, 67, 72, 77, 81, 84

Stroke Enemy 71

stroke-hungry 67

stroke(s) 3, 26, 54, 59-65, 68, 70-77, 81-85, 122, 136, 179, 186, 196-201, 224

stroke-starved 76

subtle physical power 208

subtle psychological power 209

super strokes 61

sympathy 39-40

Synanon 64-65

T

Ten Commandments of Emotional Literacy 202
thanatos 230
training process 49
transactional analysis 24-26, 83, 102-103, 122, 126, 130, 207, 229
transcendence 219-222
trauma 9, 11, 232
trust 113, 119, 121
truth(ful) 188, 228-229
types of power plays 207

U

uncontrolled emotion 6
unwanted strokes 79-81

V

validating an intuitive hunch 109
validation 109, 112
verbal barrier 33, 45
verbal strokes 60, 84
Victim 125-136, 144, 148, 152-153, 157, 167, 207, 210, 216
Victim script 123
Violence 13, 206, 222, 229, 232

W

Warm Fuzzy Tale 63
work(ers) 193-194, 198
workplace 193, 194, 200, 201
Hogie Wyckoff 49